A DAY AT A TIME

Also by Guy H. King

A DAY
AT A TIME

Guy H. King

London
MARSHALL, MORGAN & SCOTT
Edinburgh

LONDON
MARSHALL, MORGAN & SCOTT, LTD.
1–5 PORTPOOL LANE
HOLBORN, E.C.1

AUSTRALIA AND NEW ZEALAND
117–119 BURWOOD ROAD
MELBOURNE, E.13

SOUTH AFRICA
P.O. BOX 1720, STURK'S BUILDINGS
CAPE TOWN

CANADA
EVANGELICAL PUBLISHERS
241 YONGE STREET
TORONTO

U.S.A.
CHRISTIAN LITERATURE CRUSADE
FORT WASHINGTON
PENNSYLVANIA

This edition 1956
Second impression 1957
Third impression 1960
Fourth impression 1962
Fifth impression 1965

MADE AND PRINTED IN GREAT BRITAIN BY PURNELL AND SONS,
PAULTON (SOMERSET) AND LONDON

DEDICATION

TO

DR. DONALD GREY BARNHOUSE

"Mr. Great Heart"
to many a traveller along the Pilgrim's Progress.

A token of high regard
and warm affection.

FOREWORD

"TAKE care of the pence and the pounds will take care of themselves." I suppose that old proverb is true. Is this also true: "Take care of the days and the years will take care of themselves"? Anyhow, the Good Book breaks life up like that—"*As thy days* so shall thy strength be" (Deut. 33: 25).

Well, that is what this little volume is meant for—*a Day at a Time*.

A Shaft to lighten the day's journey,
A Key to unlock the day's programme,
A Morsel to quicken the day's appetite,
A Tonic to energize the day's doings.

We are grateful for permission to reissue in volume form, these talks, which originally appeared in *Revelation*, in response to requests from both sides of the Atlantic. If the Lord can bless them, how happy we shall be.

Christt Church Vicarage,   G.H.K.
Beckenham.

6

CONTENTS

JANUARY

ON STARTING RIGHT

January is the genesis of the year, so we do well to start our daily thoughts with the Book of Genesis. It is hoped the first few Meditations especially will help us to begin the year aright.

"In the beginning God . . ." (Gen. 1: 1)

AND what a beginning; whether for a world, or for a year! The words refer to the fact of His being there before all time, but they apply also to His being there before all things; God first. Because of this, what a beautiful world it was. What peace and joy and blessing abounded for the happy pair, until they were tempted to oust God from His rightful primacy, and to put self first. So shall it be for us, that if God be put first, in every day, every plan, every choice, richest blessing shall be ours this year. "Not as I will, but as Thou wilt" (Matt. 26: 39), "Not I, but Christ" (Gal. 2: 20). I wish you a very happy New Year, and with the wish I give you the secret. "In the beginning God . . ." Begin every month, every week, every day, every thing, with God!

PRAYER.—*Gracious God, take Thou the first place in all my days, and have the first choice in all my decisions.* AMEN.

". . . Where art thou?" (Gen. 3: 9)

THE question was asked of a man who was not where he had been. He and his wife were, out of shame and fear, hiding from God. The old, happy, unclouded relationship had gone. Well, we are at the start of another year, and while our first inquiry must be as to His position, the next shall be concerning our own position, that is in our relationship to God. Have we been growing cold, slipping back, getting slack, losing ground? Where are we? Has anything come into our lives to cause us to be not so keen as we used to be to meet with God, in the garden of communion, worship, prayer? Shall we let God Himself search us out with this challenging question; though it be with judgment, it shall also be with mercy. Shall we get right back again to the old place of trust, obedience, and fellowship?

PRAYER.—*"Lord, may no earthborn cloud arise to hide Thee from Thy servant's eyes."* AMEN.

". . . Where is . . . thy brother? . . ." (Gen. 4: 9)

HERE is a man who cared so little about his brother that he murderously compassed his death and hid the body. Then he impudently inquired what business his brother was of his. Well, "where is thy brother?" It is, of course, of infinite concern to us Christians. Where does he stand in respect to physical, to mental, to spiritual welfare? These first three New Year days have challenged us to examine, in relation to ourselves, God's position; then our own position; and now our brother's position, our broader brother, of the slum area, of the heathen country, of the Christless world, of the house next door; our blood-brother and family relations; our blood-bought brother. "Let us do good unto all men, and especially unto them who are of the household of faith" (Gal. 6: 10). Shall we dedicate our New Year to an all-out endeavour to get our brother just "where" he ought to be?

PRAYER.—*God, who hast taught me that I should love Thee with all my heart, help me to love my brother also, and so show the reality of my love to Thee.* AMEN.

". . . Enoch walked with God . . ." (Gen. 5: 22)

THAT was a very lovely thing to do, but too difficult for us, do you think? Well, humanly speaking it couldn't have been easy for Enoch. He had great responsibilities as the leader of his clan, exercising the vexed and varied functions of judge, priest and ruler. And look at the moral condition of his time, if Jude 15 is any inkling of it. Was it these difficulties that impelled him to walk with God? No. Look at this curious thing: of each of those early fathers it is said he "lived" after he begat his son. But of Enoch it is that he "walked with God" after he begat his son, Methuselah. What a difference! That's when, and why, the "walk" began. It was the responsibility of his boy, rather than of his clan, that drove him to it. And what a rewarding experience he found it (Heb. 11: 5). Though this be a special message to parents, it is also a word to us all. Whatever our station, let us walk with God, till He takes us home with Him.

PRAYER.—*O God, may I this day and all the days keep in step, and keep in line with Thee right to the end.* AMEN.

"And God saw . . ." (Gen. 1: 31; 6: 5)

Two utterly contrasted things God saw, and separated by only a page or two. I wonder if He sees us at either end of the picture? First, God saw "everything that He had made, and behold it was very good." It gave infinite pleasure to Him, as does His new creation (2 Cor. 5: 17) when all is well between us and Him. But then, God saw "that the wickedness of man was great in the earth, and that every imagination of the thoughts of his heart was only evil continually." How quickly man had declined, and from what a height to what a depth! Lay open your heart and life to the searching gaze of God. What does He see? "Very good," or "only evil," or something in between; thank God not too evil, but alas not too good. By the grace of God, there is no height of holiness we may not reach, but for the grace of God, there is no depth of wickedness we may not touch. Christians, be watchful! His eye upon us is a solemnizing thought, but it can be a comforting thought, as Hagar found: "Thou God seest me " (Gen. 16: 13).

PRAYER.—*Thou Holy God, may the Holy Spirit make me holy in Thine eyes as I walk in Thy ways.* AMEN.

". . . the Lord shut him in" (Gen. 7: 16)

How safe he was then. If Noah himself had shut the door, the lock might not have quite closed, or he might have forgotten to shoot the bolt; the flood waters might have forced a way in. But God saw to all that, and the family of the "righteous" (7: 1) was completely safe. The storm of judgment could not touch them. My fellow-believer, tell your soul, for its own peace and delight, that the moment you put your trust in the Saviour, He shuts you in. A storm of judgment there shall be, but not for you (John 5: 24). Your Ark of Salvation is Jesus Himself, and since you are "in Christ," as the Epistles so often express it, you may be at perfect rest as to the future. Be concerned, during the waiting time, only to get others in, to share not only the security but all else that is ours "in Him."

PRAYER.—*We thank Thee, Lord, for the security of salvation and the satisfaction that we have. May we live as those who know they can trust Thee wholly.* AMEN.

". . . a mighty hunter before the Lord . . ." (Gen. 10: 9)

I WONDER what Nimrod hunted. All sorts of game, probably, to satisfy his hunger. Well now, God has a hunger for the souls of men; and He wants a hunter who will go out after them. May He make you "a mighty hunter," a great soul winner, to "satisfy" His "travail" (Isa. 53: 11). The weapons of such hunting are first, prayer. We can pray for people we can't reach otherwise. We can talk to God about those who won't let us talk to them about God. Ask Him to lead you about this.

> *Lord lay some soul upon my heart*
> *And bless that soul through me;*
> *And may I humbly do my part*
> *To bring that soul to Thee.*

Make this your daily prayer. Another weapon is consistency. What a weapon is a truly Christian life. There is testimony, no preaching, but simply telling what He is to us. And then there is Scripture. We cannot get souls without an intelligent use of the Bible. So let us diligently learn to wield the sword of the Spirit. Again we pray, God make you "a mighty hunter."

PRAYER.—*Lord, I would seek this joy of joys, to lead to Thee many who are astray. Fit me increasingly for this great adventure.* AMEN.

". . . I will bless thee . . . and thou shalt be a blessing" (Gen. 12: 2)

AN old Scottish divine most truly said, "You may be a blot, you may be a blessing, but you can't be a blank." Yes, but who wants to be a blank, or a blot? Who does not want to be a blessing? That is also what God wants you to be, and if you really want what He wants, the thing's done! The strategic points in our life are the places where God's will and our will coincide. The purpose for which God promised to bless Abram was that he, for his part, might be a blessing to others. That is why He blessed you, shall we say, the other night; not merely for your own sake, but that you might pass it on. If we are to do deep, lasting good to others, we must ourselves first be blessed. But then it is uttermost selfishness, plain disloyalty, to keep it to ourselves. "Thou shalt be . . ." is for us both promise and command.

PRAYER.—*Lord, save me from a selfish Christianity, and inspire me with a great desire for others.* AMEN.

"... *he ... pitched his tent ... and ... he builded an altar ...*"
(Gen. 12: 8)

IF you read through his chapters, you will find that this was the habit of Abram's wanderings. Wherever he pitched his tent he built his altar. This was the altar of sacrifice whose necessity, as pointing to the One Sacrifice for sins forever, had evidently been impressed upon Adam, and Abel, and now Abram, and all the others. This was the altar of worship, whose influence permeated and sanctified all his life. This was the altar of testimony, whose message spoke of Jehovah, the True God, as opposed to all the little altars of the little so-called gods. So Abram kept a sanctuary of God alongside his dwelling-place. Have we, too, in our homes, a spot sacred to Him, a place set apart where, morning by morning, we have our quiet time of fellowship with Him in Bible reading and prayer? And have we set up the family altar, where family prayers sanctify the day? There are two essentials then; a tent, and an altar.

PRAYER.—*O God, where I dwell with others, may it be seen that I dwell with Thee. May it be noised abroad that Thou art in the house.* AMEN.

"... *I am the Almighty God ...*" (Gen. 17: 1)

THIS was a new Name by which God here introduced Himself to Abram. He had never used it before. Of course, He had a reason for adopting it now. He had come to announce an enlargement of His promises, to give an undertaking that the man was also to have a new name, Abraham, "a father of many nations," to keep pace as it were with his prospect. But could God fulfil His plan, and keep His word? It was so big a thing as to be humanly unbelievable. Yes, but the Name? Translated "the Almighty God," it is really El-Shaddai, which means "The God Who Is Enough," a Name commensurate with His nature, and with His purpose. Never forget that you have an Enough God; loving Enough to wish you only the very best; wise Enough to know always what is the very best for you; strong Enough to secure for you that very best. What a Name, and what a God!

PRAYER.—*Almighty God, who hast ever revealed Thyself as able to meet and overcome all human needs, may I wholly trust Thee thus.* AMEN.

"*. . . I have taken upon me to speak unto the Lord . . .*" (Gen. 18: 27, 31)

HERE is a deeply moving instance of intercessory prayer. Abraham almost wonders at himself for daring thus "to speak unto the Lord." Yet, God would have it so. He has, in so many ways, encouraged His children to "speak" to Him, with becoming humility, of course, but also with holy boldness (Heb. 4: 16). So the patriarch prays, each favourable answer luring him on to further petition. Fifty, forty and five, forty, thirty, twenty, ten; then the intercessor stopped. Whatever for? Why didn't he go on? I think because at that point God closed the interview. "The Lord . . . left communing with Abraham." Remember that in prayer, our "whatsoever" is governed and limited only by His "will." Beyond that we cannot go. But what a grand and fruitful employment is this ministry of intercession. Will you not form the lifelong habit of taking it upon yourself "to speak unto the Lord" about the needy world, about the individual soul, about the far-flung mission field, about the people next door?

PRAYER.—*Lord, help me to remember that Thou dost ever answer prayer; sometimes the answer is "Yes," sometimes it is "No," sometimes it is "Wait," but always an answer.* AMEN.

"*. . . I cannot do anything till thou be come thither . . .*" (Gen. 19: 22)

SURELY the strangest anomaly in the whole universe is the impotence of Omnipotence. Yet here it is. A work of judgment was afoot, but Lot was entangled with the doomed city and God expressed Himself as unable to act until this man cut himself adrift. His unwillingness to come all out held up God's plan. That was a plan of judgment, but I am quite sure the same is true of His plans of blessings. Many a disappointed Christian is asking wistfully why God doesn't fully bless his life as He has done for many, and indeed promised to do for him. And I believe the simple answer is that there is a hold-up because of some compromise, some entanglement, with the sinful world. You think we ought not to be too narrow? All right, but you were asking why the blessing tarries, and this is the answer. When Lot was completely "come thither," the judgment fell, and just then will your blessing fall.

PRAYER.—*Gracious God, may I be willing to cut adrift from any entanglement so long as I may be brought alongside of Thee and Thy purpose.* AMEN.

". . . God remembered Abraham, and sent Lot out of the midst of the overthrow . . ." (Gen. 19: 29)

L OT was not saved because he deserved it. All the way along he had been asking for trouble, and if, as 2 Peter 2: 8 tells us, he "vexed his righteous soul," that seems all the more reason why he should have cleared out. But many another "righteous soul" has found separation a bugbear. No. Lot was saved because "God remembered Abraham," the man of His choice. Even as we were saved from our sinful estate, not for any supposed merit of our own, but because God remembered Another, the Man Christ Jesus (1 Tim. 2: 5), our sins are remembered no more because our Saviour is remembered forever. Shall it not be our soul's blest employ this day and every day to remember with deepest thankfulness God's everlasting remembrance? Shall we not praise Him continually that the "overthrow" is not for us, but the "overcome"?

PRAYER.—*Lord, we thank Thee that Thou dost ever see us in Him Who is ever in Thy sight, and we rest in the thought.* AMEN.

"And Abraham . . . went . . ." (Gen. 22: 3)

W ELL, that sounds simple enough. Does it? Remember, God has come not to "tempt" (see Jas. 1: 13), but to "test" Abraham. And what a test. He has told him to sacrifice his son on an altar, indicating the place where it is to be done. This Isaac is his only true son, the son he had long, long waited for, the son that had come to him at last by miracle. Moreover, God had promised that through this son, Abraham should have a multitudinous seed. And now, he is told to slay Isaac in sacrifice on that distant mountain. This seeming breaking of God's promise is almost as shattering to Abraham as the loss of his son. But though he just could not understand it, though he was just heartbroken over the whole thing, "Abraham . . . went." God give us such faith (note Heb. 11: 17–19) and such obedience. Would we be prepared to do what He tells us in the face of everything?

> *Trust and obey, for there's no other way*
> *To be happy* (or anything) *in Jesus, but to trust and obey.*

PRAYER.—*Lord, give me such a faith that despite all appearances and all considerations of my own, I may promptly, wholly and gladly obey Thy Will.* AMEN.

"*Huz . . . and Buz . . .*" (Gen. 22: 21)

A QUEER sort of text for devotional thought! They are the names given by Nahor to his two eldest sons. What names to go to bed with, or to get up with in the morning, or worse still, to go to school with! But the boys seem to have survived quite happily, since they evidently became rich landed proprietors, for we read that Job was born in the land of Uz (or Huz), and Elihu, his friend, was a Buzite. As to meanings, Huz signifies counsel and Buz, criticism. There are still plenty of Huzzes and Buzzes about: people who give advice and people who find fault; people who help and people who hinder. Fancy being a hinderer, making it harder for others to do right, but a helper is something different. You can tell what God thinks of such by noticing in 1 Corinthians 12: 28 the kind of people He classes them with. May every Buz become a Huz!

PRAYER.—*May I, O Lord, in all my life be nothing of a hindrance, but everything of a help.* AMEN.

". . . *I being in the way, the Lord led me . . .*" (Gen. 24: 27)

O NE of the commonest troubles among Christians is the fact that they do not seem able to get God's guidance in the affairs of life. Well, we can't deal with such a matter in the few words of this brief meditation. But we can say a little something about one fundamental necessity for guidance and that is "being in the way." All the course of this great adventure, Eliezer was travelling in the way of obedience to God's purpose, and as he took one step, he found that God "led" him on to the next. It is in the roadway of obedience that the signposts of guidance are to be found. Recall the Master's own words in John 7: 17, "If any man will do . . . he shall know . . . " In His own way and time, the loyal shall be led. They not only hope for that, they may expect it.

PRAYER.—*May I, O Lord, walk so close in the ways of Thy Will that I may catch Thy Voice, saying "This is the way, walk ye in it."* AMEN.

" . . . *Wilt thou go with this man? . . .*" (Gen. 24: 58)

BEAUTIFUL chapter, not only for itself, but for its arresting typology. Abraham desiring a bride for his son, which is the mind of the Heavenly Father for this age; Isaac waiting for the coming of his bride, the attitude of the Son of God at this period; Eliezer seeking a bride for the son, the special employment of the Holy Spirit during this dispensation, calling out the bride for the Son; Rebekah being the bride thus sought, the picture of His Bride, the Church. Each believer is a part of His bride, and the question is, when the Holy Spirit comes to hire us to Christ, "Wilt thou go with this Man?" He seeks, not only our original consent, our conversation, but the continual consequence, our consecration to Him and His interests until the glad day when the prepared bride and the Heavenly Bridegroom meet, and "the Marriage of the Lamb is come" (Rev. 19: 7). Wilt thou, then, and until then, go all the way with Him?

PRAYER.—*Our Gracious God, give me in my heart glad anticipation of the joys to come in the Marriage Supper of the Lamb.* AMEN.

" . . . *it reached . . .*" (Gen. 28: 12)

THE trouble with all man-made ladders to the sky is that like Babel's Tower, they don't reach. Man's self-esteem, self-effort, self-reliance will never get him there. But here is a ladder that "reached," and it was within man's reach, too, for it was "set up on the earth" by his side. It is absorbing to recall that in John 1: 51 the Lord Jesus said that this ladder was a picture of Himself. On Him, through Him, our supplications reach God, and through Him, His supplies reach us, an "ascending and descending." That is why we so often end our prayers, "Through Jesus Christ our Lord." But it is also only through Him that our souls can get to Heaven. If He had been anything less than sinless, anyone less than God, the ladder would never have reached, but on account of His own spotless purity and absolute deity, such was the sufficiency of His "finished" work that "it reached." There was no other good enough, long enough.

PRAYER.—*How we bless Thee, Heavenly Father, for the eternal efficiency and sufficiency of the work and worth of the Saviour.* AMEN.

". . . Jacob . . . took the stone that he had put for his pillows, and set it up for a pillar . . ." (Gen. 28: 18)

DON'T waste your sympathy on Jacob, for the hardness of his pillow. Those hardy Easterners were not accustomed to the downy ease of us softer Westerners. I'm afraid Jacob does not warrant our sympathy on any score, except that his mother spoiled him. And anyone is entitled to pity on that account. This was a thoroughly unpleasant character, until the change came. But the point here is the comfort he had found as he rested upon his stony pillow that night, as we saw yesterday, in the unexpected Presence in his loneliness, and the unexampled Promise for his life. In the morning he made the pillow a pillar, a token of gratitude, remembrance and witness. Has your weary saddened heart ever found a pillow of rest and comfort in some sweet providence of God, something He did for you, said to you? Then set up your pillow for a pillar, an open and public acknowledgment of His goodness, that others also in like case may find like comfort.

PRAYER.—*Thou Covenant God, who hast given so much to us, help us ever to bear our glad testimony to Thee that others may find Thy blessing too.* AMEN.

". . . seven years . . . seemed . . . but a few days . . ." (Gen. 29: 20)

WHAT magic alchemy was this that caused the lengthy span of weeks and months and even years to contract into the little space of days, and only "a few" at that? It was a thing called love, the most powerful influence in all the world. It was for love of Laban's daughter that Jacob engaged himself to seven years' servitude. Yet even so the years did not drag, but flew by. And hasn't the apostle the same thought in mind when, in 2 Corinthians 5: 14, he says, "The love of Christ constraineth us." Yes, even to such experiences as in the eleventh chapter of this same Epistle (vs. 23–28), gotten in the course of his servitude as "the bondslave of Jesus Christ." The love he spoke of could transform years into days, and transmute shame into honour, loss into gain, suffering into glory. Jacob would have understood that. Do you covet such love? Then consult Romans 5: 5.

PRAYER.—*Thou God of Love, all that happens to us comes from Thy plan or Thy permission, and even the harder things are the more acceptable when received from such loving hands.* AMEN.

"*. . . there wrestled a Man with him . . .*" (Gen. 32: 24)

WE miss the whole significance of this story if we imagine that Jacob began the struggle. No, it was this mysterious "Man" who started it. This was God Himself wrestling for Jacob's conversion. He had made his vows at Bethel, that night of the ladder, but they had been only human resolutions, and he did not keep them. He slipped back into being as bad a trickster as ever. Isn't that the sad history of many supposed conversions, where after-events have shown that the real regeneration had never taken place. It was only a human resolution with perhaps a little reformation, after all. They fell back into the old unregenerate ways, in accord with the vivid metaphor of 2 Peter 2: 22. But now at last came the mighty change. That night at Jabbok was Jacob's new birth night, if we may borrow the New Testament phrase. He never went back on that. So would God wrestle with every soul, but if a man will not yield, he can only perish. Let the stubborn procrastinator beware. "My Spirit shall not always strive with man" (Gen. 6: 3).

PRAYER.—*Thou God of all Patience, how many souls have cause for eternal gratitude that Thou dost not weary of them, but dost conquer them at last. Give me patience in dealing with souls.* AMEN.

"*. . . the sun rose upon him . . .*" (Gen. 32: 31)

A NEW day! Aye, but never had the sunrise looked so sweet, so bewitchingly beautiful, for everything was new for Jacob that morning after what had happened at the ford on that never-to-be-forgotten night before. He had a new name, "as a prince," even as we Christians are "made kings and priests" (Rev. 1: 6). He carried a new sign, the touch of God upon his thigh, even as we have the "seal" in our hearts (Eph. 4: 30). He was a new man, never to return to the old ways, even as we are made a "new creature" (2 Cor. 5: 17). He had a new master, self being now dethroned, and giving God place, even as now "ye are bought with a price" (1 Cor. 6: 19-20). Yes, indeed, everything was new for Jacob, as for us, when the sun rose on that first day of the new life in God.

> *Heaven above is softer blue,*
> *Earth around is sweeter green,*
> *Something lives in every hue,*
> *Christless eyes have never seen.*

Ah, what a sunrise; a new-born day to match a new-born soul!

PRAYER.—*We thank Thee, O God, that the Sun of Righteousness has risen for us with Healing in His Wings. May the glow of the sunrise irradiate all the day.* AMEN.

". . . a coat of many colours" (Gen. 37: 3)

I<small>T</small> is one of the queer vagaries of Biblical interpretation that we have fastened upon the colours, whereas it was not the shade but the shape that gave significance to the garments. The fact is that it was the coat of the birthright, and that's why the other brethren were so mad, and so touchy about the dreams. Joseph was but the youngest among them. Why should they all be passed over? They could not appreciate that he was the elder of Jacob's only two proper sons, and therefore entitled to it. We believers, "sons of God" by new birth, and "heirs according to promise," also have a coat of birthright, the spotless robe of His righteousness, in place of "all our righteousnesses," which are "as filthy rags." God help us to walk worthy of the coat we wear, and to keep ourselves "unspotted from the world."

P<small>RAYER</small>.—*Thou knowest, O Lord, how muddy is the road of life, but how glorious is the garment that we Christians wear, and how all-sufficient is Thy Grace to keep us clean and keen.* A<small>MEN</small>.

"And the Lord was with Joseph, and he was a prosperous man . . ."
(Gen. 39: 2)

I <small>LIKE</small> old John Wycliffe's translation here. "He was a luckie fellowe." So I should think, not because he had money or comfort or friends or prospects; of these he had none. But because "the Lord was with" him. That is the only kind of luck we Christians believe in; and there's no luck about that! It is a perfectly logical thing. He will not force Himself upon our company; He comes only by invitation. To have Him in our hearts, and on our side, what joy and power and victory and blessing this brings. Joseph's is one of the most thrillingly successful lives recorded in all history, and herein lay his secret. The Lord was with him. His brothers turned against him, his masters were against him, his circumstances were against him, but the Lord was with him. That's why he was such "a prosperous man." Luckie fellowe! And the grand thing is, He is willing to be "with" us, too. He only waits to be asked.

P<small>RAYER</small>.—*We thank Thee, O Lord, for this blissful possibility. Help us so to realise Thy presence and so to walk in the sunshine of Thy companionship that we too may enjoy such divine fortune.* A<small>MEN</small>.

JANUARY   **25**

"And his master saw that the Lord was with him . . ." (Gen. 39: 3)

IT was certainly true, as we saw yesterday, that the Lord was with Joseph, but I wonder how his master noticed it. Do you think it was something about the way he did his work; that he was straight and strenuous in his job, not working always with one eye on the clock? I shouldn't be surprised. After all, the Christian life, while it is vital and vocal, is also visual. If we have it, have Him, people should in some way be able to "see" it. Remember Acts 4: 13, "When they saw the boldness . . . they took knowledge of them that they had been with Jesus." The Christian schoolboy should so do his work that his teacher can see he is a Christian; the same with the Christian clerk in the office and with the Christian maid in the home and with the Christian hand in the factory. Let your master "see." Above all, let the Master see.

PRAYER.—*Lord, may I have Thy help that whatsoever my hand find to do, I may do it with my might as to the Lord, and not merely to man.* AMEN.

JANUARY   **26**

". . . Do not interpretations belong to God? . . ." (Gen. 40: 8)

JOSEPH got a great reputation for showing the meaning of dreams, but he said, "It is not in me." Daniel had the same gift, but note his confession, "There is a God in heaven that revealeth secrets" (Dan. 2: 28). That, too, was Joseph's acknowledgment. "Do not interpretations belong to God?" There are other riddles to be resolved besides dreams. We are quite persuaded that life is a rational thing, but why then is our experience so riddled with problems? Why does God allow war, evil, suffering? To be more personal, why has that sorrow, that disappointment, that loss come to you? What is the meaning of it all? Do you know God well enough to trust Him even in the dark? Be sure there is a meaning, a purpose; and if, for His own best reasons, God doesn't let us see the interpretation yet, remember that "what I do thou knowest not now, but thou shalt know hereafter" (John 13: 7). And "blessed are they that have not seen, and yet have believed" (John 20: 29).

PRAYER.—*Our Gracious God, we so readily trust the Mind that ever cares and the Hand that never makes a mistake, and we gladly await the Time when we shall understand.* AMEN.

". . . *a man in whom the Spirit of God is*" (Gen. 41: 38)

PHARAOH spoke better than he knew, for this is a New Testament conception. Certainly, by his understanding and advice here, Joseph displayed much of the manifold gift of the Spirit as outlined in Isaiah 11: 2, and the Egyptian monarch is to be congratulated on his recognition of the right "man" for the moment. It is a wonderful thing that every true believer is "a man in whom the Spirit of God is." He may not be consciously aware of the marvellous fact, any more than were those unsatisfactory Christians of 1 Corinthians 6: 19, who wrung from Paul the surprised comment, "What? Know ye not . . .?" They ought to have known it, and if they had known it and had acted accordingly, they never would have occupied such a low level of Christian attainment. However, the fact remains that every real Christian, of however poor a quality, has the Spirit in him. The reason for the poverty of his life is that the Spirit, though resident, is not president. With Him in control, let us like Joseph rise up and serve well our generation.

PRAYER.—*Heavenly Master, help us, when we complain that we can't, to remember that Thou canst. Through the indwelling Spirit fulfil Thy purpose for us, in us, through us.* AMEN.

". . . *How old art thou?*" (Gen. 47: 8)

AT 130, Jacob was a mere chicken compared with some of the old worthies of an earlier day, but Pharaoh was so struck with his appearance that he was moved to inquire his age. The old man's life had been so full of adventure, disappointment, anxiety and trouble that the years had probably set their mark upon him. But what a marvel we should hold a man who has reached such a tale of years. By the way, "How old art thou?" I mean now, in second birthdays. Asking a small boy once how old he was, I found him in a truculent mood, and all I got out of him was, "I ain't got any old." Is it like that with any of my readers spiritually? Haven't you got any old? Haven't you yet been born again? "Ye must be . . ." (John 3: 7). Isn't it time you were (John 1: 12)? Once born, twice die; twice born, once die, and not even that if the Lord come again in your lifetime.

PRAYER.—*Blessed be Thou, O Lord, who hast revealed the truth of the new birth through the operation of the Holy Spirit. Help all newborn people to show in their lives the splendour of their royal birth.* AMEN.

"The Angel which redeemed me from all evil . . ." (Gen. 48: 16)

THE happy fact of angel ministry is often seen in Genesis and else-where, but this one is spelled with a capital "A," and must be the One who is so often described as "the Angel of the Lord," the last two words printed, in the King James Version, in capital letters. It is now widely accepted that this Angel of Jehovah is none other than the Blessed One who came afterwards to be known on earth as the Lord Jesus. What a fascinating study to mark all those Old Testament appear-ances of His as "the angel" where "the Lord" follows in capitals. So this is the "Man" who wrestled with Jacob by Mahanaim, and there "redeemed" him "from all evil." The very same One who, praise His Name, has redeemed us from all iniquity by His precious blood. May He indeed "bless the lads," and the lasses, too!

PRAYER.—*And may I, dear Lord, help to bless the lads and lasses by leading them to come with their love and lives to their Redeemer.* AMEN.

". . . his hands were made strong by the hands of . . . God . . ."
(Gen. 49: 24)

A LITTLE child's hands holding the reins are made strong enough to drive that restive team by the over-covering hands of the father, who knows just how to handle them. A small boy's hands are made strong enough to lift that heavy hammer by the over-covering hands of the blacksmith, to whom it is child's play. Well, do you sometimes find yourself confronted with tasks that are beyond you; a burden per-haps too heavy for your limited strength, a team of circumstances liable to run away with you, since you scarce have skill or strength enough to handle the reins? Joseph had problems big enough to overwhelm him ever since he set foot in Egypt, a poor young friendless slave in an alien country. But how successfully his hands tackled and solved them all. And how so? His old father spoke truly, "His hands were made strong by the hands of the Mighty God." So ask that as your hand takes up your task, His hand may take yours, and do the task through yours. Thus, "O God, strengthen my hands" (Neh. 6: 9).

PRAYER.—*Thou Mighty God, blessed be the Hands of the Master wounded to save us, wide-spread to welcome us, wonder-working to undertake our life's tasks. We would put our hand in Thine.* AMEN.

"*. . . but God . . .*" (Gen. 50: 20)

WHAT a world of difference those two little words can introduce into a situation. No other two words in the dictionary can so transform a man, or a matter. They come over and over again in the Bible, and a study of their occurrences will demonstrate the truth of what I say. The world may do its worst, the devil may try his utmost, "but God" can overturn the whole evil conspiracy. The retrospect may be black, the aspect may be bleak, the prospect may be blank, "but God" can transfigure the whole scene. Joseph was "sold . . . but God" overruled it all, not only for his own advancement, but for the world's advantage. How difficult for the believer to be a pessimist, how reasonable for him to be an optimist, not because of his circumstances, his resources, his abilities, "but God." We began the month's meditations with God; so do we end with God.

PRAYER.—*Thou God of all the beginning and the ending in all Christian life, help us so to rest on Thee that we may ever see the wondrous change Thou dost bring to pass.* AMEN.

FEBRUARY

DRAUGHTS FROM AN UNFREQUENTED WELL

Ezekiel is a book largely neglected, not often read. Of course, it bristles with difficulties, yet it abounds in treasures. It is a deep well of truth, to which this month we shall come for a refreshing draught day by day.

FEBRUARY   1

"*. . . among the captives . . . I saw visions*" (Ezek. 1: 1)

So did John the Beloved on Patmos Isle, so did John Bunyan in Bedford Gaol, so too in spiritual manner have many of God's children. Perhaps you are one of the "captives" of ill-health, or of crippling circumstance; you feel hemmed in, restricted, frustrated. Well,

> *Two men looked out through prison bars,*
> *One saw mud, the other saw stars!*

It all depends on whether, when we look out, we look down or look up. Our prophet had "visions of God" in his place of captivity; and so if we look up He will show us visions of Himself, and of His purposes which will indeed refresh our spirit and quicken our service.

PRAYER.—*Lord, we thank Thee for eyes to see. Whatever our immediate circumstances, may we always endure as seeing Him who is invisible.* AMEN.

FEBRUARY   2

"*. . . they had the hands of a man under their wings . . .*" (Ezek. 1: 8)

WHAT a suggestive detail! There was no mistaking the fact that these glorious cherubim had wings, but it might easily have escaped notice that underneath the wings were hands, "the hands of a man." In spite of all the heavenly quality of these dazzling beings, there was beneath it all a human touch. We are vividly reminded of One who being the Son of God, was Son of Man. How we rejoice in those Hands, with their tenderness and skill and power so abundantly manifested when He was here in the flesh. Yet we have heard of Christians so filled with heavenly aspirations that they seemed to lose all human feelings. They appeared to forget that alongside of love to God was set love to neighbour. The more heavenly our character, the more earthly, in a right sense, should be our conduct. There is rare influence in a person of whom it may be said, "What a saint, but how human!" Wings, and hands!

PRAYER.—*Lord, keep us ever mindful of others around us, and keep us faithful in all our earthly contacts with them and with Thee.* AMEN.

"*. . . when . . . they let down their wings . . . there was a voice from the firmament that was over their heads . . .*" (Ezek. 1:24–25)

THESE "living creatures" are symbolical of God's messengers in every age. How busy they were, as we are all meant to be, flying hither and thither upon His errands. While there are some, idle Christians, who never use their wings, there are others, restless Christians, who never fold their wings. Both are great losers. Be sure that if we are too busy to be quiet with God, we are busier than He wants us to be, and sometimes He has, by allowing sickness, to force us to be quiet a while. Wingfolded time is not wasted time, for it is then that there comes "a voice" from above; some needed message of encouragement, of rebuke, of guidance, of challenge, always of love. There, and thus, shall damaged wings be repaired and readjusted, slothful wings be quickened and inspired with loving eagerness, and so outspread wings all speed forward once more on missions for Him.

PRAYER.—*Give us, we pray Thee, minds for communion with Thee, ears to hear Thy voice, lips to speak Thy messages, and so wings to be about Thy errands.* AMEN.

"*. . . I went in bitterness of spirit . . . but the hand of the Lord was strong upon me*" (Ezek. 3: 14)

WE may be quite sure that if we are depressed and oppressed by the condition of things around us, God Himself is no less burdened, and furthermore that He desires that something should be done about it. Nothing is easier than to settle down in dumb acquiescence, to adopt a craven, defeatist attitude, to go "in bitterness of spirit," giving no place and no chance to the prophet's "but!". The state of his world was evil, "but the hand of the Lord was strong." Evil may be strongly entrenched, and ever encroaching, but let us face it and fight it, not however with our own hands but with His strong hand. That mighty grasp and grip was on this prophet for this purpose, and it will be "upon me," and you, if we will in unflinching faith sally forth to His adventure. The best cure for "bitterness of spirit" is bigness of soul.

PRAYER.—*We recall, O Master, how Thou didst face the buffetings of this world with uttermost triumph. May we be so in Thy Hand that we shall never be under the circumstances but on top of them.* AMEN.

" . . . I sat where they sat . . ." (Ezek. 3: 15)

THERE had been begotten of God in the heart of Ezekiel a great love and longing for his people; a yearning comparable to Paul's in Romans 10: 1: "My heart's desire and prayer to God for Israel is that they might be saved." I wonder if we have an earnest passion for the salvation of people, even our own people, primarily those of our own family and then of all people. Well now, in order to work for them in understanding and sympathy, our prophet went and "sat where they sat," shared their life and experiences, got right down next to them. When the Saviour came down to rescue us from our sorry plight, He, for all His deity, lived and moved amongst men, not aloof but alongside. He, the pre-eminently Good Samaritan, "came where he was" to save the poor derelict. You can't exercise this kind of saving ministry from a distance. If we aim to be soul-winners, let us pray for a very tender, understanding sympathy.

PRAYER.—*May the Holy Spirit shed abroad in our hearts that love of God which is ever near to the needs of men.* AMEN.

" . . . ye shall know that I am the Lord" (Ezek. 6: 7)

WHEN we come across this phrase, we are perhaps inclined to pass it by without much notice until we find it again at 7: 27, and yet again and again and again, running like a refrain right through the book. Ye, or they, shall know that I am the Lord. Such knowledge is to be conveyed, and attained, through the happenings of circumstances, sometimes striking, sometimes ordinary, and also through observance of a fellow creature. This knowledge of Himself is what God is concerned to teach these people and us people through every possible channel. What a glorious privilege and happiness if, by our behaviour and demeanour, we are enabled to bring those who know us to a real knowledge of what His Lordship means in everyday life, remembering for our own part that if He is not Lord of all, He is not really Lord at all.

PRAYER.—*Lord, we pray that we who know so much about Thee may indeed be privileged to know Thee more and more and so to honour Thee.* AMEN.

FEBRUARY 7

". . . thus saith the Lord, . . . An end . . ." (Ezek. 7: 2)

IT is for our spiritual health that these draughts we take at our un-
frequented well should be not all of the same nature. Its tonic waters
are at times bitter to the taste to balance any possible overindulgence
in what is sweet to the taste. The Bible is the sole exception to James'
general rule (3: 11) that a fountain does not "send forth at the same
place sweet water and bitter." Today our text brings us the sharp reminder
that you can't play with sin, or trifle with God. He has borne the evil
ways of sinners with wondrous patience, He has for long withheld judgment, but enough! An "end" to all this! The stroke of his wrath and
judgment is about to fall. We are so accustomed to dwell upon His love
that we tend to overlook the sterner qualities of His holiness and justice.
Do not let His mercy blind you to His majesty. Have we, in anything,
been presuming upon His kindness? "An end" to that presumption,
lest the stroke fall!

PRAYER.—*Our Heavenly Father, keep us so careful of our beginnings, so
mindful of our ends, that through all our experience we may rejoice in
Thee, who art the Beginning and the End.* AMEN.

FEBRUARY 8

". . . the chambers of . . . imagery . . ." (Ezek. 8: 12)

THIS is indeed a terrible picture; the elders of Israel in some secret
room painting the walls with animals and then, after the manner of
heathen rites, bowing down and worshipping them. We all have
our secret room, our "chambers of imagery," whose walls are figured
with what our imagination has pencilled there. Outwardly orthodox
enough, inwardly we may be esteeming and worshipping unholy things
"portrayed" on the walls of memory. It is in the "chambers of imagery"
that the real man is found. D. L. Moody once said that "character is
what a man is in the dark." It is vain to think nobody knows, or to say,
"The Lord seeth us not," for He does see, He does know. If there is
no "hole in the wall" of our souls for our fellows to know what is going
on in "the chambers of imagery," God needs no hole to see through.
It is all open to His eye. Oh, then, to turn His promise in chapter 36: 25-26
into our prayer.

PRAYER.—*Wilt Thou, O Lord, be complete Master of our outermost and
innermost being, that all through we may be pleasing in Thy holy sight.*
AMEN.

" . . . *come not near any man upon whom is the mark* . . ." (Ezek. 9: 6)

FIVE angels have gone forth to execute judgment upon the people, but a previous angel has gone forth first to place a mark upon the foreheads of the godly remnant among the nation. They had not been party to the prevailing idolatry, they had been greatly troubled and saddened by it all. They had remained utterly loyal to their God. So now the slaughtering angels were bidden to spare them. They were "marked" men, as were the servants of God in Revelation 7: 1–3, and as were the firstborn in Israel's houses in Exodus 12: 13. Let me remember that it is also blessedly true that if I am a real believer, the Holy Spirit has

> *Set His mark upon me,*
> *Sealed me for His own.*

Sin's avenging judgment cannot come near "any man upon whom is the mark." So let us be at peace, let us enjoy full assurance, let us be praisefully grateful, let us live as "marked" men.

PRAYER.—*Lord, we thank Thee for the Holy Spirit's seal and that for us there is no condemnation. May His zeal also be upon us to bring others for the sealing.* AMEN.

" . . . *they went every one straight forward*" (Ezek. 10: 22)

WHAT a pattern in this are these creatures to all His creatures. Alas, we are not always as straightforward in our dealings as we might be. It is credibly reported among us that even we Christians and church members are not invariably as "straight" in our words and works as we should be; in our home life, our business life, our social life, even our church life. And are we as straightforward in our progress as the Master expects? That is, of course, the point of the text here. All too often we turn aside from the path of Christian duty, seeking our own gratification or ease with some of the unpleasant consequences of John Bunyan's Bypath Meadow. Or we turn back from the road, like the man at his Slough of Despond. Oh that, having got straight at the Cross, we might keep straight by His Spirit, and so "make straight" (Heb. 12: 13), lest we cause weaker souls to stray.

PRAYER.—*We mourn, O Lord, that so often we Christians, by our inconsistency, bring discredit upon the worthy Name wherewith we are called. Help us to do better.* AMEN.

"... *the manners of the heathen* ..." (Ezek. 11: 12)

A CERTAIN lecturer, being announced to speak on the manners and customs of a native tribe, summed up the matter by saying, "Manners none; customs beastly!" Shall I be lynched by the readers of these notes if I dare to record that as I move about among Christians I find not a few who unfortunately answer to the first part of my lecturer's description? They have "the manners of the heathen." The way some of us Christians behave toward our fellow church members and toward outsiders—in the shops, in the buses, in the world—is too sad for words. When you think of the exhortations of Scripture to such things as gentleness, selflessness, kindness, it really is surprising that worldlings are all too often better mannered than we are. An S.P.G.M., a Society for the Promotion of Good Manners, is in some quarters long overdue. Will you join? "Only let your (behaviour) be as it becometh the Gospel of Christ" (Phil. 1: 27). What peerless manners were His!

PRAYER.—*We thank Thee, Lord, that Thy word deals with homely as well as Heavenly things, and we pray Thee that Thou wilt give us grace to see to our manners, that we may be as He is in the world. AMEN.*

"... *I will be to them as a little sanctuary in the countries where they shall come*" (Ezek. 11: 16)

D O you not admire those clever little creatures, the water beetles, who have the wonderful gift of surrounding themselves with a bubble of air, and so are able to go and live awhile at the bottom of a pond? They take their enveloping atmosphere with them. So it was with those early Christians in Corinth, for example, who were able to exist in such a fetid moral atmosphere because they were "in Christ." He was their enveloping Atmosphere. So it was with Ezekiel's friends, who found sanctuary in God from the world's encroachments and enticements. So it shall be with any believer in the inimical surroundings of a godless workshop, office, foreign country, or even home, who shall find in his faithful God both a place of shelter and a fane of worship.

PRAYER.—*We thank Thee that we have a spiritual heredity in Thee, O Lord, and also a spiritual environment in Thy presence. May the blessings of both be our strength and joy. AMEN.*

"Though . . . Noah, Daniel and Job were in it . . ." (Ezek. 14: 14)

GOD has sometimes spared or blessed for the righteous' sake. He would have spared the cities of the plain "for ten's sake." He blessed the house of Potiphar for Joseph's sake. He saved a shipload for Paul's sake. But even if these three godly men were in this guilty city God would not spare it, so great was its wickedness. I suppose the three were mentioned as being conspicuous examples of obedience; Noah, the obedience of faith; Daniel, obedience under opposition; Job, obedience in suffering. But what especially intrigues me here is that Daniel was yet alive when Ezekiel was writing. He had been fourteen years in Babylon, and nearly ten in important posts, and the fame of his upright life had spread, so that God was able to include his name in such distinguished company. Truly, all the saints are not dead. There were great men in those days, Noah, Job and others. But so there are today, God's Daniels. Then and now, men of obedience. Are you one?

PRAYER.—*Thou, Lord, art our Governor. Help us so to live in Thy governance that we may be able to be the greatest influence for good that Thou canst make us.* AMEN.

". . . I have not done without cause all that I have done . . ." (Ezek. 14: 23)

GOD never does anything without a reason. Whether His active will or His repressive will or His permissive will, there is always an underlying cause, which if we could discover it would explain and justify everything. Why does God do this? Why doesn't He do that? Why does He allow the other? Well, He doesn't work by whim, and if for the nonce the reason is not apparent, let us not suppose that there is none. Rather, let faith rest upon the truth that infinite wisdom, infinite love, infinite holiness, infinite justice and infinite resource lie behind all His dealings. There are always conditions regulating His works of judgment, as in our present passage, on His works of blessing. Faith is a poor thing if it cannot trust in the dark the hand and heart of such a God as ours, whether we understand or not.

PRAYER.—*O Lord, help me to rest in Thine Omnipotence, Omniscience and Omnipresence, in all the circumstances and conditions of my life.* AMEN.

FEBRUARY 15

". . . thy beauty . . . was perfect through My comeliness, which I had put upon thee . . ." (Ezek. 16: 14)

Is there anything lovelier than this story of the Abandoned Child? It refers to Jerusalem, but it applies to every saved and born-again child of God. Passing by here the recital of that infant's blessings of life, health, food, clothing, growth and progress, each of which has its spiritual counterpart in the believer's experience, we stay to emphasize the gift of beauty, which was the very crown of all else. Is it not sadly true that some of us Christians, who have been blessed in so many things, are strangely lacking in this beauty of character? We are perhaps spiritually wise and strong and dependable, and even successful, but our behaviour has little beauty about it. May our prayer be, "Let the beauty of the Lord our God be upon us" (Ps. 90: 17), and may its answer be that the Holy Spirit put His own "comeliness" upon us, even within us.

PRAYER.—*Yes, Lord, may I grow more and more like Thee that my character may serve to bless many.* AMEN.

FEBRUARY 16

". . . a sign between Me and you . . ." (Ezek. 20: 20)

THE proper keeping of the Sabbath, or of the Lord's Day, may be regarded as a matter of plain duty, or as an opportunity for worship and service, or as a bit of practical wisdom, for even physically man does need a regular rest. When Sunday golf was under discussion, a Scottish greenskeeper said, "If the players do not want a rest the greens do!" But perhaps the most blessed way of regarding it is to recognize it as a "sign" between God and His own. The time is, I believe, fast approaching when to keep the Day will, even to the world, be the mark and token of our loyalty to Him. Anyhow, as the divinely given "sign," let us ever keep it as the Different Day, as the Lord's Day, not ours, as the Day of days for the Lord of lords.

PRAYER.—*The Lord be praised for all that earthly Sabbaths have meant to us, and for the Eternal Sabbath that lies beyond. May I be a different being for my observation of the different day.* AMEN.

FEBRUARY 17

". . . until He come whose right it is . . ." (Ezek. 21: 27)

THERE is a vacant throne on this earth which awaits the coming of its rightful Occupant, and to which all other and lesser thrones will be subservient. This is not just figurative language, but literal fact. The crown shall be taken off the heads of all rivals and placed upon that one Head that wore the crown of thorns to prepare the way for the crown of gold. Oh blessed Coronation Day! But meanwhile there is one little bit of this earth which each of us is responsible for, and in that bit there is a throne. This bit is you, and the throne is in your heart. Because He has created you, and more, because He has bought you with His blood, that throne is His by twofold right. Has He, or may He, come to occupy it? Blessed indeed is that life in which He has come to exercise that sway which is His by right.

PRAYER.—*May every heart prepare a Throne and every voice a Song for Thee.* AMEN.

FEBRUARY 18

". . . thy songs . . . cease . . ." (Ezek. 26: 13)

WHAT an arresting instance of fulfilled prophecy is the experience and eventual disappearance of this city of Tyre, of which these chapters speak. It is all very fascinating, but we can just now dwell only on one little point, "Thy songs . . . cease"; little, but large in significance. The truly godly and holy life is a singing life. The "songs of Zion" are in heart and voice; that is a thing noted in both Old and New Testaments. When singing stops, there is something wrong. Sinning and singing don't agree! The wickedness of Tyre effectually dammed the stream of song. What an uplift is the song to our own heart, "The joy of the Lord is your strength" (Neh. 8: 10). What an advertisement is it to others, "He hath put a new song in my mouth . . . many shall see it . . . and trust in the Lord" (Ps. 40: 3). See that nothing is allowed in your life which shall cause your song to cease.

PRAYER.—*We recall that "prisoners heard" a song Thy servants sang and were blessed. May my life even in uncompromising circumstances thus sing to bless.* AMEN.

". . . they hear thy words, but they will not do them . . ." (Ezek. 33: 31)

SUCH was to be the fate of the prophet's fervent utterances. Doubtless there was a good deal of vocal appreciation, for "with their mouth they show much love." "Amen," they would say; "Hallelujah," perhaps; "Hear, hear," if they had spoken English. "Loud applause" might even have punctuated the more eloquent periods. Yes, yes, but they didn't "do" anything. And the words of God always demand action, as well as attention and appreciation. "If ye know these things, happy are ye if ye do them," says the Master. The truth is something not merely patronized and applauded, but to be done. Note 1 John 1: 6, "We . . . do not the truth." Said a very late comer to someone just inside the church, "Is the sermon done?" "No," was the reply, "it has now got to be done." Verily, as the practical James says, "Be ye doers of the word, and not hearers only."

PRAYER.—*Lord, I have heard again this truth. Help me to do it and always to be a doer.* AMEN.

"I will feed My flock, and I will cause them to lie down . . ." (Ezek. 34: 15)

IF you see a sheep lying down, you may be quite sure that it is satisfied. It never lies down unless it is. So does the Good Shepherd undertake not only to give His sheep some food but to give them all the food they need. The under-shepherds may starve the flock, but the Chief Shepherd will satisfy the flock, if they follow His leading into what is here called "a fat pasture," the precious Word, the fattest of them all. How sad it is to see those who have become His sheep neglecting the Scriptures, the heavenly food that satisfies all needs of the soul, and so becoming undernourished and delicate sheep, unable to stand up to the winds of circumstance, or to the attacks of the enemy wolves that are on the prowl to spoil the flock. The reason for the thin sheep is the neglect of the fat pasture.

PRAYER.—*Blessed Lord, who hast caused all holy Scripture to be written for our learning, grant that we may in suchwise hear them, read, mark, learn and inwardly digest them . . .* AMEN.

"*. . . there shall be showers of blessing*" (Ezek. 34: 26)

YES, indeed there "shall be," in that season of millennial blessedness of which the passage speaks, but why not now? Yes, indeed there "shall be" for the ancient people to whom the passage refers; but why not for us, the people of God? I believe that on God's side there is no reason at all. I believe that, in Malachi's figure (3: 10), He is only waiting to "open the windows," and that as soon as ever we fulfil His condition He will throw wide the casement and cause the flood of blessing to descend in such profusion that we shall not be able to contain it ourselves, we shall just have to overflow it to others. The condition? "All the tithes," a full, complete, joyous surrender. Oh, the sadness that some of us are content with something so far less than those "showers"; unwilling to pay the price, we are satisfied with but drops and trickles.

PRAYER.—*Lord, beget in me here by Thy Spirit a great appetite for all, that Thou canst bestow.* AMEN.

"*. . . I am for you . . .*" (Ezek. 36: 9)

IN the course of our Christian life and service, we often find that so many things are against us. Some of us may have re-echoed old Jacob's despairing cry, "All these things are against me." Certainly the people of this passage had plenty against them. Yet, when you have put down all those things on what you might be tempted to regard as the wrong side of the account, there is one item for the other side which would put the account right, giving you a fine balance in hand. "All these things are against me"; well, but "I am for you." So run the debit and credit sides of the account of Ezekiel's people, and of many other people; but so much is included under that one head of the assets, that all liabilities are adequately covered. And one may say, with Romans 8: 28, "We know that all things work together for good to them that love God." Are you one of these latter? Then, "I am for you."

PRAYER.—*We thank Thee, O God, that we "know" that all things work together for good to the godly. Whether we understand it, or think it or feel it, we "know" it.* AMEN.

FEBRUARY 23

"*. . . I . . . will do better unto you than at your beginnings*" (Ezek. 36:11)

THE promise refers to the land which, whatever people think or rulers plan, is bound to become again the house of Israel, for God purposed it so. It will be fascinating to watch as history unfolds, how He brings it about, for come to pass it certainly will. But our text is not only an historical allusion, it is also a spiritual illustration of God's dealings with His own. He always plans to do better for us than at the beginning. If we be conscious of a dimming of the brightness of our first Christian experience, if love grow a little bit cold, if we wistfully inquire, "Where is the blessedness I knew when first I saw the Lord?", we may be certain that we are falling short of His purpose for us. It is all to be "better . . . than at your beginnings." Or, as Proverbs 4: 18 has it, "The path of the just is as the shining light, that shineth more and more unto the perfect day."

PRAYER.—*What cause we have to thank Thee, Lord, for the "more and more" of Thy purpose and provisions. Help us to live the "more than conquerors" life.* AMEN.

FEBRUARY 24

"*. . . I the Lord build the ruined . . .*" (Ezek. 36: 36)

MULTITUDES of people in war devastated areas know all about ruined places. But you will notice the word "places," being italicized in the King James Version, is not actually there in the original. The translators were doubtless right in assuming that was what the passage was intended to convey, yet the absence of the noun leaves the way open to include any sort of ruin. Do you suffer from ruined prospects; home gone, business gone, loved ones gone, everything gone, hope gone? Will you let Him plan your future prospects? And ruined souls, how ruinous is the power of sin, and how sadly we find poor, wretched creatures wallowing in the very gutter of wickedness. If only they would turn, and trust the delivering power of the Saviour! Our ruined lives; has anyone made a mess of his life, years spent but nothing to show for it? Let him but bring it to Him who will "restore . . . the years that the locust hath eaten," and so convince even the heathen that He can build up the ruined.

PRAYER.—*Keep us ever mindful, O Lord, that what we have ruined Thou mayest redeem, not for our blessing only, but for Thine own great glory.* AMEN.

"And I will lay sinews upon you . . ." (Ezek. 37: 6)

Is that not what some of us Christians badly need? Like those once dead bones, we have been born again, and the Breath of God, the Holy Spirit, is in us, yet there seems to be so little vitality or virility about us. There is but small evidence of moral muscle, or spiritual sinew. The atmosphere of the world is vitiating and we must needs be strong to stand up to it. The task envisaged for us is heavy, and we must needs be strong to tackle it. The enemy up against us is subtle and mighty, and we must needs be strong to overcome him. The present purpose of God for our lives is magnificent and enthralling, and we must needs be strong to fulfil it. "They stood up upon their feet, an exceeding great army." That's it; an army on its feet, ready for marching orders. Even more, an army on its toes, eager to be off!

PRAYER.—*Lord, we pray for more sinewy Christians devoted to Thy cause, eager to capture souls for Thee and to plant Thy flag in other lives.* AMEN.

". . . still upward . . . still upward . . . still upward . . . from the lowest . . . to the highest . . ." (Ezek. 41: 7)

It is a description of part of the decorative architecture of Ezekiel's temple, but we may surely find in it a typical application to the experience of those whom Paul speaks of as "the temple of God" (1 Cor. 3: 16). Starting from the "lowest," where first we began, we are to mount ever higher, being never content to remain at the lower. When we get in the Christian life, we are expected to get on, which means to get up. Ever the call comes to the heights of knowledge, how often Paul speaks of them; and to the heights of victory, "more than conquerors through Him"; and to the heights of service, the bond-slavery of Jesus Christ; and to the heights of fellowship, the blessed communion and intimacy with Himself which He so graciously allows. "Still upward" is the believer's motto. Not easy is the path, and many voices call us to turn back, but "Excelsior!"

PRAYER.—*Lord, save us from becoming creeping, crawling, cringing Christians, but make us ever to be climbing up and up.* AMEN.

"... *waters* ... *to the ankles* ... *to the knees* ... *to the loins* ...
to swim in ..." (Ezek. 47: 3–5)

HERE is a great river which whatever be its literal significance is most certainly a great spiritual type. Is it a picture of the river of salvation, ever flowing full and free; or the river of grace, "which is full of water"; or the river of life, bringing health and fruit in its wake; or the river of the Spirit, flowing water being ever a type of Him in Scripture? Whichever we select, it is anyhow a sacred symbol of God's blessing coming from the sanctuary of the temple, from the altar of the sacrifice, emanating from His loving heart. In fact, it flows fuller all the way, but in experience we Christians all too often are content with the shallows. Every quarter of a mile or so, the water deepens, reaching from ankles, to knees, to loins, to swim in. In spiritual counterpart, where are we in this great river; still paddling, or wading perhaps, or swimming in its lovely depths?

PRAYER.—*Lord, teach me how to swim and lure me to the depths wherein I can launch out, whether downstream or upstream.* AMEN.

"... *by the river* ... *shall grow all trees*" (Ezek. 47: 12)

SINCE the river is a picture of God's grace, God's life, God's Spirit, we are not surprised at the enormous influence for good; for example, its effect upon the fish in its waters and upon the trees on its banks. By the way, believers are likened to trees in the Bible—"he shall be like a tree planted by the waters" (Ps. 1: 3); "that they might be called trees of righteousness, the planting of the Lord" (Isa. 61: 3). Are we that sort of trees? Because of the life-giving waters, maintaining a freshness of spiritual experience, a beauty of character, a shade for others from winds and heats of circumstance; a healing influence ("medicine," verse 12; Rev. 22: 2) for stricken souls; a fruitful life that shall sustain others ("meat"). All this shall be "that He might be glorified".

PRAYER.—*Thou Holy God, make all the godly holy, and by the Holy Spirit do this for me to Thy praise.* AMEN.

". . . *the name of the city . . . shall be, The Lord is there*" (Ezek. 48: 35)

EVERY city has a name. In this case it is dictated by its outstanding feature. The most important characteristic of the place is not its dimensions, nor its dwellings, nor its denizens, but the fact that the Lord is there. So its name, Jehovah-Shammah, is derived. After all, that, if it is the fact, is the pre-eminent thing about any life, and in His presence lies all our hope of peace, of protection, of provision. Is it, then, true of your city, a City of Mansoul, that its real name is "The Lord is there"? We cannot exaggerate the importance of our having His residence within us, but let it never be forgotten that if we are to enjoy the wondrous benefits of His presence, He must be in every sense in full charge and control of the city. Then what a clean city it will be, what a prosperous city, what a happy city, what an honourable city; "Christ in you the hope of glory" (Col. 1: 27).

PRAYER.—*Thou Prince Emmanuel, how great a City of Mansoul my life should be, since Thou art there to take control.* AMEN.

MARCH

IDYLLS OF THE KING

The four Gospels give us four presentments of our Lord Jesus, and the first, by its especial emphasis on sovereignty, and on the kingdom, is a revelation of His kingly quality and station. Let us this month browse in this royal demesne.

". . . *born King* . . ." (Matt. 2: 2)

YES, He is a "born King." It is natural to Him to reign. Luke 2: 11 says that He is a "born . . . Saviour." It is natural to Him to save. He is, if we may put it so, every inch of Him a King, every inch of Him a Saviour. It is in this latter relationship that we must first come to know Him. This is the reason for His very Name (1: 21). This being satisfactorily settled, the question then arises, "Where is He . . .", in respect of our hearts and lives? Is He but only over the threshold, or is He truly on the throne?

PRAYER.—*May Thy Kingship be a constant spur to me to Christian adventure, to worthy living and to utter loyalty.* AMEN.

". . . *Follow Me, and I will make you fishers of men*" (Matt. 4: 19)

BETTER catch souls than soles, and Peter and Andrew, two members of the famous firm of fishmongers, Messrs. Zebedee, Sons and Partners, are here bidden forsake the latter form of angling for the former. Who that is a true believer does not long to be a soulwinner? Many a Christian has laboured to make himself one. Let him go on reading his books and learning his texts, but let him first and foremost get hold of this: "I will make you . . ." That is better than trying to make himself one. "Follow Me" is the all-embracing secret. The word for "follow" means "come behind." A prime rule of fishing is to keep yourself out of sight, but if the light be behind me, my shadow is cast. So let the Light be in front, and you "come behind" Him. As we obey Him day by day, step by step, point by point, we shall get our success in the Royal Fishing Rights. Oh, to come home with a great haul!

PRAYER.—*Thou Great Fisher of Men, lead me to go where the fish are, teach me to bait my line and give me the joy of many a catch.* AMEN.

MARCH 3

"Ye are the salt of the earth . . . the light of the world . . ." (Matt. 5: 13, 14)

LET us ponder the familiar words. When a person becomes a Christian he is not removed from this sphere, but is left here to fulfil a noble function. The world is subject to moral corruption and the believer is to act here as "salt." The world is enwrapped in spiritual darkness, and the believer is to act here as "light." In that bit of the world in which we find ourselves, we are to help keep it right and bright. There is a threefold activity to that end, which is open to all Christians of every sort and size. There is the ministry of prayer, which we can all exercise, whether in other ways gifted or not. There is the ministry of example; the evidence and influence of a godly life is of great effect. There is the ministry of testimony; we can't all preach, but we can all, if we will, say what He is to us.

PRAYER.—*Thou, O Christ, who art the Light of the World, help us that with nothing between we may so reflect Thee as to be in our measure the light of the world.* AMEN.

MARCH 4

". . . first be reconciled to thy brother . . ." (Matt. 5: 24)

THAT raises the whole question of restitution. If we have done some wrong to our brother that can be put right, we are expected so to do. God is only too ready to pardon, but the reality of our repentance towards Him must be demonstrated by our restitution to him whom we have injured. Debts must be paid, quarrels and grudges must cease ("as much as lieth in you," Rom. 12: 18), sin must be acknowledged and, so far as may be, repaired. The reason why I have strayed to note this text for today is that many Christians are held up on account of this very thing. They long to enter into fulness of blessing, but they never get it because this must "first" be done. They never seem to grow in the Christian life. They remain stunted in stature because this must "first" be done. Is this holding you up, my reader?

PRAYER.—*Lord, I pray that to this end I may have all-sufficient courage, all-embracing tact, and all possible success.* AMEN.

"Be ye therefore perfect . . ." (Matt. 5: 48)

W HAT a perfect child, we say; or, what a perfect specimen of young manhood; or, what a perfect old dear. This is not final perfection, but stage perfection; each perfect for his stage and station. As God is perfect "Father in heaven," so be you the perfect son to Him, at each age and stage of your Christian life and experience, whether in the language of John's first epistle as "little children," or as "young men," or as "fathers" in spiritual growth. A1, 100 per cent, do we make the grade as we take the gradient? Let us test ourselves by such a standard as the "love, joy, peace, longsuffering, gentleness, goodness, faith, meekness, temperance" of Galatians 5: 22–23. That is Christian perfection, against which "no law" can find cause to prosecute, and the secret of which is that it is "the fruit of the Spirit." Perfection of character depends on the Person in control.

PRAYER.—*Lord, may I be content with nothing less than the best—Thy best, that I may in all things give Thee pleasure.* AMEN.

". . . use not vain repetitions . . ." (Matt. 6: 7)

M ARK well that this is no forbidding of repetitions as such. The Master indeed goes on to give a form of words which is to be employed when we pray, and He Himself, in one of the deepest and darkest moments of His own human experience, offered a repeated prayer, "saying the same words" (26: 44). It is the uttering of the same thing over and over again, just as a formality, as a matter of routine, as an irksome habit, which makes the repetitions "vain." Let us beware of all such unreality and insincerity in our prayers. It is a fault all too easy to slip into. When the King graciously grants us audience, let us take care that our petitions come not merely off the printed page, but out of the earnest heart. When there is heart, there is hearing.

PRAYER.—*Lord, teach me ever more and more this and every secret of effectual, prevailing prayer, seeking that Thy will be done in earth as it is in Heaven.* AMEN.

"Thy kingdom come . . ." (Matt. 6: 10)

THE kingdom is in the universal sense in abeyance, though in the individual sense it can even now be a very real thing. Well, here is a guide for our prayers, that while we plead for the former, we ask, too, for the latter; that in our world, our country, our town, our office, our circle, our home, hearts may offer Him the crown. Here also is a cause for our gifts. What better object for the dedication of our gifts of money and gifts of character could there be than this grand project of seeking a throne for Him in others' lives. And it is an adventure for our lives. If Jesus be King in our hearts, we are thereby committed to the task of extending His Kingdom. By what we do and what we say and what we are, we contribute to the answering of our own prayer. What a glorious adventure for any life, to go forth to plant His flag in other lives.

PRAYER.—*Thou Universal Sovereign, make me ever a dutiful subject, a devoted soldier and a dedicated servant of Thy Kingdom.* AMEN.

". . . Why are ye fearful . . . ?" (Matt. 8: 26)

BUT there was a tempest raging! And the mountainous waves were breaking over the boat. And it looked as if the little craft could not possibly weather the storm. Yes, I know, but the King was on board, and He marvelled that these subjects of His were afraid of anything. He proceeded to show that "the winds and the sea" were His subjects too, and stilled them to a "great calm." But He quite evidently expected an inward great calm in spite of the outward great storm. The plain fact is that our outward circumstances, the storms of life, are subject to His control, and if He allows the tempest to arise, He is able to keep the ship in safety and on her destined course. Even if the boat should flounder, it will not founder. So after John Newton we sing,

> *Begone unbelief . . .*
> *With Christ in the vessel,*
> *I smile at the storm.*

There is to be peace within even when there is little without.

PRAYER.—*Lord, when Thou art in the ship, wilt Thou be in control of the ship, bringing us to our desired haven.* AMEN.

"Pray ye therefore . . ." (Matt. 9: 38)

THAT would be the Master's recipe for all difficulties and perplexities. Perhaps some may find it a little surprising in its present context. It touches the state of things in the mission field. On the one hand opportunities are great, enquirers are many, doors are open, "the harvest truly is plenteous." On the other hand, there are not nearly enough workers, "the labourers are few." What is to be done to make up the shortage? Why, let us organize missionary meetings, distribute missionary literature, get out missionary boxes. Yes, all very good; but the Master's injunction is, "Pray ye therefore." That is the primary and always the principal source of missionary recruits. Are we all faithful in this prayer ministry for the missionary fields at home and abroad? Do you pray with a map in front of you? Of course, if we prayed more, we might begin to feel that He was wanting to "send forth" us, as part answer of our own prayers.

PRAYER.—*Lord, lay upon my heart a greater burden for other lands and other people. Help me by every means, but especially by this chief means, to do my part for Thee and for them.* AMEN.

". . . freely ye have received, freely give" (Matt. 10: 8)

THERE is no question about the first part of that text. The magnificence and munificence of His royal bounty is the continual wonder of our deeply grateful souls. What He bestows is always after the superlative degree: "abundantly pardon," "eternal life," "perfect peace," "more than conquerors," "fulness of joy." Such is the King's side of the matter, but what of ours? "Freely give." What we receive enjoins us to give, encourages us to give, and enables us to give. Unhappy is the prospect of the Christian who has ceased to "give out" to others. Stand at the northern end of the Dead Sea. As you watch Jordan's turbulent waters rushing in you say, "Freely ye have received." Why, then, a Dead Sea? Only because it does not "freely give," it has no outlet. That is why there are some dead Christians. If we don't give out, we shall soon give out!

PRAYER.—*Truly, O God, we ought to remember the words of the Lord Jesus when He said "'Tis more blessed to give than to receive."* AMEN.

"Take My yoke upon you, and learn of Me . . ." (Matt. 11: 29)

WHEN a young student entered the school of a Rabbi, he was said to take upon him the Rabbi's yoke. That, I think, is what the Master is here referring to; not the oxen's yoke, but the rabbi's yoke. And this opinion seems to be endorsed by His subsequent words, "And learn of Me." What a royal school is this, and how highly privileged are they who are "yoked" to His direction and discipline. What apt, and assiduous pupils we should be who have the chance to profit by the "light" and "easy" burden of His scholarship! To sit at His feet is to imbibe rich fare indeed; to benefit from His words and His example is responsibility indeed. Meeting a small boy in the street on his way home from school I asked, "What have you learned today?" May I put the same question to you now?

PRAYER.—*Thou Greatest of the Teachers of men, give to me the grace of humility and of teachableness, that I may become an apt and profitable scholar and a worthy exemplar of Thy teaching.* AMEN.

". . . is a man better than a sheep? . . ." (Matt. 12: 12)

THERE are quarters in which horses are accounted more valuable than men, and greyhounds more important. There are people who assign Children's Homes second place to Cats' Homes. Indeed, pigs were more thought of than people in Matthew 8: 30-34. But seriously, how shall we answer our text's question? Well, man is a good deal of a sheep. "All we, like sheep, have gone astray" (Isa. 53: 6). But man is a good deal more than a sheep: physically ahead and intellectually apart and spiritually alone. Yet, man is a good deal in need of a shepherd, as David knew when he wrote Psalm 23 and as our Lord knew when He uttered John 10, offering us salvation and shelter and sustenance. A little child, put up to recite that Shepherd Psalm, became suddenly shy and nervous and could get no further than the first five words. She tried again, but the next words wouldn't come, though she knew what the sense was. At last, as she ran off the platform in fright, she said, "The Lord is my shepherd; that's all I want!" Yes, indeed.

PRAYER.—*Thou Great Shepherd of the Sheep, may I rest in the joys of protection from the enemy, of provision for my needs and progression in the Way.* AMEN.

". . . the good seed are the children of the Kingdom . . ."
(Matt. 13: 38)

W HAT a wealth of symbolism is stored up in this figure of the Christian! In the previous parable, he sows the seed; in this one, he is the seed. It is no easy thing to be a seed. It has to encounter underneath the cold damp weight of earth and the attacks of unfriendly insects. And above ground it must meet the winds and the rains and the frosts. But it has all sorts of things to help it grow, even as we Christians, faced with much difficulty, are aided by all the means of grace. Oh then, that for the Royal Gardener's (John 20: 15) delight and glory, we might produce and display the flower of a beautiful character, the fragrance of a sweet influence, the food of a helpful life, the fruit of a successful service. To this end there must be utter sacrifice of self. The seed must "fall into the ground and die" (John 12: 24).

PRAYER.—*Lord, how I depend upon my Divine Husbandman. As the seed lies held of earth for its nurture, so may my faith lie held of Thee for abundant harvest.* AMEN.

". . . Lord, save me" (Matt. 14: 30)

T HERE is something telegrammic about that, isn't there? Certainly Peter, "beginning to sink" as he was, could not have knelt down on those "boisterous" waves and made a long prayer. All he could do was to send off a sky telegram. And be it noted that the reply was received "immediately." I wonder if you are a regular user of sky wires? It is a fine habit to acquire. Whatever may be our surroundings at a given moment, when fear arises or temptation or sudden emergency, we can get into instant communication with God and "obtain . . . grace to help in time of need" (Heb. 4: 16). Without kneeling down, without even shutting eyes or moving lips, the thought is winged heavenward and the response is winged back usward. Happy the believer who has such happy recourse to the Court of the Royal House.

PRAYER.—*Lord, I thank Thee that Thou knowest my circumstances and my instant needs, and art never surprised to receive my telegrams, and never failest to return a speedy answer.* AMEN.

MARCH 15

" . . . *O thou of little faith . . .*" " . . . *O woman, great is thy faith . . .*"
(Matt. 14: 31, 15: 28)

WHAT sort of a faith is ours? Let us not dwell on the "little faith" man. There are far too many of him about; there are others in 16: 8. Let us rather consider the "great faith" woman. There are all too few of her, and we would greatly delight to join her company. In seeking the great boon for her little girl, what obstacles her faith had to surmount. That is what made it so great. She was a foreigner, and normally in those days of antagonisms, she would not dream of getting anything out of a Jew. Then, she found the disciples so unfriendly: "Send her away." And, worst of all, the Master Himself just ignored her: "He answered her not a word." Yet her faith broke through all these barriers to secure the blessing as well as the Master's praise. Is our faith big enough to trust God, even when we can't understand, or when He seems to make no response, or when the matter appears well nigh impossible?

PRAYER.—*Our Heavenly Father, we thank Thee that the faith required for personal salvation needs but little faith, but how abundant is the blessing open to ever greater faith, for we have such a Mighty and Loving God to trust in.* AMEN.

MARCH 16

" . . . *But whom say ye that I am?*" (Matt. 16: 15)

IT is very interesting to hear what people said about the Lord Jesus, particularly so as different folks had such variant, almost contrary, opinions of His personality as to think that either He was Elijah or else Jeremiah. Two entirely opposite natures, yet Christ was reminiscent of both! How many-sided was the Son of God who was made, not a man merely, but Man, the complete Representative of all men, and of each man. However, what others say about Him is not enough; we have each to say what we think, "but whom say ye . . .". Peter, taught of God, gave an answer that greatly gladdened the Saviour's heart. "But whom say ye," my reader? How He would rejoice if He heard you, unafraid and unashamedly, in the presence of all say of Him with Mary, "My Saviour" (Luke 1: 47), and with Thomas, "My Lord and my God" (John 20: 28).

PRAYER.—*My Master, lead me on to an increasingly intimate apprehension of Thyself, that by Thine Infinite Grace I may know Thee as a personal friend and companion along the road.* AMEN.

"*. . . they came down . . .*" (Matt. 17: 9)

Iᴛ had been a grand time up on the Transfiguration Mount; and Peter was all for staying there. "Let us make here three tabernacles." Don't you sometimes wish that you could stay up on the mountain top after a great Sunday, or a great Conference, or any great spiritual experience? But you can't; you must get down to Monday's humdrum, to the ordinary ways of everyday life. Watch those three as "they came down." Behind them, all the wondrous experiences of the Vision and the Voice. What an inspiration! Before them, all the needs and anxieties of father and boy, of beaten disciples and critics. What a problem! Ah, but beside them, for there were not three only descending, "the Form of the Fourth" (Dan. 3: 25) was with them. He came down with them to help them in their contact with the work-a-day world. The mountain is meant to prepare us for the valley. We must come down, but we do not come alone.

Pʀᴀʏᴇʀ.—*Lord, may I ever be ready to do Thy work in the ordinary ways of life and to realize Thy presence for the doing of it, that the vision may irradiate the valley.* Aᴍᴇɴ.

"*. . . little ones which believe in Me . . .*" (Matt. 18: 6)

Tʜɪs eighteenth chapter is verily the Children's Charter. By the way, do you believe in child conversion? If not, test any gathering of Christian workers to see how many came to the Saviour as children. You will have the surprise of your life! Anyhow, I personally can have no doubt about it, for I was myself "saved" when I was a boy of fourteen. In any case, the matter is settled for us, because the Saviour here Himself states that even "little ones" can believe on Him. The King has many little loyal subjects in His realm. Carry on, then, all you Sunday School teachers, and add to their number. Yours may not be an easy task, but it is a highly privileged one, and a highly strategic one in the interests of the Kingdom. And let us all be carefully and prayerfully on our guard that we do not "offend" any one of them, lest we put, or prove, a stumbling block in their way.

Pʀᴀʏᴇʀ.—*We seek from Thee, the children's Friend and Saviour, Thy love for little people, that we may be privileged to teach them for good and for God.* Aᴍᴇɴ.

"*. . . Why stand ye here all the day idle?*" (Matt. 20: 6)

IN the spiritual sphere, as in the physical, there is a close connection between idleness and illness. And besides, the New Testament has no conception of an idle Christian. It would regard that as a contradiction in terms. Nevertheless, there are not a few lazy believers about. I am afraid the excuse of the men in the parable was not quite honest. The fact is when the "householder" went into the market place "to hire labourers" in the early morning, and again at the third, sixth and ninth hour, these eleventh-hour people were just not there. Perhaps they got up late and dawdled over the meal and lounged about the house. But they certainly need not have been "all the day idle." Neither need any of us. There's plenty of work in the King's Vineyard, and if any of us has done nothing yet in His service, let us, even at this "eleventh hour," begin, and perchance of His grace, the King's "penny" shall be ours.

PRAYER.—*We thank Thee, O God, for the exceeding privilege of being labourers, not only for Thee, but together with Thee, for Thou shalt choose what and where our work shall be, and what our joyous reward.* AMEN.

"*. . . bring them unto Me*" (Matt. 21: 2)

ONLY a couple of donkeys, but because they were brought to Jesus, they were of great service to Him and became forever famous. If they had not been "brought," you would never have heard of them. You are not a big donkey, nor a little one, but I am going here to presume that at some time, someone brought you to Jesus. Well then, are you now allowing Him to "ride" you, which is to tide you over every obstacle, and to guide you to share in His kingly triumph? And now He says of those ordinary days of yours, "Bring them unto Me," and of those ordinary gifts of yours, "Bring them unto Me," and of those ordinary words of yours, "Bring them unto Me." I keep saying "ordinary" because those donkeys were ordinary enough. It only shows what He can do with ordinary things, and with ordinary people, if they are brought to Him and yielded to the royal control.

PRAYER.—*Lord, we acknowledge with such gratitude, and even hope, that Thou canst do so much with so little. Thou didst feast five thousand with five little loaves, canst Thou not then use even us, who put ourselves in Thy Hands.* AMEN.

MARCH 21

"*. . . a man which had not on a wedding garment*" (Matt. 22: 11)

THE Royal Banquet, the Gospel feast, is open to all who have the wedding garment. How came this man to imagine that he could dispense with the proper dress clothes? Owing to certain reasons, the invitation was extended to "both bad and good," referring I suppose to financial status, poor and rich; but applying also to moral condition. Was this man rich, and did he think his clothes good enough as they were? Was he poor and unable to afford the garment? It matters not, for the garment was not to be bought but was offered free upon entrance to poor and rich alike, but it was obligatory upon all. Some think they are good enough as they are, but only the spotless robe of righteousness is really good enough. Let us not think that when the King comes in to see the guests we shall be acceptable without it. Men may abound in excuses now, but they will be "speechless" at His challenge, if unprepared then.

PRAYER.—*Lord, take from me all idea that I am good enough, and lead me to see that only Thy righteousness is covering enough to sit at Thy board.* AMEN.

MARCH 22

"*. . . how often would I . . . and ye would not!*" (Matt. 23: 37)

HERE we see man's refusal of God's proposal. God offered to make them His children and to take them under His wing, but they actually refused such high and wondrous privilege. Then we have man's obstinacy against God's persistency. "How often" did He come, and in such different ways, but all to no purpose. One is reminded of Revelation 3: 20, where the Greek is, so poignantly, "Behold, I keep on standing at the door, and I keep on knocking . . ." But no, they would not have Him. All because of man's blindness to God's kindness. As if He planned to rob them of any good or blessing, overlooking that the very hand that knocked was scarred with wounds gotten in procuring their highest good, and deepest blessing. I wonder if by any chance there is some blessing that He has for long been pressing upon our acceptance, and that we will not take from His hands, because we shrink from the cost or because we are preoccupied with and satisfied with lesser and lower things. "Ye would not"; how sad and how stupid!

PRAYER.—*May I ever be, O Lord, so ready to welcome each offer of Thine without any doubt or delay, that fulness of blessing may be mine for Thy service.* AMEN.

MARCH 23

> *". . . Tell us when . . . and what . . ."* (Matt. 24: 3)

SO by these queries is raised the matter of the King's return, and there follow upon these, the arresting statements of this tremendous chapter, some of it having primary and partial fulfilment in the devastating experiences of the Fall of Jerusalem, but awaiting full and final accomplishment in the Day of Christ. Of course we cannot in this short note explain or expound the passage, but have you noticed that while the Master, in some detail, tells them "What," He doesn't tell them "When." The truth is that in dealing with His Second Coming, He is always occupied with facts, never with dates; and they do His cause disservice who go date-hunting. Verse 36 tells us that no one but the Father knows "When." Any day may be the Day. Let us be ever on the *qui vive*. Such is the reason for the Master's deliberate disregard of one part of His disciples' enquiry. Keep on the lookout: "live . . . looking" (Tit. 2: 12–13).

PRAYER.—*Our Gracious Lord, we thank Thee that although Thou hast not given us a calendar of Thy coming, Thou hast given us a programme. May the joys and glories of the programme ever make our hearts to glow with happy expectancy. Make us and keep us ready for The Day.* AMEN.

MARCH 24

> *". . . opportunity to betray Him"* (Matt. 26: 16)

JUDAS, having struck his bad bargain, began to scheme and plot that he might deliver Christ into the chief priests' hands. That, I believe, was the reason for all the secrecy surrounding the place where the Passover was to be eaten. The Lord was anxious to have that last Feast and Fellowship with His disciples, which, if he had known, the traitor would have broken into with the arresting party, as happened later in Gethsemane. But you and I have not to seek opportunities to betray Him. Every day at business, every social contact, every occasion of recreation, every home activity, bristles with circumstances which, if we are not on our guard, will lead us by the way we speak, or the way we behave, to deny Him. It is not that, as Judas, we plan to do it. The enemy gets us off guard, that's all. But, thank God, every opportunity to betray is also an opportunity to be true.

PRAYER.—*O Thou who art so faithful to us, may we on our part ever be faithful to Thee, may no cowardly thought, no difficult situation, cause us to depart from uttermost fidelity and loyalty.* AMEN.

". . . could ye not watch with Me . . . ?" (Matt. 26: 40)

I THINK the emphasis is on that "ye," as if to say, "Could you, Peter, not watch with Me, you, after all your boasts and promises? But a brief while ago you were professing such devotion, and now you have already failed Me!" There is something deeply moving in the Master's craving for the disciples' companionship in that Night Watch. How intensely human it shows Him to be! Suppose He were to say that "ye" to you, perhaps about the Morning Watch. You promised to give that early morning time to Him. You would spend it in prayer and in the study of the Word. It was going to make all the difference to the quality of your Christian character and the quality of your Christian service. And, besides, you did so long for such fellowship with Him. You meant every word of it, as Peter did; but, like him, you have failed your Lord. Well, why not begin again? And remember that the secret of getting up in the morning is going to bed at night.

PRAYER.—*Lord, Thy watchfulness over us has ever been our deep delight, yet Thou dost even ask of us to watch with Thee in fellowship. May we learn the blessedness and the secret of keeping tryst day by day.* AMEN.

". . . thy speech bewrayeth thee" (Matt. 26: 73)

IT was the North Country accent that gave this Galilean away, and by the way he spoke he was adjudged to be one of the King's men. What a challenging thought! Going up to some offices one day in the city of London I sensed, rightly as I afterwards discovered, that the lift operator was a Christian. It was not anything he said, but simply the way he spoke. His speech betrayed him. Now, when we are in a shop, or in a bus, or in a sports crowd, or in any place or company, is there a something about the way we speak that would cause anyone to look rather closely at us, and surmise that we are one of His? Have we the King's accent? It will have a sympathetic quality, a gentle note, a clear tone, a kindly character, a joyous hint. "Never man spake like this Man" (John 7: 46). No, but let us speak something like Him.

PRAYER.—*Thy Word has often taught us, O Lord, how much depends for good or for ill upon our speech. May we be enabled by the Holy Spirit ever to speak Christly.* AMEN.

". . . What shall I do then with Jesus . . . ?" (Matt. 27: 22)

PRIMARILY, there are only two things that can be done with Him; to accept Him, or reject Him. There is no further alternative, for to neglect Him is to reject. But this note is addressed to those who, by His grace, have accepted Him. "What shall I do *then* with Jesus?" Many things; these three for instance. Put Him first. Someone comes first in every life; all to often it is self. But He has bought us with His precious blood. Surely He has a right to the first place in the life He has redeemed. Publish His fame. Tell others what He has done for you, and what He is to you day by day. "Let the redeemed of the Lord say so" (Ps. 107: 2). Portray His face. The Christian is meant to be a portrait of the Christ, "like Him," and 2 Corinthians 3: 18 shows us how. Let us face the challenge. If we do not portray Him, we betray Him.

PRAYER.—*O Lord, we know that what Thou canst do with us depends so much upon what we shall do with Thee, yet how we long that Thou shalt use us to the uttermost in Thy service. Help us, then, to afford Thee the pre-eminence in our lives.* AMEN.

". . . Hail, King . . ." (Matt. 27: 29)

THE rough and ribald soldiers were having great sport with this Jesus in their common room before they led Him out to His crucifixion. They staged a mock coronation, for in the course of the so-called trial, they had heard His claim to Kingship. How absurd it sounded in their ears. Hence, this horseplay. An old faded scarlet military cloak, looking now a pale purple, was used for the Royal Mantle; a sprig of thorn from the garden was twisted into shape for the Crown. A reed from the river bank did service for the Sceptre. A mocking bow stood for the Homage. Only one thing now was missing, the Anointing Oil. Well, they just spat on Him; that would do for that. "Hail, King!" Yes, but a real coronation is coming when He returns in Advent Glory to take His power and reign. Meanwhile, shall we not give Him a personal coronation in our own hearts, and seek to secure it for Him in other lives. "Make Christ King!"

PRAYER.—*Thou Majesty Divine, take Thou Thy Power and reign in this poor heart of mine, that I may know and show that the Kingdom is really Thine.* AMEN.

"He saved others . . ." (Matt. 27: 42)

THIS is a message of love; "He saved others," He didn't save Himself. His enemies said He couldn't. Of course He could, but thank God He didn't. What love was in His mighty self-sacrifice. It will, for some, be a message of despair, "He saved others," but He didn't save me! Many, alas, in the Last Day will have to say that; but it will be their own fault. He would have saved them if only they had "come" to Him. Yea, it is a message of hope; "He saved others," then why shouldn't He save me! He does not pick and choose in this. He is ready to rescue "whosoever believeth on Him." And shall it not be a message of challenge, "He saved others"; I ought to be doing the same. Out of gratitude that He has saved me, out of loyalty to Him as my King, out of concern for the lost condition of unbelievers, I should rejoice to spend and be spent in bringing others to His saving grace and mercy.

PRAYER.—*Lord, teach me the secret of the happy order of Jesus first, Others next, and Yourself last.* AMEN.

". . . Come, see . . . go quickly, and tell . . ." (Matt. 28: 6–7)

HOW vividly the words recall the first impact of Easter truth. When once we have for ourselves come to "see" the glorious fact of the resurrection, we should be ready to pass on the news to others and that right "quickly." When an old Indian Chief was being told about the crucifixion and resurrection he asked, "When did all this happen?" "Nineteen hundred years ago," he was told. "But," he replied, "why haven't you come to tell us sooner?" Why, indeed! Surely the truth of the living Christ has not yet captured our mind and captivated our heart. Have you ever noticed how, on that first Easter Day, everybody started running about? Bad news gives pause to the feet, but good news gave pace to the feet. So gripped were those first believers by this tremendous news that they just couldn't keep still, or keep silent. Having come to see, they went quickly to tell. Verily, "the King's business required haste" (1 Sam. 21: 8).

PRAYER.—*Thou Living Christ, may I never cease to be thrilled by this great news, so thrilled that I must perforce tell it out by lip and by life, and may I ever know the power of Thy Resurrection in my own experience.* AMEN.

"Go . . . and lo . . ." (Matt. 28: 19, 20)

IT is often said that the second is dependent upon the first, as if to teach that we cannot expect His company unless we obey His command. Personally, I do not accept that. I believe rather that the reverse order is true; that the "lo" is the precedent word, and is intended to be an encouragement to us to "go." The King says in effect, "As you have My presence alongside, you need not fear to go anywhere I send you." Is the "go" to a hard task, a lonely road? It is all right, go ahead; the "lo" is yours. He is with you. When David Livingstone was found dead, kneeling at his bedside, there was there in front of him his little pocket Bible, open at this closing page of Matthew, and in the margin he had written alongside our 20th verse, "The word of a gentleman!" Yes, "go" is the King's command, His last command; and that we may obey, "Lo" is His last promise. He will keep His word.

PRAYER.—*How we praise Thee, Living Lord, that we ever have Thy abiding Presence to guide us, to guard us, to gird us, and to goad us.* AMEN.

APRIL

HYMNS ANCIENT AND MODERN

We call it the Book of Psalms, but it is really the Hymn Book which was compiled for the synagogue services. The book was ever a delight to our Lord Himself. Hymn No. 22 was in His mind at the very last moments of His life in the flesh (Matt. 27:46). Hymn No. 118 was, in accordance with Passover usage, sung ere they left the Upper Room (Matt. 26:30). Let us browse awhile in these ever-hallowed pages. How Ancient some of these hymns are—for instance, No. 90 is reputed to have been written by Moses; yet how Modern some of them are in their application to our everyday circumstances, needs, and aspirations.

"Blessed is the man . . ." (Ps. 1: 1)

WHAT man? Negatively, a separate-living man, who neither walks, stands nor sits with the ungodly. It was Peter's folly that first he "stood" (John 18: 18), and then "sat" (Luke 22: 55). No wonder he "fell!" Positively, this is a Scripturally minded man, delighting in "the rivers of water." The Bible man is ever the blessed man. Comparatively, this is a specially safeguarded man, who in contrast to the ungodly has his way protected and prospered. Thrice blessed is such a man.

PRAYER.—*Lord of Every Blessing, teach me and help me to walk in the blessed Way, that fulness of joy may be my daily experience.* AMEN.

"If the foundations be destroyed, what can the righteous do?" (Ps. 11: 3)

HOW shall we describe that "if"? Undoubtedly it is a tremendous "if," for the righteous have risked all on those foundations; such fundamentals as the inspiration of the Bible, the deity of Christ, the efficacy of the atonement, the truth of the resurrection, the coming of the Spirit, the necessity of the new birth. It would be a breath-taking moment if such were proved unstable, or untenable. It would become a tragic "if," were it to be substantiated. A novelist who wrote a story about a supposed discovery which showed the falsity of the resurrection called his book, "When It Was Dark." It was only fiction, but if it were fact, how tragically dark all would be. But, thank God, it is a triumphant "if," put up hypothetically only to be knocked down like Paul's "if" in 1 Corinthians 15: 14. We turn with uttermost rejoicing to the triumphant assertion of 2 Timothy 2: 19, "Nevertheless the foundation of God standeth sure." The "if" is slaughtered by that "nevertheless."

PRAYER.—*We bless Thee, Lord, for the certainties that we Christians have, the assured truths upon which we stand, the inalienable facts upon which our hearts rest.* AMEN.

APRIL 3

"Who have said . . . Our lips are our own . . ." (Ps. 12: 4)

D ON'T you say that, for it isn't true. "Ye are not your own" (1 Cor. 6: 19), so no part of you is your own. By blood-bought right you belong wholly to God. Like everything about you, your lips are His. He is Lord over us, and therefore over our lips. For this among other reasons, our lips must not criticize others. I am afraid the critical habit has got hold of a great many of us, and we are gravely guilty of unkind judgment of others, even of our fellow believers. And if only we knew all the facts, our opinion of the person might be very different. Moreover, our lips must not hurt others. What a lot of harm they can do; the hasty word, the unkind word, the angry word. James 3: 1–12 tells us that the tongue can be a fire, a beast, a poison. How greatly we need to use this Psalmist's prayer, "Keep the door of my lips" (141: 3); what comes out, and dare I say it, what goes in!

PRAYER.—*May my utterance, O God, be ever in Thy control, whether consciously or unconsciously. "Take my lips and let them be filled with messages for Thee."* AMEN.

APRIL 4

". . . He hath dealt bountifully with me" (Ps. 13: 6)

G OD always gives to a superlative degree. He is not content just to pardon; it must be "abundantly pardon" (Isa. 55: 7); whatever that adverb is intended to cover. The life He offers is "eternal life" (John 10: 28), beginning here, but not ending here. The peace He imparts is "perfect peace" (Ezra 7: 12), which persists in spite even of adverse circumstances, and which passes all human understanding (Phil. 4: 7). The joy we may experience is not a pale, fleeting thing, but "joy unspeakable" (1 Pet. 1: 8), which can be tasted to the full but can never adequately be described. The conquest open to us is not merely the bare margin, but we are to be "more than conquerors" (Rom. 8: 37); getting not only the victory but the spoils of victory. The measure of grace available for our Christian life and service can only be stated as "all grace abound" (2 Cor. 9: 8), that is, all kinds and all degrees of grace, to overflowing. Verily, "He *hath* dealt bountifully with me!"

PRAYER.—*Lord, since Thou hast blest believers so overwhelmingly, how can we do otherwise than yield up to Thee all that we have, all that we are, all that we do. Freely we have received, may we freely give.* AMEN.

". . . remember the Name . . ." (Ps. 20: 7)

THREE times it is mentioned in this Old Hymn. There is its protective value, "the Name of the God of Jacob defend thee" (v. 1). Have you ever tested its delivering efficacy in times of temptation, or wandering thoughts, or fear? Use it, not of course as a sort of lucky charm, but as the secret sign of your absolute trust in Him. There is its aggressive value; "some trust in chariots . . . horses, but we will remember the Name of the Lord our God" (v. 7). Old Testament saints knew its victorious power, as David here, and against Goliath. New Testament apostles used it thus, as Acts 16: 18. Modern Christians find the same, as on many a mission field. It has power in heaven and in hell. There is too its suggestive value; " in the Name of our God we will set up our banners" (v. 5). How suggestive is the banner; of a point of rally, a pledge of loyalty, a promise of victory, planting His flag in other lives. Very well then, "we will remember the Name."

PRAYER.—*Give us grace, O Lord, that besides all this, we may walk consistently in that worthy Name wherewith we are called, that being Christians we may be Christians.* AMEN.

"My God, My God, why hast Thou forsaken Me?" (Ps. 22: 1)

PAUSE for a moment on these words, at this heart-rending spot. It was no fancy, begotten of His tortured and weakened body. It was actual fact. God *had* forsaken Him. In this He touched bottom in His comedown to the depths to rescue us; in this He came to the "uttermost farthing" of His payment of our debt. We who are sinners cannot assess the soul agony of the Sinless in being thus God-forsaken. It will be the ghastliest element of the hell of the impenitent; and He bore it in the stead of the penitent. And oh, the joy of it, the wonder of it, He was forsaken of God that we might never be forsaken of Him (Heb. 13: 5). The Master had an earlier and lesser experience; though a deeply painful one, of being forsaken when "all the disciples forsook Him . . ." (Matt. 26: 56). Disciples, mark you! May we never thus disgrace our discipleship. Let us, on this solemn point, renew it at the foot of the Cross.

PRAYER.—*Our Heavenly Father, in the face of such a cry of desolation for us, we can ask for nothing, but only pause in amazement at such love for such unlovely creatures as we are.* AMEN.

APRIL 7

"Mine eyes are ever toward the Lord; for He shall pluck my feet out of the net" (Ps. 25: 15)

HERE is the grand secret of victory in time of temptation. Three attitudes are open to us at such a time. There is the attitude of looking at the net, the temptation spread for our downfall. How attractive and alluring it often is. "When the woman saw" (Gen. 3: 6) was the moment of her defeat. "When I saw" (Josh. 7: 21) was Achan's own account of his first step downward. When the moment is upon you, eyes off the net! There is the attitude of looking at the feet, at yourself; either belauding your strength or bewailing your weakness. To be occupied thus is to court disaster. No, when temptation assails, eyes off the feet! There is the attitude of looking to the Lord. This is the only way of safety and victory. The very moment you are conscious of the evil, turn at once, without a second's delay, to Him. You may not have time to pray, but He will understand what your instantaneous look means, and He shall pluck your feet out of the net. This then is the secret: Eyes Right!

PRAYER.—*Our Gracious God, we thank Thee for a multitude who have proved the efficacy of this divinely revealed secret, and we pray that we, in our own case, may be of that glad number who are in all circumstances "Looking unto Jesus."* AMEN.

APRIL 8

". . . God . . . thundereth . . ." (Ps. 29: 3)

THIS arresting phrase comes in the Hymn of the Thunderstorm. Every time "the voice of the Lord" is mentioned we are to imagine a mighty clap of thunder. As we read the verses we follow the track of the storm; coming up from the sea, reverberating among the mountains, accompanied by vivid lightning flashes, working havoc on its way, until at last it blows itself out, and "the Lord will bless His people with peace." One recalls that in John 12: 28–29, His voice sounded to people like thunder. Sometimes God whispereth, as in 1 Kings 19: 11–12. Sometimes He thundereth, when it is the only way. How effective it then proves. It "breaketh" (v. 5), as some need to be, from their pride, opposition, prejudice. It "shaketh" (v. 8), as some need to be, from their self-complacency, inconsistency and sloth. It "maketh" (v. 9), as some need to be, from their inability to bring forth souls to new birth. As revival tarries, we are constrained to pray,

> *Speak with the voice that wakes the dead*
> *And* make *Thy people hear.*

PRAYER.—*Yes, Lord, whatever be the voice we need, speak it to our innermost being, that we may accord it our utmost response.* AMEN.

"I will extol Thee . . ." (Ps. 30: 1)

YES indeed, and this Hymn No. 30 reminds us of many reasons why we should. "Thou hast lifted me," says verse 1. Down in the horrible pit of sin He found us, and instead of passing us by, He stopped and stooped to bring us up. "Thou hast healed me," says verse 2. This is the positive aspect of His salvation, for His love has brought us not only from disease but unto health. He has made provision for our soul's well-being; the precious blood, to keep us clean; the Holy Scriptures to make us strong; the indwelling Spirit to work in us true holiness. "Thou hast kept me," says verse 3. We have read of keeping, and if we are to remain loyal and true, it is not we, but He that must do it. "Thou hast girded me," says verse 11. Here it is "with gladness." Elsewhere we are shown the other attractive pieces of the Christian's extensive wardrobe: "the garment of praise," "be clothed with humility," "the whole armour of God," "above all (what an overcoat) put on love."

PRAYER.—*Give to us, O Lord, such an understanding of the realities of these great benefits that our hearts may be ever attuned to the song of grateful praise for it all.* AMEN.

". . . like a green bay tree . . . like a green olive tree" (Ps. 37: 35, 52: 8)

WHAT a contrast! The one a picture of the wicked; the other of the righteous. In this striking metaphor is shown the believer's stability. A sore problem in the Psalmist's day was the prosperity of the wicked, but David sees him as a bay tree, slender rooted, with no staying power. The olive, with its great spreading roots, is well stablished, as is the Christian "rooted in Him" (Col. 2: 7). Here too is the believer's locality. The Revised Version translates our first as a "tree that groweth in his own soil," as if somehow dependent upon itself; but the other is planted "in the house of God" even "in Christ," beautifully situated for enjoyment, enlargement, and enrichment. And the believer's utility is also suggested. That of the "bay" is practically nil, "which produceth all leaves and no fruit," as Matthew Henry says. But the "olive" is the most useful tree in the Holy Land; berries for food; oil for food, light and healing; branches for fuel; timber for ornamental articles. I would rather be olive than bay, wouldn't you?

PRAYER.—*Lord, I would covet the Prophet's description of the "Trees of Righteousness, the planting of the Lord, that He may be glorified."* AMEN.

". . . how frail I am" (Ps. 39: 4)

IT is well that I should continually recognize this; yet the remembrance does not in the least depress me, though it does humble me. For my Bible teaches me that God chooses such for His purposes. Look at 1 Corinthians 1: 27–28 and see how to combat the wise and mighty of this world, even the "things that are," the powers that be. He has deliberately "chosen" such frail creatures as the absurdities, the inadequates, the inferiorities, the contemptibles, and even the nonentities. Having chosen them, God infuses such with His own all-sufficient strength. Think of such men as Peter the boaster, Thomas the doubter, Philip the ignorant, John the fiery; how frail they would have remained if they had not been "endued with power from on high" (Luke 24: 49). Being thus infused, God uses such in His service. A great Christian once said, "I continually wonder at the way God works with such poor tools." Well, the frail shall not fail if filled.

PRAYER.—*Lord, it is not difficult for us to recognize the truth of our own frailty, but we rejoice in our utter dependence upon the strong Son of God. May my hands be made strong by the Hands of the Mighty God of Jacob.* AMEN.

". . . O God, my God" (Ps. 43: 4)

THE movement of that "O" to that "my" is fraught with enormous significance for the one who has made it. We go from the vocative to the possessive. He is not just One who, from a distance, is to be addressed upon the throne of His deity, but He has graciously allowed me by faith to call Him my own, and to offer Him the throne of my heart. We go from the universal to the individual. True, He reigns over a vast universe, but now He is conceived as ruling the life of the least believer. We go from the aloof to the alongside. "O God" is so far off; "my God" is just near by. He does not aid us from a distance, but is "a very present Help" (Ps. 46: 1). He is not an absentee Benefactor, but a very Resident in our hearts. Blessed be God who, of His sovereign grace, has allowed His creatures such intimacy as belongs to those who through faith can address Him as "my God"!

PRAYER.—*Lord, with what gratitude, with what humility, we take that "My" upon our lips and hide it in our hearts, and because Thou art mine, may I be truly Thine.* AMEN.

"*. . . attend unto my prayer*" (Ps. 61: 1)

Bᴜᴛ why should He? We are so small. In a crowded shop there was one customer who couldn't get attended to. He was a little boy; grown-ups kept usurping his place at the counter and the grocer didn't notice him, he was so small. Remember, "God heard the voice of the lad" (Gen. 21: 17). None is too small to gain His ear. We are so sinful. A much more formidable barrier is this, but God has dealt with that from His side, and we may even with "boldness enter into the holiest by the blood of Jesus" (Heb. 10: 19). Wonderful that the all-holy God deigns to attend to us. We are so stupid. "We know not what we should pray for as we ought" (Rom. 8: 26), but even here God comes to our rescue, for "the Spirit . . . helpeth our infirmities"; both as to the "what" and the "as," the matter and the manner. We are so selfish. "Ye ask amiss, that ye may consume it upon your lusts" (Jas. 4: 3). It is a secret of gaining His attention to our prayer that we ask only for His will.

Pʀᴀʏᴇʀ.—*Moreover, Lord, we find our introduction to Thee in the Name of Thy dear Son, and ask for the supply of all our needs, not in our own name, but in His, "Through Jesus Christ our Lord."* Aᴍᴇɴ.

"*God hath spoken once; twice . . .*" (Ps. 62: 11)

Iᴛ is amazing enough that God should deign to speak to man at all, but that after man's disregard of, or disobedience to, His word, He should say it again and yet again; this is condescension, and patience and grace indeed! The recorded reiterations of God are very moving. "The Lord called Samuel again the third time" (1 Sam. 3: 8). "The word of the Lord came unto Jonah the second time" (Jonah 3: 1). "How often would I . . . and ye would not" (Matt. 23: 37). "Behold, I stand at the door, and keep on knocking (Gk.)" (Rev. 3: 20). I wonder if it is true to say that today, throughout the whole worldwide church and to each member, God is urgently reiterating a call to repentance, which must come first; a call to readjustment, to put God back into the first place in all our plans and considerations; a call to receive His best, even the revival rain which He longs to give, and a call to realize for it all "that power belongeth unto God."

Pʀᴀʏᴇʀ.—*Lord, may I walk so closely with Thee that there shall be no need for Thee to say things over and over again, but that I may catch Thy every whisper, and rejoice to do Thy every wish.* Aᴍᴇɴ.

APRIL **15**

". . . the river of God . . . is full of water . . ." (Ps. 65: 9)

IN spiritual application we may think of this as the river of His grace, and it is of vital concern that the believer should realize that this river is ever at the flood. The life of faith is full of need. What difficulties arise, for example, out of the uncongenial atmosphere in which we have to live, and out of the powerful enemies we have to meet, and out of the spiritual service we are called to undertake, and out of the holy ideal we are expected to reach, and out of the unsatisfactory self we have to deal with. Oh yes, indeed, we are full of need but the river of God is full of water. So we should expect, for His gifts are ever on a lavish scale. There is nothing niggardly about His supplies. In the light of our great need, how refreshing is the "all grace . . . all sufficiency . . . all things" of 2 Corinthians 9: 8. Thus our need and His great fulness meet!

PRAYER.—*Give me understanding, O Lord, of how immeasurable and how immediate is Thy provision for my life. May I dip deep into the fulness of the inexhaustible supplies of the river.* AMEN.

APRIL **16**

". . . Thou didst march through the wilderness" (Ps. 68: 7)

WHAT, God did? Yes. He trod the wilderness. Why? Well, why, in Daniel 3: 25, is He walking in the fire; why, in Matthew 14: 25, is He walking on the sea; why, in Psalm 23: 4, is He walking through the valley? Every time because His people are there, and need Him. So, with Israel, and so with you, if you are called to tread a wilderness, He will tread it with you. He transformed the wilderness. Unexpected things happened there for these people. A guiding pillar, a miraculous manna, a supply of water, a healing serpent; such things and many such, transfigured their journey. And spiritually "He turneth the wilderness into a standing water" (Ps. 107: 35), and "the desert shall rejoice and blossom as the rose" (Isa. 35: 1). He terminated the wilderness. He intended eleven days of desert for them, but they incurred forty years. He doesn't plan your life to be all wilderness; the text doesn't say He did "march in," as if there were no end of it, but "march through." There's a Promised Land ahead.

PRAYER.—*We know, O Lord, how full of change our journey is, but we know, too, that there is no change with Thee, but that, always the same, Thou dost still accompany Thy children every step, every mile, of the road.* AMEN.

". . . summer and winter" (Ps. 74: 17)

SUCH is life! Its experiences are so varied; one time hot, one time cold. Who does not know the sunny days, when all is bright and all goes well? Who does not know the dark times, when all seems frost-bound, and all is under a cloud? Gladness and sadness; yes, that's how it is with life. Its varied experiences are all under God's control. "Thou hast made summer and winter." It is a comfort to know that winter can fall upon our life's barometer only by His permission. If life is hard and harsh for you, it is not haphazard, it is allowed for a purpose. Its varied experiences are conducive to our good. The Arabs have a proverb, "All sunshine makes a desert." So, "summer and winter," all is well, for "we know that all things work together for good to them that love God" (Rom. 8: 28). That is not something we hope or think but something "we know."

PRAYER.—*Come sunshine, come shadow, if Thou, O Lord, art there we will not complain or fear, but know that all is well. Give us at least a sunny heart where no shadow is.* AMEN.

". . . my sore . . . in the night . . . my song in the night . . ."
(Ps. 77: 2, 6)

WELL, if you have a sore, whether of body or spirit, it is certain to feel worse in the night, when you are likely to be at a low ebb. The writer of this Hymn says of it, "My soul refused to be comforted," "my spirit was overwhelmed." Ah, but later he remembered a song, to counter the sore. It has often been so in the dark experiences of men. Some of the loveliest things in poetry, in music, and in literature, have come out of the "night" of sorrow and suffering. Job 35: 10 speaks of "God, my Maker, who giveth songs in the night." Yes, God gives them; and if you are passing through a "night" time, and are inclined to be "sore" about it, ask Him to give you a "song" instead. Paul and Silas in the Philippian jail might have moaned and groaned for their "sore," but instead they "sang praises." Better than the hoot of the owl is the song of the nightingale.

PRAYER.—*Many of Thy Saints, O Lord, have taught us that Thy Presence brightens even the dreariest places. Shall we not then mount above the clouds where the morning stars sing together, that earthbound travellers may hear us and be blest.* AMEN.

APRIL 19

"Can God . . . ?" (Ps. 78: 19)

YOU will notice that in asking this, "they spake against God," so we may say at once that this is a question which should never have been asked. A heathen man may be expected to ask it. "Is thy God able?" (Dan. 6: 20). A distracted man may be constrained to ask it. "If thou canst?" (Mark 9: 22). A truly believing man will not ask it, for he knows that God "can," whatever be the purport of the matter concerned. If, therefore, God does not, there will be some good, and wise reason. But this is a question which will easily be answered. In our verse, the question refers (a) to the usual, "furnish a table." His provision of our daily needs and His production of the yearly harvest are evidences that He "can." Our question refers (b) to the unusual, "in the wilderness." Even in impossible circumstances, God always "can," for "He Himself knew what He would do" (John 6: 6).

PRAYER.—*We thank Thee, O God, for the revelation of Thyself as El-Shaddai, "The God Who Is Enough." May we, like Thy Saint of old, rest content and happily satisfied.* AMEN.

APRIL 20

". . . a doorkeeper in the house of my God . . ." (Ps. 84: 10)

LET me ask you three questions. First, Are you in? Have you by faith entered into life; are you "in the faith" (2 Cor. 13: 5), "in Christ" (Col. 1: 2), "in the house of my God"? If so, you are ready for my second question, Are you far in? Strangely enough, the word seems to mean, not a keeper of the door, but a keeper at the door, and the sentence might more happily be rendered, "I had rather be just inside the door of the house . . . than to dwell in the tents . . ." Yes, of course, but you surely won't be content to remain only just inside? How far, then, are you getting in, getting on, in the Christian life? And now for my third question: Are you getting others in? We must be often coming to the "door" that we may stretch out our hand to fetch others "in" to share the joys and blessings we ourselves have found "in Christ."

PRAYER.—*O Lord Christ, we bless Thee that Thou art Thyself both the Door and the Dwelling place. May we not keep to ourselves the wonders, the beauties, the graces, the blessings, that are in Thee, but go all out to get all in that we can, to share them.* AMEN.

"*. . . salvation from day to day*" (Ps. 96: 2)

H IS salvation is an eternal thing, but it is also a diurnal thing. We may "show forth" its effect in personal experience and behaviour "from day to day." It stands up to the day's demands, the relationships, the circumstances, the temptations, the responsibilities, the anxieties. How, some days, they crowd in upon us and threaten to strangle spiritual life. It links up with the day's work, enabling one to be a better tradesman, a more skilled mechanic, a more dependable clerk, a more efficient housewife. Speaking to this point, C. H. Spurgeon once said, "It were a pity indeed if Paul's tents were the worst in the store and Lydia's purple of the poorest dye." It brightens up the day's monotony. Life is a dull affair for many, day after day the same dreary round of humdrum duties. Well, but what joy should enter with the realization that the Master is alongside. A children's chorus used to run:

> *I have a Saviour who's mighty to keep*
> *All day on Sunday and six days a week.*
> *I have a Saviour who's mighty to keep*
> *Fifty-two weeks in the year.*

PRAYER.—*Blessed be Thy Name, O Lord, for all the special joys of Sunday night, but no less for all the needful strength for Monday morning. Because the Strong One remains with us, may our week-days never be weak-days.* AMEN.

"*Let the redeemed of the Lord say so . . .*" (Ps. 107: 2)

T HERE are three reasons for this injunction. The health of the soul is the first. No believer is spiritually healthy who has not learned to "say so." He is as bereft of living experience as is the Dead Sea, which is for ever taking in and never giving out. Romans 10: 10 is concerned to teach us that "mouth confession" is essential to a living experience of daily salvation. The health of others is also linked up with this our personal testimony, for this is His appointed method of disseminating the Gospel. We shrink from the judgment of 2 Kings 7: 9, "This is a Gospel day and we hold our peace"! Famishing souls need what we have found in Christ. Let us "say so." The honour of the Master is moreover involved in our witness to Him. As therefore He shall give us opportunity and grace, let us speak a glad and grateful word for Him, as a "legion" of others have done (Mark 5: 9, 19–20).

PRAYER.—*Our Master, give us courage that we may speak, give us tact that we may speak without offence, give us joy that we may speak with winsomeness, give us fruit that we may speak to honour Thee.* AMEN.

"I believed, therefore have I spoken . . ." (Ps. 116: 10)

TRUE faith is a vital thing, being essential to eternal life and salvation. It is also a visual thing. People should be able to see it by our Christian behaviour and demeanour. The point here, however, is that it is a vocal thing. "Therefore have I spoken." So we return, for emphasis, to yesterday's theme. If we believe, we have something to speak about, for our very belief has been the master key which has let us into all the treasure house of His royal bounty. Verily, "we speak that we do know" (John 3: 11). What good news it is! If we believe, we have Someone to speak for. After all, our belief has brought us not merely into touch with a thing, a blessing, but with a Person. Things cannot satisfy persons, but this Person satisfies in all things. Therefore, we surely must ever be on the lookout for the chance to say a word for Him who can so marvellously satisfy.

PRAYER.—*Because of our experience of Thy Grace, O Lord, we are entitled to speak; because of the blessing that may come of it, we are encouraged to speak; because of the power of the Holy Spirit we are enabled to speak; so may we speak.* AMEN.

"This is the day . . . we . . . rejoice . . . in . . ." (Ps. 118: 24)

THE joy of a great Fact; the empty tomb which, linked as it always is in the New Testament with the empty Cross, makes it the greatest fact in all human history. The joy of a great Friend; not a beautiful memory only, but now a living Companion in life's pilgrimage. The joy of a great Force; "the power of His resurrection" (Phil. 3: 10) as an indwelling reality for daily experience. The joy of a great Faith; that we have such an One to trust in, whom even the shut doors of fearful circumstance cannot keep from our side. The joy of a great Future; for He "hath abolished death, and brought life and immortality to light" (2 Tim. 1: 10). His resurrection is the pledge and pattern of ours; "because I live, ye shall live also" (John 14: 19), and is the promise of our glad reunion with our loved ones in Christ, for the expectation of those "raptured greetings" is based (1 Thess. 4: 14) upon the happening of this gladsome Day.

PRAYER.—*Thou Risen Christ, may all our days be tinged with the glow of that first day of the week.* AMEN.

APRIL   25

"Teach me . . . the way . . . Make me to go . . ." (Ps. 119: 33, 35)

THE interrelation of these two things is most important. The going is dependent upon the knowing. Lots of people get lost through ignorance of the right way. In the spiritual realm, there is a right and a wrong way of salvation, a right and a wrong way of holiness, a right and a wrong way of service, a right and a wrong way of guidance, a right and a wrong way of experience. At every step we need to pray, "Teach me the way." But remember that the knowing is dependent upon the going. If we do not take the one step He shows us, we may be sure that He will not disclose a further step. The Master put it in John 7: 17, "If any man will do . . . he shall know." At every step, then, we need also to pray, "Make me to go." Knowing and going are the two stout legs upon which the believer pursues his pilgrimage.

PRAYER.—*We thank Thee, Lord, that Thy Word speaks of the Christian life as The Way. May we not lose The Way or loiter therein but ever tread it alongside of Thee, who art Thyself The Way.* AMEN.

APRIL   26

"Thou art near, O Lord . . ." (Ps. 119: 151)

BLESSED truth for all believers! Near enough to guard us, like those "horses and chariots of fire" in between Elisha and the Syrians in 2 Kings 6: 17. "The Angel of the Lord encampeth round about them that fear Him, and delivereth them" (Ps. 34: 7). Nothing, and no one, can touch us unless He gives leave to pass. Near enough to guide us too, is He. He is not a guide post that merely shows the way, but a Guide who shares the way. So does He undertake to guide us into all truth, in paths of service, in the ways of His commandments, in the line of His purpose. He is near enough to goad us, for we are oftentimes so slow and need to be urged on to do and to say, and to be what He requires. He is near enough to gird us, for the work His servants must do, and for the war His soldiers must wage. So blessedly near is He!

PRAYER.—*Since Thou art so near to us, O God, may we never in heart follow afar off, but ever know the blessed intimacy that Thou dost so graciously allow.* AMEN.

APRIL 27

"He that goeth forth . . ." (Ps. 126: 6)

OUR religion is a "going" concern! When we have answered His "Come," we are faced with His "Go"; even though it be with a heavy heart (weepeth), on account perhaps of the hardness of the ground, or the difficulties of the task, or the lack of response. Anyhow, we shall go with a laden hand, "bearing precious seed." Some have gone forth with other things, but they have not worked. This "seed is the Word" (Luke 8: 11). If some criticize the seed, let us cast it. For we go with a blessed hope; "shall doubtless come again with rejoicing." All the tears and toil will prove to have been abundantly worthwhile. Without a doubt, if we are faithful, we shall be fruitful. For we shall come home with a golden harvest; "bringing his sheaves with him." What a contrast to those who can show "nothing but leaves" (Mark 11: 13). Here's to a happy Harvest Home for us all!

PRAYER.—*May we heed Thy injunction, O Lord, to "look on the fields for they are white already to harvest." May we indeed be quick to respond and be quite sure of the result.* AMEN.

APRIL 28

"Happy is he that hath the God of Jacob for his help . . ." (Ps. 146: 5)

YOU see, He is a God of surprising love. His love for faithful Abraham, for blameless Isaac, for meek Moses, yes; but surely not for Jacob! Yet, "I loved Jacob" (Mal. 1: 2). Recall the words we sometimes sing, "Jesu, what didst Thou find in me that Thou hast dealt so lovingly." The God of Jacob can teach us how to love the unlovely. He is a God of abiding companionship. Jacob's sense of loneliness, that first night away from home, was corrected by the Ladder Vision; "the Lord is in this place, and I knew it not" (Gen. 28: 16). Yes, He is there, whether we realize it or not. He is a God of infinite patience. Over and over again Jacob disappointed Him, until at last He conquered him, at the wrestling. He is ever the same, "I am the Lord, I change not, therefore ye sons of Jacob are not consumed" (Mal. 3: 6). He is a God of transforming grace. What a change came over Jacob at Jabbok; a new man, a new name, a new power, a new day. "A new creature" (2 Cor. 5: 17).

PRAYER.—*How we bless Thee, Almighty Lord, that the God who loved in Jacob's time is just the same to-day, so ready to deal graciously with us if we will only surrender ourselves and yield to Thy all-conquering might.* AMEN.

". . . His understanding is infinite" (Ps. 147: 5)

W HAT a comfort is in this fact! He understands you. How trying it is to be misunderstood. He will never do that. We rejoice in the intimate understanding of His humanity; "touched with the feeling of our infirmities" (Heb. 4: 15). We rejoice in the infinite understanding of His deity; "Thou knowest all things" (John 21: 17). He understands your problem. The "what" of it, the "why" of it, the "whither" of it, are all open to Him. However big it may be, however inscrutable it may appear, take it to Him. He understands your capacity; just what you can and cannot do, and He will not expect you to do what you can't! He will want you to do something in His service, and He knows the place you can best fill, and the grace you will most need. So be assured that as He understands so He undertakes.

PRAYER.—*We thank Thee, O God, for so comforting an assurance. Oh, that we on our part might understand more of this and of all Thy precious truths, and where we do not understand, may we rest in Thy revelation.* AMEN.

". . . He will beautify the meek with salvation" (Ps. 149: 4)

W HAT a wonderful thing salvation is; what a powerful thing, but what a beautiful thing! It takes a black heart and makes it white. "Wash me, and I shall be whiter than snow," says this same hymn writer in No. 51 of his collection, and he knew how black a heart could be. Salvation goes to the root of the matter. It doesn't whitewash, but washes white. It takes a drab life and makes it radiant. "They looked unto Him and were radiant," says the American Revised Version of Psalm 34: 5. Salvation brings an interest, a hope, an adventure, even a Presence, into life which make it so different from the dreary thing which perchance it used to be. It takes an ugly character and makes it sweet. "The image of His Son" (Rom. 8: 29) is its plan even for a selfish, hard, critical, sour person. Could anything be lovelier? What a portrait of beauty is the Christian character in Galatians 5: 22–23. It takes a gloomy prospect and makes it golden. "It is appointed unto men once to die, but after this the judgment," says Hebrews 9: 27, but what a change for the believer. "The path of the just is as the shining light that shineth more and more unto the perfect day" (Prov. 4: 18). Beautiful!

PRAYER.—*Lord, make us to be among the meek ones, that by the working of the Indwelling Spirit we may be made more and more like Thee, causing others to feel how wonderful Thou art in Thy transforming grace and power.* AMEN.

MAY

THE BUILDERS

Such is the title which suggests itself for the Books of Ezra and Nehemiah; the one, building the Temple; the other, the Wall. We, too, are to be builders, as I Corinthians 3:11-15 makes clear. May our meditations this month help us to build aright.

F

MAY 1

"*. . . The Lord God . . . hath charged me to build Him an house . . .*"
(Ezra 1: 2)

HOWEVER did this heathen king know anything about the Lord God, and however did he acquire that conviction that he was to build His temple at Jerusalem? Do you think it was the faithful Daniel who taught the king about Jehovah, and showed him the Isaiah passage (44: 28) which 170 years before had, thus long before he was born, actually named Cyrus for the task? God chooses all sorts of people for His purposes. Though he be a king, like this Cyrus, whose will runs supreme, he must bow to God's will. Though he be a heathen, with many so-called gods, he must subserve the One God. God chooses all His own people to build for Him. Are we as ready to take up the work as was this heathen monarch?

PRAYER.—*Lord, wilt Thou give us plans to build to, tools to build with, skill to build well, and zeal to build earnestly for Thee.* AMEN.

MAY 2

"*. . . the vessels of the house of the Lord . . .*" (Ezra 1: 7)

THE risen Lord said of Paul, "He is a chosen vessel unto Me" (Acts 9: 15). And the same Paul used the like figure of a good Christian. "He shall be a vessel . . . meet for the Master's use" (2 Tim. 2: 21). Let us then employ the chequered career of those old vessels as a guidance for ourselves. Four words sum it up. (1) Dedicated: "Solomon brought in the things which David . . . had dedicated, even . . . the vessels" (1 Kings 7: 51). Do you recall the day when you dedicated yourself to the Lord? (2) Deported: "Nebuchadnezzar . . . carried . . . the vessels . . . to Babylon" (2 Chron. 36: 7). What a sorry picture of the back-slider, now in the wrong hands, and in the wrong place. (3) Desecrated: "They brought the vessels . . . and drank in them" (Dan. 5: 3). That heathen crowd, in that drunken feast! How backsliders can go from bad to worse. Thank God, that isn't the end; backsliding never is, for "I will heal their backsliding" (Hos. 14: 4). So we find these vessels. (4) Delivered: "Let the . . . vessels . . . be restored . . . everyone to his place" (Ezra 6: 5). If any backslider read these words, may he turn back to the Lord, that he may be delivered and restored to his proper place in the service of what Paul calls the "Great House."

PRAYER.—*May I be for Thee, O Lord, a clean vessel, always meet for the Master's use, and wilt Thou employ me to carry the Water of Life to thirsty or dying souls.* AMEN.

MAY 3

"They gave after their ability . . ." (Ezra 2: 69)

GOD never expects anyone to do more than that. Our financial gifts are reckoned thus. You are expected, if you are His, to give of your substance for the maintenance of God's House and work, as these in Ezra. If you are a person of but slender means, you are not expected to give as much as one of large means. Of one who offered a "farthing," the Master spoke in terms of highest praise, because she gave to the limit of her ability. Of another He said, "She hath done what she could" (Mark 14: 8). Do we support the Cause thus far? Our personal gifts are also called for. You may not be a person of many gifts, but has the Lord got the "gifts" you do possess? You are not expected to do, or to be, or to give, what you can't, but "after their ability"; and He has a wonderful way of multiplying the gifts thus given (John 6: 9ff.).

PRAYER.—*"Take my love, my Lord, I pour at Thy feet its treasure-store. Take myself and I will be, ever, only, all for Thee."* AMEN.

MAY 4

". . . the duty of every day . . ." (Ezra 3: 4)

THE words refer to the daily routine regarding the burnt-offerings, but we may assuredly apply them to the ordinary, regular duties of every day's life. The Christian must be faithful about his daily duty. A servant girl gave it as a sign of the genuineness of her conversion, "I always sweep under the mats now." The way we do our daily duty isn't a bad test. Some seem to be prone to attend meetings to the neglect of daily duties, but that of course is all wrong and is a shockingly bad witness to the world, which is so quick to notice. The Christian must also be mindful that his Master is with him in his daily duty, no less than in his daily prayer, as Brother Lawrence found in "The Practice of the Presence of God," as he did his ordinary humdrum work in the kitchen. Let us then do our duty, and our duties, as in His sight and as unto Him (Col. 3: 23).

PRAYER.—*Our Master, we recognize that our duty to Thee is but another expression for our debt to Thee. How great is that debt. How careful then to do that duty, whether it be what we owe to others or what we owe to Thyself.* AMEN.

MAY 5

". . . why should damage grow . . . ?" (Ezra 4: 22)

How easily and often imperceptibly it happens. The question here was asked by the Jews' enemies, who affected to believe that the building of the Temple would damage the king's reputation and revenue, and had better be stopped. That was of course all nonsense, but damage to the King of kings is all too frequent. How does this damage come? As a business agent may, by improper behaviour, damage the firm's name; as a member's failure to send his subscription may damage the club's finances; as a servant's negligent ways may damage the employer's property; as a son's unkindness to his brother may damage the father's heart; as an ambassador's unwise words and actions may damage the king's empire. Are we conscious of doing any damage to our King? Why should this damage grow? If He put His finger on any such dark or doubtful spot, let us put it right at once, lest it grow worse. And let us seek His grace to help us that "the king should have no damage" (Dan. 6: 2). A worthy purpose for all loyal subjects of the King.

PRAYER.—*Our Lord and Master, how sadly we have to acknowledge that so often we do let Thee down. Wilt Thou forgive all our disloyalties and strengthen us to love Thee more and so to serve Thee better.* AMEN.

MAY 6

". . . prepared . . . to seek the law of the Lord, and to do it and to teach . . ." (Ezra 7: 10)

THIS man Ezra was a wonderfully all-round, full-orbed believer. He was especially renowned as a teacher, and here we see how he set about preparing himself for that so important ministry. To know is the first thing. When it speaks here of "seeking the law" it means getting to know it; not only its words, but its meanings, and its spirit. How infinitely worthwhile it is to get a real acquaintance with the Word, not just by reading the daily portion but by real study. To do is the next stage. "If ye know . . . happy are ye if ye do . . ." (John 13: 17). This teacher set himself to carry out in his own life the things that "the law of the Lord" said. To know the way, and to go the way (Ps. 119: 33, 35), should be simultaneous, and even synonymous. To sow is the last point; to scatter in other minds and lives what we have come to know for ourselves; to seek, to do, to teach; mark the stages, and mark their order.

PRAYER.—*As Thou, the Great Husbandman, hast shown the way, help us that in our degree we may come to know the precious seed and go to scatter it far afield.* AMEN.

". . . perfect peace, and at such a time" (Ezra 7: 12)

IT is but the conventional phrase of a polite letter writer, but how wonderful if the wish be a reality. Our Lord's "Peace be unto you" is another formal greeting, but on His lips how full of meaning. Our own "Goodbye," too, may imply so little, or so much if it really says, "God-be-wi' ye." So today's text may speak of (1) eternal peace, the "peace through the blood of His Cross" (Col. 1: 20) which avails "at such a time" as the Judgment, because we are at peace with God. Or (2) external peace, when outward circumstances are awry; to display "perfect peace" in our demeanour and behaviour "at such a time" is a blessed possibility and a glorious testimony to the keeping power of God. It is rooted in (3) internal peace, like the mighty sea, which while stormy on the surface is calm deep down. So even "at such a time," our hearts may be garrisoned (Phil. 4: 7) with the "perfect peace," beyond understanding, but not beyond experiencing, in Christ, for "this Man shall *be* the peace" (Mic. 5: 5).

PRAYER.—*Thou Prince of Peace, wilt Thou so control our hearts and lives that we may know the Peace of God because we have the God of Peace in the ship to whisper "Peace, be still." AMEN.*

". . . a man of understanding . . ." (Ezra 8: 18)

HERE is a list of the leading people who went up with Ezra to Jerusalem, and those who helped him with his great rebuilding task. Among all these who were "expressed by name" (v. 20) one is singled out as "a man of understanding," a man particularly useful to the enterprise. Ezra specially thanks God for him; it will be a great strength to have such a man always at hand. This is surely one of those "best gifts" which we may "covet earnestly" (1 Cor. 12: 31). This is an understanding not our own; "lean not unto thine own understanding" (Prov. 3: 5). This is an understanding taught of God; "the eyes of your understanding being enlightened" (Eph. 1: 18), "understanding what the will of the Lord is" (Eph. 5: 17). This is an understanding which is worth its weight in gold; "with all thy getting, get understanding" (Prov. 4: 7). Understanding precedes undertaking.

PRAYER.—*May we walk so close to Thee, O Master, that we may come to see things as through Thine Eyes, and to recognize Thy purposes along the way and at Journey's End. AMEN.*

"For I was ashamed to require of the king a band of soldiers . . . the hand of our God was upon us . . ." (Ezra 8: 22, 31)

THE returning exiles had back to Jerusalem a long and dangerous four months' journey before them. They were an ill-armed caravan, all the more vulnerable for the women and children who formed part of their company. They would be peculiarly open to attack from the robbers which infested the route. Little prepared, two means of protection were available. There was first the king's band. Artaxerxes, so favourable to the expedition, would readily grant a company of soldiers as escort and none would blame Ezra for adopting this sensible course. Instead, however, he chose to rely on the Lord's hand. "The hand of our God" comes often in these books. Ezra often extolled its protection. He felt now he must match his conduct with his creed; ashamed to seek the king's band when he had taught trust in the Lord's hand.

PRAYER.—*O Lord, some trust in horses and some in chariots, but we will remember the name of the Lord of Hosts, our Guard and our Guide.* AMEN.

". . . The people . . . have not separated themselves . . ." (Ezra 9: 1)

SEPARATION is an unpopular word. Many Christians shrink from the idea of being different in behaviour from those around them, of being thought narrow; or maybe their hearts retain a sneaking fondness for the things of the world. Or perchance, like Ezra's people, they are sadly and strangely entangled with some definitely sinful thing and do not wish for freedom. Separation is a key word. Unless prepared, as the Church of England Catechism says, to "renounce the devil and all his works, the pomps and vanity of this world, and all the sinful lusts of the flesh," we must be prepared to forgo the richest blessings of God and lose all likelihood of real advance in the Christian life. Separation is a positive word. Ezra's informants use it here of their people in a negative sense; but it is in reality never merely a going from, but a going to. Paul puts it, "separated unto the Gospel of God" (Rom. 1: 1).

PRAYER.—*Lord, may no kind of compromise deprive us of the joy of being the best for God, and having the best from God.* AMEN.

". . . Hanani . . . said . . . the wall . . . is broken down . . ."
(Neh. 1: 2, 3)

THAT lit a flame in Nehemiah's heart. It was as if he were a Torch, set ablaze by this sad news of the beloved city's condition. From that moment the Torch would lead an eager crusade back to set up that wall again. It is grand to be a Torch, to light the way of some great Christian enterprise. The names of Torches are held in high esteem. We can't all thus be great lights, yet we can each be a Match to set the Torch alight. Their humble service is scarcely recognized, but what honour is properly theirs. Have you ever heard of Maria Millis? No, she was only a Match, but she set alight the Torch which was Lord Shaftesbury. Have you ever heard of Edward Kimball? Perhaps not, he was only a Match, but he set alight that Torch which was D. L. Moody. So if you can't be a Torch, be a Match, as Nehemiah's brother, Hanani, was.

PRAYER.—*Humble though we be, O God, wilt Thou take hold of us and ignite us to set other lives alight for Thyself and aflame in Thy cause.* AMEN.

". . . So I prayed . . ." (Neh. 2: 4)

IT is perfectly evident, from even a cursory reading of this book, that Nehemiah was a man of prayer. But the point here is his use of ejaculatory prayer, the Sky Telegram. The regular prayertime is more like the sending of a letter, but there is not always time, or opportunity, for that. The matter is so urgent that it calls for a swift and brief message, like Peter's, "Lord, save me" (Matt. 14: 30) when he could not have knelt down and offered a long prayer. It was thus when Artaxerxes suddenly gave his "cupbearer" a great chance, and a great hope. "For what dost thou make request?" That instant Nehemiah sent off his wire, asking for immediate guidance. Happy the believer who has learned to use this method of getting help. Those who are habitually people of prayer may employ this particular habit of prayer with great effect.

PRAYER.—*We know too, O Lord, that Thou wilt immediately send a reply to every wire from godly men. Not always the thing they want, but always the thing they need.* AMEN.

"*. . . a man to seek the welfare of the children . . .*" (Neh. 2: 10)

D IVORCED thus from their context, the words are made to carry a meaning not originally intended, yet they do, in the way quoted, convey a message of great importance. The children's need is undoubted; throughout the world they are an increasing problem. The children's welfare is not only physical, mental, social, but spiritual. And it is linked up with their personal relationship to the Saviour. The children's friend is the "man," or woman, who will "seek" to reach, touch, and fetch them for Him. Who will dedicate his life to this strategic service? Be sure our Sanballat will be exceedingly "grieved" at such a decision, but that will only strengthen the call. What hope would be kindled if in every place there should arise "a man to seek the welfare of the children." We have wrested the phrase from the context in the Word that we might ponder it in the context of the World need.

PRAYER.—*Thou Children's Friend and Saviour, wilt Thou not in these days call out those who shall give their lives to this great work, and to this end wilt Thou beget in them a great love for the little ones, and so help to build the walls of the New Jerusalem.* AMEN.

"*. . . I . . . viewed the wall . . .*" (Neh. 2: 15)

T HAT was of course a sensible and even essential thing to do. The subsequent story will disclose the vigour of the people, who put their whole hearts into the job, and the valour of the workers, who had to carry on in face of strenuous opposition from the enemy, and the victory of the cause which saw the wall joyfully completed. But it all began with the vision of the task, which here came to Nehemiah. He saw for himself that night the "broken down" condition of the wall that must be built up, somewhat as Joshua, years before, had seen the mighty wall of Jericho that must be broken down. Note that in both cases it was a private view, with the crowd shut out, when it could be seen in the quiet what must be done and what resources were available. That is the way to commence any work for God: a secret view of it, and of Him.

PRAYER.—*Our Master-Builder, give us eyes to see the task that lies ahead, give us hands to do the work that it entails, give us minds to understand that we may count on Thy help, give us hearts to do it all for Thine own Glory's sake.* AMEN.

MAY   **15**

"_. . . Let us rise up and build . . ._" (Neh. 2: 18)

IN the previous verse, Nehemiah proposed the resolution, "Let us . . ."
Now here the meeting carried it unanimously, "Let us . . .". In
support of his resolution, Nehemiah spoke of the challenge of the
hour: the city "lieth waste," a matter causing "great distress." Perhaps
the state of our city, or country, causes deep heart-searching and is a
great challenge to our faith and endeavour. Mark the other circumstances
of the situation, not only the sad condition of the place, but also the hand
of God, obviously directing, and the word of the king, promising every
help. So observe the commencement of the work, "So they strengthened
their hands for this good work." Truly, if God's hand be in the matter,
our hand had better be in it too. "Let us rise up and build."

PRAYER.—_Give us a great desire, O God, and an ever-growing enthusiasm
for Thy cause in our day and generation. May we build safely and surely
and build for ever under Thine Eye._ AMEN.

MAY   **16**

"_. . . they builded the sheep gate . . ._" (Neh. 3: 1)

SO they began to build the wall. But where did they start? At "the
sheep gate," the entrance nearest the Temple, through which at Passover the sacrificial lambs went to their death and through which the
"Lamb of God" probably passed, that Holy Week, from Bethany when
He went to His atoning sacrifice. It was at that spot they began. So, too,
at the building of the Temple, they started by setting up "the altar . . .
and they offered burnt offerings thereon" (Ezra 3: 3). That "gate," and
that "altar" were typical figures of Him in His sacrifice, and as 1 Corinthians 3: 11 says of our building, "Other foundation can no man lay
than that is laid, which is Jesus Christ," the crucified. So let us build on
Him, and His "finished" work.

PRAYER.—_May I indeed found all my hopes, all my service, all my experience, all my salvation, all my strength, on that "Rock of Ages, cleft for
me." Verily may I enter the City of my Blessings through the Sheep
Gate._ AMEN.

MAY   **17**

"*. . . their nobles put not their necks to the work . . .*" (Neh. 3: 5)

THE ordinary Tekoites worked like slaves, indeed not content with the bit of the work assigned to them, they repaired "another piece" (v. 27), so absorbed were they in the undertaking, but their leaders did not share this fine enthusiasm. The majority were "up to their necks" in it, but these few "put not their necks" into it. Many of God's builders are equally slack; though not completely idle, they are not continuously industrious. How distasteful to "their Lord" are those who are "neither cold nor hot" (Rev. 3: 15). These ignobles of the text were woefully lacking in zeal for the Cause. Do you not think that this quality of enthusiasm is sadly missing from the make-up of many of us modern Christians; that we are not all out, all in, for God.

PRAYER.—*Seeing, O Gracious God, that Thou hast given Thine All for us, may the Holy Spirit inspire us to give our little all to Thee, to spend and be spent in Thy great cause, that at the last we may hear Thy "Well Done."* AMEN.

MAY   **18**

"*Next . . . repaired . . . the goldsmiths . . . the apothecaries . . . the merchants*" (Neh. 3: 8, 32)

BUT these were not bricklayers; theirs was more delicate work than building walls. Yet they lent a hand. The fact is, of course, that whatever may be our everyday employment, we are expected to take some share in that other work which is eternal, building for God. How greatly has that cause been advanced by the laymen of the Church; men of fine craftsmanship like "goldsmiths"; men of scientific mind like "apothecaries"; men of business capacity like "merchants," who have conceived it their duty to engage in God's service and to use their gifts and distinctive testimony for Him. The clergy may be the professional bricklayers (is that why they drop so many?), but the merchants and others are called to add their quota to the rising wall, if only by mixing the mortar, or carrying the hods. Are we active members of this Labour Corps?

PRAYER.—*Lord, whatever else we are, may we also be labourers with Thee however humble or however high the task allotted to us, and may we build close to Thee.* AMEN.

". . . over against his house . . ." (Neh. 3: 10)

IN this Log of the Job, several are spoken of as building on the spot immediately in front of their own home. And assuredly that is the place where we should begin. It is something of a tragedy that many Christians are prepared to build for God anywhere but at their own dwelling, and in front of their own household, forgetting the primary rule of spiritual Building Construction, "Learn first to shew piety at home" (1 Tim. 5: 4). Perhaps you have not a home of your own and live in lodgings. Well, you can "build" even there for God, like the man at the end of verse 30, who built "over against his chamber." Whether the house, or only the room, it is a fine plot for erecting a testimony for the Lord that all can see. Put a bit in today.

PRAYER.—*May our nearest and dearest have the clearest evidence that we are Thine, O Lord, and if it is difficult because there we are offguard and they know us so well, yet do Thou guard us that we may not fail them or Thee.* AMEN.

". . . the king's garden . . ." (Neh. 3: 15)

I WONDER whether, like the wall, it had been allowed to go to pieces. We don't know, but in spiritual significance our heart is "the King's garden," and we do know something about the condition of that. When, on the Resurrection morning, Mary supposed He was the gardener (John 20: 15), she was spiritually near the truth. Well, how does your garden grow? Does it need weeding, from noxious habits? Or digging, turning over with the spade of repentance? Or planting, with seeds from the Nurseries of Heaven, and slips from the Tree of Life? Or hoeing with continual watchfulness? Or pruning, with the knife of adversity? Or watering, with the rain of Heaven, the showers of the Spirit? All these it will get if its greatest need of all is met, the unfettered control of the Gardener. What lovely bud, and blossom, and beautiful fruit will spring out of this unpromising soil if He have charge.

PRAYER.—*Lord, if Thou canst take pleasure in the garden of our soul, and if others can find beauty and refreshment therein, how grateful we shall be, and how well aware that it has not been we who have done it, but He, the Holy Spirit.* AMEN.

"*. . . we made our prayer . . . and set a watch . . .*" (Neh. 4: 9)

ALL God's builders have satanic enemies that seek to frighten them and to frustrate their endeavours. So are we counselled to adopt these counter-measures. "Watch and pray that ye enter not into temptation" (Matt. 26: 41). Watch before you pray, lest the enemy get you into the wrong frame of mind, that ye "ask amiss" (Jas. 4: 3). Watch while you pray, lest the enemy weaken your purpose with sleepiness or sidetrack you with wandering thoughts. Watch after you pray, lest the enemy rob you of that rest in God's will which is one of the priceless by-products of true prayer, and prevent your looking out for the answers to your prayers which would fill your heart with thanksgiving, prayer's natural twin brother.

> *Watch, as if on that alone*
> *Hung the issue of the day;*
> *Pray, that help may be sent down;*
> *Watch and pray!*

What a sane leader Nehemiah was! We may very properly follow his lead here.

PRAYER.—*Strengthen us, O Lord, that in both these spiritual endeavours we may become faithful and fruitful practitioners, that the devil may get no advantage in us, but that Thou mayest be able to use us to much advantage in Thy Kingdom.* AMEN.

"*. . . there is much rubbish . . .*" (Neh. 4: 10)

NO one has ever started to build the wall for God without soon discovering, as these did in Old Jerusalem, that "there is much rubbish." When Nebuchadnezzar destroyed the city, he did it thoroughly, and the passage of the years, seventy of them, completed the wreck. So before they could begin building, they had to clear "much rubbish." So it is with our spiritual endeavour. What heaps of rubbish hinder the task; those sad grudges that spoil many lives; those corroding envies that sour many hearts; those false ideas that sow wrong impressions of good and God; those bad habits that sink many a fair promise of youth; those foolish superstitions that strangle many a good intention at its birth; those evil tempers that stab fond affections to their death. The old Greek, Heracles, cleansed the filthy Augean stable by turning Alpheus on to it, and our only hope of clearing this "rubbish" is by using the "fountain opened for sin and uncleanness" (Zech. 13: 1).

PRAYER.—*Lord, let none of this remain a day longer in my own heart and life, that it may no more choke Thy purposes of love for me. May the pure Waters of the Spirit rid me of all rubbish, and fit me for good service.* AMEN.

MAY 23

". . . *ought ye not to walk in the fear of . . . God because of the . . . heathen?*" (Neh. 5: 9)

THERE are several reasons why we should be careful to live a holy life. One is for the Lord's sake, who bought us to that end. Another is for the Church's sake, that we may pull our weight in her testimony and service. The next is for our own sake, seeing that happiness and helpfulness in the Christian life are such close companions of holiness. A fourth is for the world's sake, lest we mislead them, and put stumbling blocks in their way. If you make profession of being a Christian, "many eyes are watching, taking note of you." Therefore, "walk in wisdom toward them that are without" (Col. 4: 5) and "make straight paths for your feet, lest that which is lame be turned out of the way" (Heb. 12: 13) and "as ye have received Christ Jesus the Lord, so walk ye in Him" (Col. 2: 6). Let us seek to walk like that today, if only "for their sakes" (John 17: 19).

PRAYER.—*Help me, O God, thus to walk circumspectly today, that I may fully discharge my fourfold responsibility, and so honour Thee in my Christian progress.* AMEN.

MAY 24

". . . *so did not I, because of the fear of God*" (Neh. 5: 15)

DO as others do is the majority's rule of conduct. When Nehemiah became Governor, Tirshatha, of this little colony, he found that his predecessors in office had been in the habit of requisitioning from the people provisions to keep the Governor's table well laden. Our friend felt that was not right, and he says, "So did not I." It was customary, but conscience rebelled. How ready we are to fall in with custom, right or not! "Everybody does it!" "When in Rome, do as Rome does!" It is so much more comfortable and convenient than being peculiar. That was not good enough for this early, robust nonconformist, Nehemiah. Do as God would have you do; that is the implication of "because of the fear of God." We may happily follow others, unless and until there comes a point of contradiction and controversy with the way of God. Then "the fear of God," or "the love of Christ" (2 Cor. 5: 14), will constrain us to nonconformity.

PRAYER.—*Prevent us, O Lord, from becoming chameleon Christians taking on always the colour of our surroundings, following always the habits of our companions, walking according to the course of this world, but rather wilt Thou help us, O Lord, to keep close to our Great Example.* AMEN.

". . . I am doing a great work, so that I cannot come down . . ."
(Neh. 6: 3)

THEN to "come down" would indeed be a come-down! You see, Sanballat and his crew were doing everything they could to stop, or hinder, these builders of the wall. And here we have one of the ruses they adopted: to try to get Nehemiah to come to a conference, blessed word! There is a place for conferences in Christian work, of course, but there is danger these days of overdoing them. To meet the modern situation we need not a great talk but "a great work." All work for God is "great." Let us, having set our hands to it, carry on and resist every effort, whether of the world, the flesh, or the devil, to deflect us from the task. Nehemiah was too wise a man and had too clear an understanding of the work to be caught that way. May we be given like wisdom, and like tenacity of purpose.

PRAYER.—*O God, keep us on the alert against all temptation to be fickle-minded, or faint-hearted or feeble-willed in Thy work. Grant us the grace of steadfast perseverance.* AMEN.

". . . Should such a man as I flee? . . ." (Neh. 6: 11)

ANOTHER of Sanballat's ruses to ruin the rebuilding was this. He sent Nehemiah an underhand message, which seemed to be the urgent advice of well-wishers who were only afterwards unmasked as being in the enemy's pay. His life was threatened, it said, and he had better make a bolt for it and find safeguard in the Temple sanctuary. But it didn't come off! You couldn't frighten "such a man" as Nehemiah. A man with a vivid sense of God's Person cannot be scared. It would be said of him, as of Lord Shaftesbury, that "he feared man so little because he feared God so much." A man with a vivid sense of God's Presence cannot be scared. He knows that "not a single shaft can hit, till the love of God sees fit." A man with a vivid sense of God's Purpose cannot be scared. He feels, with David Livingstone, that "man is immortal till his work is done." Let us each seek to be "such a man," or woman, quite unmoved by the jeers and jeopardies of the enemy.

PRAYER.—*Give us that needful courage which shall cause that we never take flight, but ever show fight for the right.* AMEN.

MAY 27

" . . . eat . . . drink . . . send portions . . ." (Neh. 8: 10)

THE words exhort us to think of ourselves. A great company gathered to hear God's Book read. There were things therein that greatly humbled them, but also much to cause them to lift up their hearts. It was a holy yet happy day. The appropriate celebration was not a fast, but a feast, so they were bidden "eat the fat, drink the sweet." So, if we are to be healthful and helpful Christians, we must feast our souls on the Word which is bread and water, meat and milk and honey, to the spirit. But then we are to think of others; "send portions unto them for whom nothing is prepared." In the spiritual application, God has "prepared" for all to share in the Salvation Feast (cf. Luke 2: 30–31), and it is our happy privilege to "send portions" to all whom we can reach. Fed ourselves, we are led to others.

PRAYER.—*Whenever we sit down to partake of Thy bounty, may we be mindful of the needs of others, and so become caterers of the Word.* AMEN.

MAY 28

". . . the joy of the Lord is your strength" (Neh. 8: 10)

THE happy man is always in a strong position and when his joy is not merely earthly but spiritual, when it is of heavenly origin, then it has a power all its own. It makes for the strength of his spiritual constitution. Joy makes for physical well-being, as any doctor will tell you and as Proverbs 17: 22 says, "A merry heart doeth good like a medicine." It is no less a tonic for spiritual health. It makes for the strength of his spiritual service also. The idea of "Music While You Work" is that happiness makes the wheels go faster, just as in Christian service joy sweetens labour. So John Keble in "St. Matthew's Day":

> *There are in this loud stunning tide*
> *Of human care and crime,*
> *With whom the melodies abide*
> *Of th' everlasting chime;*
> *Who carry music in their heart,*
> *Through dusty lane and wrangling mart,*
> *Plying their daily task with busier feet,*
> *Because their secret souls some holy strain repeat.*

It makes too for the strength of his spiritual appeal. Tenfold force is added to a Christian's argument if it is obvious what joy his Lord brings to his own life.

PRAYER.—*What cause we have, O Lord, to be joyous Christians, for though the outlook be sometimes dark, the uplook will always pierce the clouds.* AMEN.

"Thou gavest also Thy good Spirit to instruct them . . ." (Neh. 9: 20)

IF that were true of the people of Israel, during their wilderness experience, a fact for which amongst many other blessings these returned exiles are here praising God, how much more richly real is it for us who now live in the very Dispensation of the Spirit. Think especially of the coming in fulness of Him concerning whom the Master said, "He shall teach you all things" (John 14: 26), and of whom John declares, "Ye have an Unction from the Holy One, and ye know all things" (1 John 2: 20), that is, all ye need to know. And this, be it noted, is said not of the "fathers" nor of the "young men," but of the "little children" in the faith. The moment we are in the Family, we have Him at hand for our Tutor. His usual textbook is of course the Bible, of which He is Author and Authority.

PRAYER.—*While we grow in grace, may we also grow in the knowledge of Thy Word, Thy Truth, Thyself, and to this end may we be apt scholars of our great Teacher, the Holy Spirit, and what we come to know, may we go out to do.* AMEN.

". . . Pethahiah . . . was at the king's hand in all matters concerning the people" (Neh. 11: 24)

HERE is a thumbnail sketch of one who is a wonderful picture of our Ascended Lord. Note who he was. As to nationality, a "son of Judah," a real representative of the Jewish people, who could share their interests, understand their viewpoint, interpret their thoughts. How like Him who is "like as we are" (Heb. 4: 15). As to name, it means "Jehovah hath set free," so like the "God raised Him," so often spoken of Jesus. Note where he was, "at the king's hand," reminder of the Ascension truth. "This Man . . . sat down on the right hand of God" (Heb. 10: 12). And note why he was, "in all matters concerning the people." The people's representative he was, they in Jerusalem, he in Babylon; and One "in the presence of God for us" (Heb. 9: 24). The people's advocate he was, to answer Sanballat's slanders. "We have an Advocate" (1 John 2: 1). The people's intermediary he was, through whom their need reaches the king's ear, and their supplies return, even as ours "ascending and descending upon the Son of Man" (John 1: 51). How good to have such a Friend at Court!

PRAYER.—*We thank Thee, O God, for all that the Ascension Glory of our Saviour means for us, and not least, that "He ever liveth to make intercession for us." How shall we ever know what we owe to His prayers.* AMEN.

". . . they were counted faithful . . ." (Neh. 13: 13)

WHAT a theme with which to finish this month's meditations! The Master once said, "Well done, good and faithful servant" (Matt. 25: 23), and that, if no further honour accrued, would surely be reward enough for our service. It is a prize open to us all, but we must earn it. Some have said that while we can all be faithful we can't all be fruitful, but I firmly believe that if we are faithful we shall be fruitful. We may not see the fruit here, but we shall "know hereafter." Oh then, to be "counted faithful," as Nehemiah's treasurers were. Great treasure has been entrusted to our care and use, and forasmuch as "we have this treasure in earthen vessels" (2 Cor. 4: 7), let us pray that the earthly part of us may be so controlled by the heavenly that we may not fail of this "good report." Now may God be able to rely on us; and then may He be able to reward us.

PRAYER.—*Our Master, give to us the quality of fidelity, that Thou mayest know that Thou canst depend on us to do Thy bidding at any seeming cost to ourselves.* AMEN.

JUNE

STORIES FROM THE DIARY OF A DOCTOR

So we may entitle Luke's Gospel and the Doctor's other volume, the Acts. Some of what he writes (in his second Book) is matter of his own personal experience. Most is the outcome of stories which reached him from those intimately connected with the occasions recorded, or gleanings from reports carefully checked and sifted by that "perfect understanding," which came to him "from above" (see Greek), that is by inspiration of God, the Holy Spirit.

JUNE 1

"That thou mightest know the certainty of those things, wherein thou hast been instructed" (Luke 1: 4)

MODERN scholarship has almost unanimously come to acknowledge what it did not always allow: the accuracy of Luke as an historian. The worthy doctor has dedicated all his painstaking investigation to the task of reporting correctly the sayings and doings of those wonderful years. Like a true physician, he knows the unsettling effect of uncertainty, and he labours to bring to his friend that certainty about spiritual foundations which he himself has so happily come to know. We also should, and may, have this blessed assurance, and Dr. Luke is the very man to help us to know it.

PRAYER.—*While we bless Thee, O God, for all that this "Beloved Physician" has done for believers through the ages, we do not forget that he owes it all, as we do, to the Holy Spirit who inspired him. May He give us true understanding of all that through those pages shall be revealed.* AMEN.

JUNE 2

". . . I . . . stand . . . and am sent to speak . . . and to shew . . ." (Luke 1: 19)

YOU may not be a Gabriel, you certainly are not an angel, but for all that you may exercise a ministry for God which bears the Gabriel touch, the fourfold touch. (1) "Stand," in His presence at His disposal, ready for anything. (2) "Sent," on His errands wherever He shall wish me to go, relying always on His supplies for my journey and my task. (3) "Speak," not my own message but His, entrusted with the word for the crowd, or the few, or the individual, as He shall appoint, bearing the glad tidings of His love and grace. (4) "Shew"; Gabriel was to show by speaking, we are to show as well as to speak; to show in our lives a practical illustration of what we speak with our lips, the former being often the more convincing testimony of the two. Here are, then, the four marks of a promising and profitable service, for which may God call and equip us all!

PRAYER.—*We may shrink, indeed, from our responsibility of being Thy messengers, O Lord, were it not for the blessed truth that Thou wilt never send us at our own charges, but with the full supply of Thy all-sufficient grace. "Here am I, Lord, send me."* AMEN.

JUNE 3

". . . My soul . . . my Saviour" (Luke 1: 46, 47)

THE matter of my eternal welfare, the nature of my spiritual experience, the degree of my life's usefulness, all depend upon the relationship between "my soul" and "my Savioulr." Introduction is, of course, the beginning of it all; that blessed moment of repentance and faith when the Saviour became "my" Saviour. Increase in the knowledge of Him is to mark our lives from that first moment. A continually growing acquaintance with Him and with His mind is the happy experience of every truly healthy Christian, an ever-deepening fellowship through the diligent use of the means of grace. Intimacy then, and thus, becomes a privileged possibility, arising out of a walk of trustful obedience. "Trust and obey, for there's no other way . . ." He has no favourites, but He has intimates, even those who are prepared to walk with Him step by step, and day by day.

PRAYER.—*How can we ever estimate Thine amazing condescension in allowing us unworthy Christians to say "My" of Thee. May we on our side become wholly Thine.* AMEN.

JUNE 4

". . . unto you is born . . . a Saviour . . ." (Luke 2: 11)

UNTO whom? "Unto you" shepherds, though they were but lowly folk. None are too lowly, too weak, too insignificant, indeed too sinful to receive His message, or to enjoy His salvation. "Unto you" Jews, though they did not recognize, nor receive Him, their long-promised Messiah. Still the word runs, "to the Jew first." "Unto you" worldlings, though millions do not even yet know about Him. People of every clime, colour and condition are included in His offer of salvation. What a challenge to us believers to go out after those others, to reach and touch and fetch them for Him. "Unto you" individuals; though "God so loved the world that He gave His only-begotten Son," it is also and more intimately true that "the Son of God loved me, and gave Himself for me." Have we each, have you, received Him thus as your own personal Saviour? If so, then let your whole life be lived "unto Him" (2 Cor. 5: 15).

PRAYER.—*We thank Thee, O Father, that this One "born Saviour" was also "born King." May we who have enjoyed His Saviourhood live henceforth under His Sovereignty, and enrol as heralds of His Saving Grace and Reigning Glory.* AMEN.

JUNE 5

"*. . . Prepare ye the way of the Lord . . .*" (Luke 3: 4)

PREPARING the way for His coming to earth, and preparing the way for His Second Coming to earth, are the natural thoughts which emerge from such a text. But preparing the way for His present coming to human hearts is the thought I want to suggest just now for today's meditation. Note how Andrew prepared the way for Him to reach Peter, and how Philip prepared in the case of Nathanael. Don't you think we could make the "way" easier for people around us to find Him and be found of Him, by our earnest prayer for them, by our faithful witness to them, and perhaps most of all by our consistent life before them? Alas, all too many of us Christians are a hindrance, rather than a help, to His coming to other hearts. God save us all from being a stumbling block to anybody, and enable us, by sheer goodness, kindness and Christ-likeness to "prepare the way of the Lord" to them.

PRAYER.—*We feel, O Lord, if we can show to others what a difference Thou dost make in our lives, they will the more readily seek Him who so lovingly seeks them. May the Holy Spirit make us good advertisements.* AMEN.

JUNE 6

"*. . . as His custom was . . .*" (Luke 4: 16)

HOW great is the force of habit, for good or for ill, enabling or enslaving. Even the word has a strange stickability. Habit: take away the "h," and you still have "a bit." Remove the "a," and a "bit" remains. Without the "b," you find that "it" is still there. The thing itself is a boon or a bane in any life. It is an immeasurable blessing to form good habits; the habit, for instance, of the daily prayer and portion, the habit of the constant thought for others rather than ourselves, the habit of the weekly worship which the text tells us was our Lord's "custom." Some professed Christians are very lax about this, as if the servant were above his master! By the way, do you think the Master always approved of everything that was done in the synagogue worship? Was the preaching always to His liking? I trow not, but He still went, "as His custom was," to worship with others.

PRAYER.—*How dear has been Thy House, O God, to many. May we never "forsake the assembling of ourselves together as the manner of some is," even if everything in the Church is not completely to our liking, for "Thou, O Lord, art there Thy chosen flock to greet."* AMEN.

JUNE 7

". . . let down your nets . . . and he let down the net" (Luke 5: 4, 5)

Two things are here for our instruction. First, here is the lesson of obedience. Peter learned that it always pays to obey the Master. That is, as a matter of fact, the key to all spiritual advancement. We may sometimes feel that we would choose otherwise. Here, for example, is One who humanly was a carpenter, telling a fisherman to do what was obviously out of order. "Launch out into the deep, and let down your nets for a draught," but in that Sea you don't catch fish in the daytime, nor in the deep, but at night and in the shallows. Peter the fisherman knew that, "nevertheless" he was ready to do as the Master told him. But note here also the limit of obedience. The Lord said "nets," both of the two that were always on those boats, but His disciple dropped the "net," only one of them. If he had obeyed completely there would have been no "break!" Let us learn to obey Him right up to the hilt!

PRAYER.—*Thou, O Lord, art Master in our ship. May we heed Thy commands and may our obedience be full and prompt and glad, and so be truly blest.* AMEN.

JUNE 8

"And why call ye Me, Lord, Lord, and do not the things which I say?"
(Luke 6: 46)

It is a most proper thing to call Him Lord, but is it the confession merely of the lips and not really of the life? I have sometimes heard it said that Christianity is a religion of "done," not "do," inasmuch as "it is finished," and we have but to accept what is done, and trust the divine Doer of it. Yes, I know what is meant, and wholeheartedly I agree, but surely it is false to put it, "Do *or* done," when it is not truly a question of alternative, but of inclusive, "Do *and* done," being careful however to get the order right. First the Done, and then the Do. If His lordship be a reality, it will disclose itself in a daily walk of complete obedience to His will. "Ye say, and do not" was His rebuke of the Pharisees. May it never be true of us. Luke would know the importance of obeying the doctor's orders. How much more important the Saviour's!

PRAYER.—*Lord, when we pray "Thy Will be done in earth," may we ever remember to apply it to that part of the earth which is ourselves, realizing that Thy commands are always enabling, so that we can "do" if we will "do."* AMEN.

"... *he that was dead* ..." (Luke 7: 15)

"WAS" because "dead" no longer, but now alive. Physically so in the context; spiritually so in its application. How shall people know that we are no longer "dead in trespasses and sins," but "alive unto God through Jesus Christ"? Ponder the following signs of life. The sign of vision, "she opened her eyes" (Acts 9: 40). Things are seen in a new way; there is new outlook, new inlook, new uplook, new onlook. The sign of appetite, "He commanded to give her meat" (Luke 8: 55). What about our appetite for the Bible, and all Christian things? Beware of anything which spoils your spiritual appetite. The sign of speech, he "began to speak" (Luke 7: 15). If healthy, we shall begin to speak to Him in prayer, and speak of Him in testimony. The sign of liberty, "Loose him and let him go" (John 11: 44); freed from the "grave clothes" or the old "dead" days. The sign of progress, "arose and walked" (Mark 5: 42). The Christian will never come to a standstill. By such signs will they come to perceive that as for us that "dead" is a thing of the past.

PRAYER.—*May there abound in us so many signs and fruits of our new life that none shall doubt the reality of our new birth, and that many shall praise Him who has brought such things to pass.* AMEN.

"... *people gladly received Him* ..." (Luke 8: 40)

THAT is only what one would expect. Yet, such is the pull of the world and the perversity of the human heart that more usually people sadly reject Him. Why did these particular folk "receive" Him? In verse 37, they "besought Him to depart." Why the remarkable change that, when He was returned, "the people gladly received Him, for they were all waiting for Him"? The interesting explanation is found in the intervening verses of the chapter. Obeying the instructions of the One who had saved him, Legion went back to his own home and neighbourhood, and began to give his simple and sincere testimony to what He had done for him, a testimony backed up by the obvious changes in his own condition and conduct. That was the cause of the alteration in the attitude of the Gadarenes. Are we bearing a like testimony in our home and neighbourhood?

PRAYER.—*May we never be unmindful of the responsibility that devolves upon us when we receive Thee, O Lord, into our lives, that such a transformation shall be seen as shall cause many of our acquaintances also to receive Thee. May we never let Thee down.* AMEN.

". . . No . . . looking back. . . " (Luke 9: 62)

THE ploughman in this passage may be cutting his furrow in the face of a great storm of rain, beating pitilessly down upon him. He may be strongly tempted to look back over there at his comfortable cottage, and long to be there warm and dry. But he mustn't do that; his furrow would at once become crooked. So the Christian, once started, if he would go straight must, whatever be the difficulties and oppositions, never turn back. There will be a looking round for service. There is so much to be done for God, and there are all too few to do it. There will be a looking up for strength, that we may do our tasks well, that they may please and honour God, as well as help our fellows. There will be a looking forward to success that shall win His "well done," the highest of all awards. But if we would gain that happy portion, there will be no looking back, but a going straight on!

PRAYER.—*Then, Lord, may we be steadfast, unmovable, always abounding in the work of the Lord, forasmuch as we know that our labour is not in vain in the Lord.* AMEN.

". . . rejoice, because your names are written in heaven" (Luke 10: 20)

WE are told in Jeremiah 17: 13 about those who are "written in the earth." Any fame or honour they may have gathered is inscribed down here, their names may even be recorded in history, but if "they have forsaken the Lord," they are of no account up yonder. The Lord's "seventy" shall not covet to be honoured as those who can command evil spirits. The newspapers might then be full of their triumphs. They might, in large type, even in headlines, be "written in the earth," but this is rather their joy that, being faithful to the Lord, their names are "written in heaven," and fundamentally that they are among the blessed company of those who, by His infinite grace and mercy, are described in Revelation 21: 27 as "they which are written in the Lamb's book of life." We need not foolishly despise earth's roll. We could, indeed, use such fame for God, but our true happiness shall lie in the imperishable letters with which our names, for His Name's sake, are inscribed in Heaven's *Who's Who*.

PRAYER.—*May Thy Name, O Lord, be so deeply written upon my heart, that my name, even mine, shall find a place in Thy Book among those who have loved and served Thy Name down here.* AMEN.

". . . when I come again . . ." (Luke 10: 35)

DOCTOR LUKE would revel in this incident. That "certain man," battered, robbed, taken to the inn, would, I think, upon regaining consciousness have three surprises concerning his benefactor. Each of them we on our part may well entertain about the Lord Jesus, Himself supremely the Good Samaritan. First, then, he would have been surprised that he had done anything for him, for he would consider a Jew an enemy. Ah, it was "when we were enemies" (Rom. 5: 10), that He came where we were and saved us. Then, he would have been surprised that he had done everything for him. What a story the innkeeper told him when he woke up! And "how shall He not with Him freely give us all things" (Rom. 8: 32). And, joy of joys, he would have been surprised that he had promised to come back for him. He didn't say when, so the patient was continually on the watch, looking for the day when he could see him and thank him. So do we hear Him speak of "when I come again," and with joy we await His appearing.

PRAYER.—*When I might be dispirited or downcast, may the thought of seeing Thee cheer my heart. If I should be making little progress may the thought of Thy return spur me on that nothing may mar the joy and wonder of seeing Thee then.* AMEN.

". . . having no part dark . . ." (Luke 11: 36)

IN a terrific storm one of the lights of a lighthouse was blown to bits, and so as to stop the wind from raging in and damaging the other lights, and having no spare glass, the keeper managed to insert a sheet of tin. So the lantern had one dark part. That night a ship, misguided by the absence of light, mistook her position, and was dashed to pieces on the rocks. We are set in a dark place, to guide voyages safe home; but what if there be some part of our life unyielded, some side of our character unlit by His holiness, some bit of inconsistency that should prove a stumbling block to another, that should even shipwreck another life? What, if bright and clear in every other respect, there be one thing wrong, that should cause grievous harm to someone else? Let it be our daily prayer and endeavour, "No part dark!"

PRAYER.—*Lord, may my yielding to Thee be so complete that there shall be nothing to keep back. So may Thy Light shine through my whole being and no soul be hindered.* AMEN.

"*. . . Beware ye of . . . hypocrisy*" (Luke 12: 1)

How frequently and how vehemently our Lord spoke against this sin. How important it is then that we search our hearts lest there be any vestige of it in us. It is all a matter of pretence; pretending to be what we are not. The Greek word for "hypocrite" means "a play actor," playing a part which is not the real he. How often would Dr. Luke have patients well, but imagining themselves to be ill, or more rarely the ill feigning to be well. How all such would hate to be called hypocrites, which is what they are. Let us keep clear of imagining ourselves to be better than we are. Let us be careful not to speak beyond our experience. Let us avoid the danger of supposing we are Christians if we are not the real thing. That we may "beware . . . hypocrisy," let us ever be ready to submit ourselves to the X-rays of the Holy Spirit.

PRAYER.—*In all aspects of my being and life, may I be the genuine article, and may I eschew all false imitation. Thou, Lord, art so real, help me to be real in my degree.* AMEN.

JUNE   16

"*. . . I come seeking fruit . . .*" (Luke 13: 7)

THE language of course is spiritual and the reference is to the Jewish nation, but the application is to all God's people. Think of His expenditure in the thought on His eternal plan, in the cost of His precious blood, in the patient working of His Holy Spirit, in the abundant supplies of His grace. As He says in Isaiah 5: 4, "What could have been done more to My vineyard that I have not done in it?" Think, then, of His expectation; "I come seeking fruit." He has every right to expect it, hasn't He? The fruit of earnest service, the fruit of holy character, "fruit of the Spirit" as Galatians 5: 22, 23 calls it. But think now of His experience. Does He find what He is looking for in us? "He shall see of the travail of His soul, and shall be satisfied" (Isa. 53: 2). Does that not apply to the quality of our character, as well as to the fact of our salvation? Come now, after all the "travail" of His expenditure, is He anything like "satisfied" with us?

PRAYER.—*It is only because of Thine abundant grace that I can dare to pray, as I do pray, that I may in nothing be a disappointment to Thee. May my thinking, speaking, acting, being, cause Thee some pleasure.* AMEN.

JUNE   **17**

"He sent his servant . . . to say . . . Come . . ." (Luke 14: 17)

THE primary concern of the story is, of course, dispensational, but it has also its personal application. He has a Message to send, an invitation to "come" to the Gospel feast, and what a glorious feast it is! He wants a Messenger to take it. Are you "His servant"? Then He would send you "to say, Come," to invite as many as you can find to the Banquet. What a mighty privilege! He could have chosen angels for the task, and they would have grasped the task with joyful alacrity, but instead He offers us the honour of being His agents. We are not sent to argue, some of us could never do that; but to say, "Come." As Samaria's woman said, "Come, see" (John 4: 29), and as Philip advised Nathanael, "Come and see" (John 1: 46), for yourself.

PRAYER—*In Thy loving kindness and tender mercy Thou didst bid me "Come." Now may I go forth to distribute the great invitation far and wide that others may come to "Taste and see that the Lord is good."* AMEN.

JUNE   **18**

". . . compel them to come in . . ." (Luke 14: 23)

"COMPEL," not by force, but by gentle persuasion. And the people in the story would take some persuading! "The poor, the maimed, the halt, and the blind"; nobody in those times and lands would bother to invite them to a feast. The tramps along the "highways" and hiding behind the "hedges"; feasts are not for the likes of them. There must be some mistake. Indeed they would need some persuading, only a loving compulsion will get them to "come in." We think that only as "the love of Christ constraineth us," and as that love is evidenced in us by the loving word, the loving action, the loving demeanour, shall we be able to turn their footsteps to the feast. I know that some are "frightened" into the kingdom, and there are those who will only be won that way, but love is still the more prolific method. So let us lovingly persuade.

PRAYER.—*Indeed, Lord, may love be the keynote of all my Gospel activity. May I work for Thee, not to gain reward, not to get a reputation, but because I love Thee and love them enough to long for their salvation.* AMEN.

". . . *safe and sound*" (Luke 15: 27)

WHAT a grand description of a real, true Christian! He is safe, from the eternal guilt and judgment of sin through the trusted death of the Lord Jesus for him on the Cross, and from the daily habit and power of sin through the tapped Life of the Lord Jesus indwelling him in the heart. Oh, blessed safety, dependent not on anything in me, but for everything in Him. He is sound; I do not mean here sound in doctrine, though let that not be lightly esteemed, as if it doesn't matter what a man believes. For the moment, I think rather of that soundness of character which so well becomes a Christian and which so glorifies the Lord that saved him. Here are the two sides of the coin which can so effectually "be spent" in the Master's service, a coin both of whose sides are thus stamped with His "image and superscription," for let it be said again it is only He who can make and mark us as safe and sound.

PRAYER.—*So may it be that all who are safe in Jesus may be sound all through, that with no uncertainty we may sound forth Thy glorious Gospel.* AMEN.

"*No servant can serve two masters . . .*" (Luke 16: 13)

BUT surely he can! I have a gardener who serves me some days of the week, and who serves another man the rest. Ah, but look at the word. The Greek means more than just to give service, that would be quite a different word. This one means to give bond service, and you can't be a bond slave to two masters! The slave is only and utterly the property of his one lord. He has no possessions, no plans, no powers, no privileges of his own; he is completely devoted to his master for his whole time and talents, entirely dependent upon him for the supplies needful for his life and service. Do you remember how Paul loved to describe himself as "the servant (bond slave) of Jesus Christ," and how proud he was of that total servitude? May we, too, be privileged to serve Him as our sole and supreme Master.

PRAYER.—*So sweet have we found Thy service, Lord, that it is to us perfect freedom, and nothing shall cause us to leave or halve Thy service. Blessed be bondage to such a Master!* AMEN.

". . . as they went, they were cleansed" (Luke 17: 14)

CAN you imagine what it would mean for these poor men to have the opportunity of a possible cure? Perhaps the ten had heard of the healing of that one in Chapter 5: 12ff. Ah, blessed is it for leprous sinners that the opportunity is theirs to cry to Him who both can and will cleanse and save. So, in our story, we hear the order given which implies that He is prepared in His love and power to remove their foul disease. The men know full well the hope which is implicit in that command. In the obedience which immediately followed His bidding there came to them the boon they so eagerly sought. Their obedience was the sign of the reality of their faith. When He shows us the thing to do, the step to take, however unusual, even impossible, it may seem, if we would obtain the thing we crave, we shall find that in the stepping out the blessing is ours. Faith is always in one sense a step in the dark, but obedience discovers that it is a step on to the rock.

PRAYER.—*How often, O Lord, have we had to pull ourselves up when we have doubted some word, forgetting that it is Thy Word, and that therefore it is to be believed and done, and then experienced. Lord, we believe, help Thou our unbelief.* AMEN.

". . . up into the temple . . . down to his house . . ." (Luke 18: 10, 14)

HERE are two very important things: going to church, and going home afterwards. We were thinking of the first the other day; let us dwell now on the other. The publican here had received great blessing in church. He had seen how wrong he was and confessed himself "the sinner" (Gk.), and then he had got right with God. So he "went down to his house justified." I hope that there he behaved as a changed man ought. The sad thing is that many who go to church act so inconsistently at home, in their God's house praising and honouring Him, in their own house getting across one another. What a chance home gives us of working out in practice the truth we heard in the pulpit, and what a blessing to take home with us from the sanctuary the atmosphere of godly joy we found there.

PRAYER.—*O God, help us to recognize the sin of such sad disparity, and may we resolve that by Thy aid we shall never be like that again. May the House and the house exactly coincide in spirit.* AMEN.

". . . things which are impossible with men . . ." (Luke 18: 27)

WHAT a depressing subject! But not if it throw us back on God, with whom those very same things are gloriously "possible." The salvation we cannot win is possible with Him. "We must be saved," says Acts 4: 12, or perish, and yet we cannot save ourselves. The sin we cannot conquer is another impossibility with men and how incongruous it sounds and is that a Christian should suffer from a besetting sin. And yet we have no power to overcome the wretched thing. The service we cannot render is possible through Him. We long to serve and ought to serve, yet we feel we are unable to do our tasks for God and men as we ought. The saint we cannot be is possible in Him. We know we are called to be holy, yet how far beyond our attainment that blessed condition seems. Having said all that, we come back to the fact that it is all so gloriously possible to God. He will turn our Can'ts into Cans, if only we will let Him.

PRAYER.—*How needless, then, O God, are our fears, our faults, our falls, our failures, since nothing is too hard for the Lord and He is ours and we are His.* AMEN.

". . . What wilt thou that I should do unto thee? . . ." (Luke 18: 41)

SUCH was the question put by our Lord to a very needy man. What a chance! The man, a poor blind beggar, was always asking people for help. It was only money that he could hope for, but here was One, a "Jesus of Nazareth," of whom he had heard that He did marvellous things. Why, it was the chance of a lifetime. What a challenge! "What wilt thou . . . ?" Should he be content to ask the usual alms, or should he dare to ask the big thing, to crave his sight? Let us not be satisfied to ask little, let us not be afraid to ask big, of God. What a change! See him as he now goes on his way, seeing, and rejoicing, and praising. His whole life is there and then revolutionized. Maybe there is some great need harassing your soul, and crippling your life. The same Saviour puts to you the same question, with the same infinite possibilities.

PRAYER.—*We confess with shame, O Lord, that so often our desires are so small. We ask so little when Thou art prepared to give so much. Give us, we pray, a holy discontent, with anything less than the best, the best for God, the best from God.* AMEN.

"... he sought to see Jesus ..." (Luke 19: 3)

ONE would not normally associate such an admirable desire with such a person as this man Zacchaeus, Senior Tax Collector, sordid, grasping, dishonest, as the rest of his class. What was it that awakened such a wish in his heart; what set him off on such a quest? I don't know, but I think it was Matthew, Assistant Tax Collector, who had met Jesus, and been converted and utterly transformed. The "Chief" (v. 2) had seen the change in Matthew and been impressed, and now was consumed with a great curiosity to see the One who had wrought such a miracle in his hard-bitten colleague, with the result that he himself was caught in the same Gospel net, and was alike gloriously converted. In my view, it was an outstanding instance of the saving influence of the sight of a really saved life. I wonder if our lives are exercising any such power with our non-Christian associates?

PRAYER.—*We rejoice to know that many influences draw people to Thee, O Lord, but we covet that one such shall be the observance of a Christlike demeanour in us. May we so reflect Thee that others may be constrained to seek our Saviour, who is seeking them.* AMEN.

26

"... I will give you a mouth ..." (Luke 21: 15)

A CURIOUS expression but a wondrous experience, awaiting all those who, finding themselves surrounded and threatened by fierce opposition, cast themselves upon God for utterance. To the hesitating, halting Moses, He promised, "I will be with thy mouth" (Exod. 4: 12). This is the same truth, put in stronger form; and when He adds "wisdom" in our verse, I suppose it implies that they shall not only say the right thing, which is Truth, but say it in the right way, which is Tact. The former sometimes fails of acceptance for want of the latter, but let us pray to be delivered from the use of so much tact that we never say anything! All you shy, reserved, nervous, tongue-tied Christians, feeling that you ought to speak up for your Lord, but too frightened to begin, take our day's text for your comfort, and ask Him to give you a wise mouth that shall prove irresistible.

PRAYER.—*O God, we think of those of whom it is said "they were all filled with the Holy Ghost and began to speak." We pray that we, too, being filled with Him, may speak the Word with courage, tact and beautiful persuasiveness.* AMEN.

"*. . . I am among you as He that serveth*" (Luke 22: 27)

NOTHING could more clearly indicate the majesty of service, for it is the Lord of Glory who speaks. If He deigned to serve, how exalted in honour does service become, and how privileged are we to follow thus in His footsteps. It is a noble thing, a royal thing, to serve. And as we think again of the Master, we are struck by the variety of service. When Acts 10: 38 says that He "went about going good," what a mixture of energies and activities is covered by the phrase, and what a multitude of different kinds of work is open to those who truly desire to serve God, and their fellows, ministering to their physical, mental and spiritual needs. And what shall we say of the quality of service? Of His, of course, there is no question; there are no two opinions, but what of ours? As we serve "among" our neighbours, are we doing it to the very best because doing it as unto Him?

PRAYER.—"*Teach us, good Lord, to serve Thee as Thou deservest; to give and not to count the cost; to fight and not to heed the wounds; to toil and not to seek for rest; to labour and to ask for no reward, save that of knowing that we do Thy Will.*" AMEN.

"*. . . that was the preparation, and the sabbath drew on*" (Luke 23: 54)

THEIR Sabbath was of course our Saturday, and they made much of their Preparation Day, which was our Friday. In the New Dispensation there is a New Day, the Resurrection Day, "which the Lord hath made" (Ps. 118: 22, 24). But what a pity we don't make more of our preparatory Saturday. It is always a wise thing to prepare carefully. We see that in the foundations of a house, in the training for a race, in the qualification for a trade or profession. Does our worship need any less care in getting ready? Some people give no thought or time in any way to prepare themselves for this solemn drawing near to God. They even rush into church at the last minute, and have scarce taken their seats when the opening hymn is announced. I fancy that is almost a kind of irreverence. Do you recall those words in Joshua 3: 5, "Sanctify yourselves, for tomorrow the Lord will do wonders among you." verily believe that if we would, He would.

PRAYER.—*How full of wonder should our worship be. May we ever come to it with hearts prepared, with tongues unloosed to praise Thee, with ear attuned to hear Thy Voice, with will set to do Thy bidding. So may we go down from Sunday's Mountain to Monday's Valley finding Thee still at our side.* AMEN.

". . . Jesus Himself drew near, and went with them" (Luke 24: 15)

THAT first Easter evening two walking along a country road were overtaken and joined by a third. Those first two were talking about a dead Jesus. He, their Master and very dear Friend, had been cruelly done to death. Their hopes were dashed, their hearts broken, their lives empty. So, very sadly, they talked of Him. But now, in the coming of that third, though they did not realize it, they were walking with a living Jesus. Their hearts warmed within them as He and they went over the Old Scriptures together, but al the while "their eyes were holden," so that they did not recognize this remarkable "Stranger" (v. 18). At last, however, we find them rejoicing in a known Jesus. The Lord who died, and who lives, for you is ready to draw near and go with you along life's road, as living Saviour, Lord and Friend, turning your sadness into gladness, your defeat into victory.

PRAYER.—*Thou Risen Lord, be the road smooth or rough under our feet, be the sky blue or grey over our heads, we thank Thee that we have Thy Presence over-riding all else.* AMEN.

". . . they . . . returned . . . with great joy" (Luke 24: 52)

"GREAT joy" when they had just parted with the Lord they loved? Yes, they rejoiced (1) because of the hope He gave them that He would come again. The "blessed hope" of His return (Tit. 2: 13) has always been a source of joy to those who love Him. They rejoiced (2) because of the task He left them, that they should be responsible for carrying on the work, representing Him in the world and proclaiming the good news of His saving grace. What a joy it always is to have a work to do for Him. They rejoiced (3) because of the power He promised them, that they might fulfil their appointed task, even the Holy Spirit, who for us as for them is all we need for Christian service as the Book of Acts makes plain. It was this threefold joy, a great anticipation, a great occupation, a great galvanization, that sent them back with gladness to their life for Him. May such triple happiness be ours too!

PRAYER.—*We look forward with such gladness to the Golden Day that is coming by-and-by. May the very thought of it thrill our hearts to watch and wait and work for Thee.* AMEN.

JULY

THIS WAY OUT

The name Exodus is Greek for Way Out, and is the title of this fascinating book which tells how the enslaved Israelites found their way out from the cruel bondage of Egypt. We see in it not only the historical account of that tremendous deliverance, but also the typical picture of our redemption from sin.

JULY   **1**

"*. . . Take this child . . . and nurse it for me, and I will give thee thy wages . . .*" (Exod. 2: 9)

LITTLE though one might imagine it, "this child" was to be intimately bound up with Israel's deliverance. And that Israelite "nurse," really the child's mother, would get "wages" indeed, for herself and for her nation by her careful nurture of the future great emancipator. But, of course, it always is a richly profitable thing to care for the welfare of a child, from the personal and the national point of view, whether the one concerned be the mother, or the church, or the Sunday School teacher. "Nurse it for Me" is the divine injunction.

PRAYER.—*Give me an understanding, O Lord, of the strategic value of the little child, and help me, in any such that I touch, to foster and further its true spiritual growth.* AMEN.

JULY   **2**

"*. . . I am come down to deliver . . . Come now therefore, and I will send thee . . .*" (Exod. 3: 8, 10)

YOU see, man is God's care. He sees his affliction, hears his cry, knows his sorrow, and whether the trouble be physical, mental or spiritual, He does care so much. And so, man is God's objective. "I am come down to deliver." He promised to intervene on Israel's behalf; even as, in the Person of His Son, He came down at Bethlehem and at Calvary to work out His mighty plan of salvation for us. Luke 9: 31 tells us that in conversation with Moses and Elias on the Transfiguration Mount, He spoke of His "exodus (Greek) which He should accomplish at Jerusalem." Yes, His, but ours also, our Way Out from sin. But we see also that man is God's method. "I will send thee." Not in the matter of our soul's redemption, which is His task alone, but in so many other things when He proposes to do some work He nearly always does it through human agency. What a privilege for us! He looks not at our ability, but at our usability. He asks not for our fitness, but for our witness. Moses felt his inability, and his unfitness, but God saw to that!

PRAYER.—*Lord, may I be enabled to bring many souls out from sin by bringing them to the Saviour, for Thy Glory.* AMEN.

" . . . Who am I . . . ?" (Exod. 3: 11)

STRANGE words these in the mouth of this erstwhile prince of the Egyptian court. Forty years ago he would not have spoken thus, and if you had said disparagingly, "Who are you?", he would have told you in no uncertain terms. Forty years in Egypt he had been learning to be somebody. Forty years in Midian, minding sheep, he had been learning to be nobody, which was followed by forty years in the wilderness learning to help everybody. At the end of that second period, he advances that sense of insignificance as an excuse for refusing this high commission, while, if he did but know it, that was the first qualification for the job. God can begin to do something with us as soon as we realize that we are nothing, of ourselves. "Who am I?" Yes, but do not hold back on that account. Rather, go on with Isaiah 6: 8 to say, "Here am I." Thus in the surrender of ourselves, such as we are, we shall find our feeble insufficiency caught up in the full sufficiency of God, and shall discover as Moses did that what we cannot we can, in Him.

PRAYER.—*Help me, O Lord, to keep the thought of self at a distance, and to rest and rely on who Thou art, and what Thou art, to all surrendered selves.* AMEN.

" . . . what shall I say . . . ?" (Exod. 3: 13)

MANY a Christian holds back from saying anything because he doesn't know what to say. "When . . . they shall say . . . what shall I say?" Doubtless, they will have plenty to say, plenty of questions to put; and the divine injunction reads, "Be ready always to give an answer to every man that asketh you a reason of the hope that is in you" (1 Pet. 3: 15). As with Peter, the secret lies in our giving Him the real lordship in our hearts; and as with Moses, it is to know His Name, that is to know Him better; so as we do know and enthrone Him, we shall assuredly come to know what to say and how to say it. For, as we thus glorify the Master (John 7: 39b), "the Holy Spirit shall teach you in the same hour what ye ought to say" (Luke 12: 12). So, when He gives you the chance, don't hold back and like Moses hide behind this excuse, but throw yourself on His grace, open your mouth, and begin!

PRAYER.—*How many a feeble utterance Thou hast used and blest, O Lord, when it has come from a sincere heart, and above all, from the leading of the Holy Spirit. May we be ready for Him to teach us what to say.* AMEN.

"*. . . they will not believe me . . .*" (Exod. 4: 1)

MOSES is at it again; more excuse! It is not his responsibility whether they believe him or not. It is his to speak the word like Ezekiel (2: 5), "whether they will hear, or whether they will forbear." But will they not believe? As a matter of fact, Moses is given a power that will certainly lend impressiveness to his speech; the power that can change a rod into a serpent, that can turn a healthy organ leprous, or make the leprous clean. Let it be forever noted that nothing is so likely to awaken belief in our message as the power, and evidence, of a changed life and character. "It wasn't nobody's preaching; it was mother's practising," was a little maid's testimony concerning the means of her conversion, and when preaching and practising coincide, the word is likely to be with power. Consistency of life is the best possible argument for the truth of our message.

PRAYER.—*So, Lord, may I behave and believe, that many may believe and be saved.* AMEN.

"*. . . I am not eloquent . . .*" (Exod. 4: 10)

ONE last ingredient is now seen of this man's strange reluctance. He is conscious of a real lack of eloquence. Now Aaron, he is never found wanting for a word. May he come too as the spokesman of the deputation to Pharaoh? Yes, but Moses, what if you are not ready of speech? It is not eloquence that matters, though God can use that gift if anyone has it, but obedience. "I will be with thy mouth," God promises. He will see to that. Our part is to go where He sends, and do as He says. As things turned out, while comparatively little is heard of Aaron's oratory, what a powerful and resourceful speaker Moses became, and what a magnificent leader, all because at last Moses, yielding his all, mind and mouth and members, cast himself on God's all-sufficiency. The simple record runs, "And Moses went." How much lay behind that decision, and how much lay before it! There is no measuring the influence for God that is wielded by a yielded man!

PRAYER.—*How much we need to learn that if Thou command, there is nothing whatever in us that should keep us back from instant obedience, since all-sufficiency is at our disposal in Thee.* AMEN.

". . . *the Lord your God . . . bringeth you out . . . And . . . will bring
you in . . .*" (Exod. 6: 7, 8)

HERE is the promise. The fulfilment is recorded in Deuteronomy 6: 23, "He brought us out . . . that He might bring us in." I very much question whether God ever did a merely negative thing. Any divine action that wears that appearance will, on closer scrutiny, be found to have a very positive purpose in view. When, therefore, He planned Israel's deliverance from Egypt, He had no intention that they should wander for years in the wilderness, but that they should enjoy the fruits and joys of Canaan. And when He saved you and me from the guilt and doom of our sin, He purposed that we should enter at once into a life of complete victory over the habit and dominion of sin day by day; and into a life of peace, holiness, joy, service, power, satisfaction. Doubly blessed is His bringing out when it leads on to such a bringing in.

PRAYER.—*We praise Thee, O God, for all the blessings into which Thy deliverance introduces us. May we be eager to enter in to Thy great provision, that we may bless Thee and serve Thee to the full.* AMEN.

". . . *the finger of God* . . ." (Exod. 8: 19)

PHARAOH'S court conjurors at last acknowledged that they were beaten. They had imitated, or parodied, those earlier things. Their rod and serpent trick, their red water trick, their frogs out of a hat, no rabbits being available, were clever bits of magical mimicry, but the "lice" were too much for them. One cannot help contrasting our text with that other phrase in Isaiah 58: 4, "The fist of wickedness." A little child was overheard telling a younger brother of a bad man who got wickeder and wickeder until at last he struck God! The fist is destructive, the finger constructive (Exod. 31: 18, Ps. 8: 3). The fist is out to hurt God; the finger to heal man (Mark 7: 33), though sometimes it must first hurt as here in Exodus 8: 19. The fist is powerful; the finger all-powerful (Luke 11: 20). Oh, to be rescued out of the Fist of the devil, who imprisons us, by the Finger of the Lord, who saves us, into the Hand of the One who keeps us, and according to John 10: 28–29, will never, never let us go!

PRAYER.—*Wilt Thou have us always in Thy Hand, not only for safety, though we bless Thee for that, but also for service, since we pray Thee for that.* AMEN.

"*. . . there remained not one*" (Exod. 8: 31)

THERE had been millions and millions and millions of them, these wretched little poisonous flies, a fair plague of them! But now God has intervened to rid the land of these pests, and when He does a thing He does it thoroughly. "There remained not one." It is always in that perfect style that He performs His tasks. Our Prayer Book Version of Psalm 105: 28, referring to another of those Egypt plagues, says, "He sent darkness and it *was* dark." And Psalm 65: 9 tells us that "the river of God . . . is *full* of water," never a mere trickle, nor a bare sufficiency. How such thoughts encourage us to let God deal with our problems and difficulties! He would so completely overcome the things that vex us. He would so gloriously undertake the things that challenge us. Those weaknesses, those habits, those nerves, those inhibitions, those fears; "there remained not one." Oh, wonderful freedom that is in Him!

PRAYER.—*We have such cause to bless Thee for the assurance of all Thine undertakings, O Lord, and so we would bring Thee all our undertakings, knowing with what completeness Thou wilt undertake them for us.* AMEN.

"*. . . there shall not an hoof be left behind . . .*" (Exod. 10: 26)

THIS was to be a thorough-going separation, wasn't it? As such, it is a clear type and picture of God's plan for every Christian life. This keeps coming up in our daily notes, not because it is a pet theme of the writer, but only because it keeps coming up in our Bible. No one, I think, can read the Scriptures in an unbiased and unprejudiced fashion without realizing that so far as the way of true sanctification is concerned, "there shall not an hoof be left behind." So different is this from many of us Christians who try to manage with one foot ("hoof" sounds not too kind a word in personal application!) in heavenly things and one foot in the world. The only safe way, the only happy way, the only fruitful way, the truly strategic way is all out for God, "not an hoof . . . left behind." A salutary rule this is, not only for Israel's horses, but also for Christian lives.

PRAYER.—*May we thus prove in our own experience how wonderfully effectual, and how really joyful, is a life that is in every part and aspect of it entirely yielded to Thee. May we be both different and separate from the world.* AMEN.

". . . *the Lord doth put a difference between the Egyptians and Israel*"
(Exod. 11: 7)

HERE are two types, the unbeliever and the believer. In some respects, "there is no difference" as Romans 3: 22, 23; 10: 12, 13; Acts 15: 9 make clear. But these apart, there is a tremendous difference in God's eyes. A difference in fact; the one was under the blood. A difference in dealing; "when I see the blood I will pass over you." A difference in experience; in every house throughout the land of Egypt there was either a feast or a funeral. A difference in power; the magic of illusionists and the might of Pharaoh on the one hand, the almighty strength of God on the other. Such, then, is some of the enormous difference typified by this story, that God sees between those who are Christians and those who are not. Oh, then, to be "different," and to live "different."

PRAYER.—*We repeat, O Lord, part of our yesterday's prayer, that we may be different people, leading different lives in the different power of our God.* AMEN.

". . . *a lamb* . . . *the lamb* . . . *your lamb* . . ." (Exod. 12: 3, 4, 5)

SOMEONE has said that Christianity is a religion of personal pronouns. Knowing how that is meant, I should certainly agree. But from another angle, I should be inclined to say that it is a religion of possessive pronouns. How often do we find that one of its key words is "my." Here in today's text we have the same idea. This "lamb" is of course the type of our Lord Jesus, whom Peter calls "a Lamb" in 1 Peter 1: 19, and whom John the Baptist calls "the Lamb" in John 1: 29. But can you call Him "your Lamb"? He died to be so, but can only be so if you for yourself, individually, and personally, take Him and trust Him. He certainly came and died to be a Lamb, sacrificial and substitutionary. And inasmuch as "there is none other . . ." (Acts 4: 12), He is the Lamb, the only One. But all this is of no avail for you, His death is in vain for you, unless and until you do take and trust Him as your own. Happy you, if He be "your Lamb."

PRAYER.—"*Thou Lamb of God that takest away the sin of the world,*" *as by Thy condescending grace Thou art mine, so by Thy enabling grace may I labour to point others to behold Thee as their own.* AMEN.

"... *when I see the blood* ..." (Exod. 12: 13)

T HAT blood of the lamb was by God's ordering sprinkled "on the two side-posts, and on the upper door post" of the Israelite houses, but not, you observe, on the door step. Why not? Because it was the figure of the blood of the Lamb. God will not have that blood, even in type, trampled on. What must He think of those who today speak slightingly of it, or affect to have grown superior to it in this enlightened age! I notice, incidentally, that these same people have no qualms about speaking of their soldiers shedding their blood on the battlefield. The Holy Spirit leads Peter in his First Epistle (1: 19) to speak of His love's outpouring as "the precious blood," precious, of infinite value in God's eyes. And shall we presume, even dare, to disparage it? What glorious saving efficacy accrues in the case of the Hebrew house, or that of the human heart, "when I see the blood"! It matters not that we cannot see it. We take it in trust, knowing that He sees.

PRAYER.—*"E'er since by faith I saw the stream Thy flowing Wounds supply, redeeming love has been my theme, and shall be till I die."* AMEN.

"*And this day shall be unto you for a memorial* ..." (Exod. 12: 14)

A LL down the years it has been observed, "this day" of the Passover, bringing to mind for all Israel the recollection of its freedom from Egypt's yoke, a picture in its turn of the glorious deliverance from the bondage of sin, wrought out on the Day when "Christ, our Passover" was "sacrificed for us" (1 Cor. 5: 7), and made available and effectual for us individually from the moment of our putting our trust in Him. "Oh, happy day that fixed my choice, on Thee my Saviour and my God"; the outstanding, red-letter day in all life's memories. If that actual day be unknown to us, yet it is known up yonder, and is inscribed by the side of our name in the Lamb's Book of Life, which is also, I surmise, a Book of Dates.

PRAYER.—*We thank Thee, Lord, for Second Birthdays—if we do not know the date, we bless Thee that we are sure of the fact, since we have new life through trusting Thee. Praise be to Thee for the Day of Calvary, and subsequently for the Day of Resurrection.* AMEN.

JULY 15

" . . . *God led them not through the way* . . . *of the Philistines, although that was near* . . ." (Exod. 13: 17)

THE providence of God gives little encouragement to short cuts. They prove so often the longest way round, and are sometimes even perilous. The great danger of this particular route out of Egypt was the fortress of Zar, which had a large garrison of Egyptian troops, who would at once have challenged these fugitives from their own Pharaoh. Israel might have wondered why God took them such a long detour to reach Canaan. Well, that was the reason. There always is a reason for God's providences for His people. If we wonder why our rightful desires are so long in being realized, why our earnest prayers are so long in being answered, why our faithful service is so long in bearing fruit, "although that was near" which we thought would be the way, let us remember that if in His wise counsels God chooses such, in the longer way round is the likelier blessing found.

PRAYER.—*Save us, O God, from all hastiness and impatience, and teach us that as Thou so wilt cause what is best for us, so Thou dost know when is the best time to give it. Prevent us, Lord, from lagging behind Thee, but also from running ahead of Thee.* AMEN.

JULY 16

" . . . *go forward*" (Exod. 14: 15)

GOD's bugles never blow retreat. Always do they sound advance. But how advance in the circumstances of our text? The Israelites were in a precarious situation. They could not halt, or retreat, for the Egyptian army was behind, pursuing after them. They could not turn aside, for on either hand were mountains, impossible for the women and children and baggage which accompanied the Hebrew men. They could not advance for the Red Sea was in front. They were in fact caught in a trap, "shut . . . in" (v. 3). What are they to do? Why, "go forward"! But what about the sea? That is not their responsibility. If His command is to go forward, God will take care to overcome for them all obstacles if they will but obey His order. "He who bids us onward go, will not fail the way to show." In the very act of stepping out (cf. "as they went," Luke 17: 14), they found the waters receding at their feet, with all the miracle and victory that followed. Such shall ever be the glad experience of all who will dare to "go forward" at His word, however untoward the circumstances shall seem to be.

PRAYER.—*We thank Thee that we are under so Supreme a Head, O Lord, and we pray that we may strictly obey Thy marching orders whatever obstacles may stand in the way, knowing full well that every opposition is an opportunity for Thy Miraculous Power.* AMEN.

"The Lord is my strength and song, and He is become my salvation . . ."
(Exod. 15: 2)

THE same threefold testimony is found in Psalm 118: 14, and again in Isaiah 12: 2. And the fact of its being made three times over suggests that it is of especial importance for us. We have here the essential thing, "my salvation." That is, of course, fundamental to all else. And having "become" that to us, we find the Lord next in the everyday thing, "my strength"; a power adequate to the varying vicissitudes of each day as it comes. We remember the "as . . . so . . ." of Deuteronomy 33: 25. Then comes the extra thing, "my song." That, I imagine, is not a necessary ingredient of the Christian experience, but it is a wonderfully delightful ingredient. For our own enjoyment's sake and for our recommendation of our faith to others, the song of the Lord is greatly desirable. It is the outcome of full surrender. "When the burnt offering began, the song of the Lord began also" (2 Chron. 29: 27). May we all find all these things in Him.

PRAYER.—*We praise Thee, O God, that from the moment when Thou dost become our salvation, we may be assured that we may have daily strength for the daily life, in such measure that it will give us something to sing about. Thanks be to Thee!* AMEN.

". . . the Lord shewed him a tree . . ." (Exod. 15: 25)

THERE was there no water of life for these people. What was there was undrinkable, "bitter." How shall the bitter become sweet? How shall the taint of death be exchanged for the taste of life? Whether we think of the waters of Marah, or of the waters of Experience, the answer is the same. "The Lord shewed him a tree"; small "t" at Marah, capital "T" at Golgotha. "Whom they slew and hanged on a Tree" (Acts 10: 39), "who His own self bare our sins in His own body on the Tree" (1 Pet. 2: 24). To that Tree the Lord ever points the children of men, as the very fountain whence flows the water of life, and as the very foundation whereon rests all the subsequent blessing of lives. For the conversion of the unbeliever, for the return of the backslider, for the inspiration of the worker, for the comfort of the sad, for the sweetening of life, the Lord still points to the Tree.

PRAYER.—*May we too, O Lord, be ever mindful of Calvary's Tree; ever grateful for all that it stands for as the source of our very life in Christ, and as the constant constraint of all our godly living. May we often be found beneath its wondrous shelter.* AMEN.

JULY 19

" . . . *the bread wherewith I have fed you in the wilderness* . . ."
(Exod. 16: 32)

THIS miraculous manna-bread was to be kept in the remembrance of the children of Israel, and so a portion of it was put into a pot and placed in the Ark of the Tabernacle. Furthermore, at the Feast of the Passover, in succeeding years, at one stage, the one presiding took unleavened bread and brake it and passed it round to the others, with the words, "This is the bread which your fathers ate in the wilderness"; not the literal bread of course but a pictorial representation of it. It will be recalled that when the Master instituted the Feast of the Holy Communion at His last passover, He took the bread as usual at that point, but altered the words to "This is My Body which is given for you," meaning of course as in the original sentence, not literally so, but pictorially so. The earlier bread was a type of the Eternal Bread, broken at Calvary, partaken by Faith, remembered in Communion. Let us ever thankfully have this His loving keepsake "in remembrance" (Luke 22: 19).

PRAYER.—*Whether our life be a veritable wilderness or something very different, may we never fail to find our soul's sustenance in Thee, who art the Living Bread sent down from Heaven, that so we may be strong to serve Thee in the manifold service of our fellows, and to stand for Thee in testimony to the world.* AMEN.

JULY 20

"*Then came Amalek* . . ." (Exod. 17: 8)

WHEN did he come? Immediately after the people of Israel had acted rebelliously against Moses. Why did he come? Presumably as God's punishment of the people for their wrongdoing. So often the predicaments of history turn out to be the providences of His Story. What is to be done with him when he comes? "The Lord will have war with Amalek from generation to generation" (v. 16). It is interesting to observe here the conscription of the forces, "choose us out men." Every Christian is a conscript. The contribution of the greatest force, "when Moses held up his hand" in prayer, and it transpired that the chief factor in the victory was not so much the fighting in the valley, though that was necessary, as the fighting on the hill, which was essential. The condition of making it a force was and is personal righteousness. "Who shall ascend into the hill of the Lord? . . . He that hath clean hands . . ." (Ps. 24: 3, 4); "lifting up holy hands" (1 Tim. 2: 8). So shall the work be done, the victory won, when comes Amalek.

PRAYER.—*Teach me, O Lord, to use more and more effectually the "weapon of all prayer" for "Satan trembles when he sees the weakest saint upon his knees."* AMEN.

"If . . . God command thee so . . . thou shalt be able to . . ."
(Exod. 18: 23)

IN other words, God's biddings are God's enablings. He does not guarantee us power to carry out our own designs, though He often does help us even in those. It is a common weakness among us that we so often first make our plans, and then ask Him to bless them. Yes, and He does frequently acquiesce and bless. But the better way is to seek His plans, and then we may count on having His power to carry them out. The Bible has many a "command" of God to us, and dwelling upon our own inadequacy, we all too often feel we just can't do it. "Be ye holy." How can we? "Let the redeemed of the Lord say so." How can we? And so on. But does God command us so? That is the key point. For if He does, then the power is assured and we shall be able to. If we will undertake His purposes, He will undertake our sufficiency. That is a factor never to be found in any other religion, but it is gloriously true for us.

PRAYER.—*May I never hesitate then, to step out at Thy command, since Thou hast thus assured me that I shall prove "able to" accomplish Thy will for me, whatever it may be, or whatever it may entail.* AMEN.

". . . to meet with God . . ." (Exod. 19: 17)

THE chapter of today's text reveals how serious and how solemn and how sacred a thing it is to meet with God. And yet we are so apt to rush into His presence hurriedly, thoughtlessly, even carelessly. I note that here in Moses' day the people were even instructed to "wash their clothes" (v. 10), which I take to be something in favour of Sunday clothes about which in these days many are getting slack; just another little symptom of the modern heedlessness of the solemnities of worship. Our whole demeanour and behaviour in God's House need, I fancy, to be overhauled. All too many of us are all too slipshod. We would not act at the Great House like it, so why at the Lord's House? Of course, we would not be admitted "to meet" Him at all if it were not for our One Mediator, through whose precious blood the way into the Holiest has been opened to us. Thus we can go to meet Him without fear, but not without care.

PRAYER.—*May I never be guilty of trading upon Thy mercy or trifling with Thy grace, but while I rejoice with amazement at Thy Royal Invitation, may I tread with reverence the Royal Courts of Thy House.* AMEN.

"Thou shalt . . . Thou shalt not . . ." (Exod. 20: 3, 4)

How we thank God for the Ten Words, the great moral code for all time and for all people given to Moses in circumstances of utmost solemnity, not once but twice and written with the very "writing of God" (32: 16). Wherever there has been disregard of the Ten Commandments there has followed material damage and mental confusion, and moral degradation, and so shall it ever be. When a later Scripture says, "Ye are not under the law but under grace" (Rom. 6: 14), it does not mean that Christians have got beyond the commandments and need no longer keep His laws, but rather that they have a new reason for keeping them, since to us they are now to be looked on not merely as harsh and rigid laws but as guideposts of grace. Not legal but loyal, with the loyalty of love, is to be our attitude. To such "His commandments are not grievous" (1 John 5: 3). Let it ever be in our minds that the easy way of keeping His "thou shalt" and "thou shalt not" is "thou shalt love" (Matt. 22: 37, 39).

PRAYER.—*Give us to see, O Lord, that our wisdom lies in obeying Thy Words, not only in the letter, but in the spirit, and may the Holy Spirit so beget in us that spirit of love that shall make us glad thus to serve Thee and our fellows.* AMEN.

". . . his master shall bore his ear through with an aul . . ."
(Exod. 21: 6)

That is a noteworthy scar that this man bears. It is the sign of a great satisfaction. For six years he has been a slave. In this seventh year he can, if he wants to, claim release, but he has come to love his master. So he binds himself afresh, this time for ever, and the Ceremony of the Ear is enacted. He has found satisfaction in the service of his master. As our hymn says, "I love, I love my Master, I will not go out free." Old Polycarp, disciple of St. John, when offered the alternative of recanting or martyrdom, said, "Fourscore years and six have I served Him and He never did me wrong. How then can I revile my King, my Saviour?" This scar is the pledge of a great consecration. Not for a moment, but for the life; not for a part, but for the whole. Such is the significance of this mark of the aural aul. Shall not we who have found such joy in His service present ourselves for a like life's consecration?

PRAYER.—*Our Gracious Master, we recognize that if our service has proved unsatisfying to us in any way, the fault has lain entirely with us, yet may we come back to Thee and render Thee such complete submission that we shall find how glad it is to be now and forever, Thy bond-slave. Seal me, then, with Thy Holy Spirit.* AMEN.

". . . the names . . . upon his heart when he goeth in unto the holy place . . ."
(Exod. 28: 29)

WHAT a beautiful thing this is! The High Priest was caparisoned in rich apparel, each detail of his dress being significant of some spiritual truth. The breastplate was especially gorgeous, studded with twelve precious stones, on each of which was inscribed the name of one of the twelve tribes, with the divinely inspired suggestion that, bearing them over his heart, Aaron should thus bring the people and their needs with him into the sanctuary. How glorious it is to realize that our Great High Priest bears us by name on His heart, even as "graven . . . upon the palms of His hands" (Isa. 49: 16), in His priestly intercession. And we too have priestly prayer work to do and may bear others not only in mind as thinking of them, but in heart as loving them, when we go into the Presence. How greatly effectual is our help of others when we go in with "names . . . upon our heart."

PRAYER.—*O Lord, in all our desire to be a help to people, may we understand that our greatest help will be to pray for them. So may we intercede for people not only in general, but as individuals, knowing that as we pray for each personally, we are doing what Thou, our High Priest, art already doing for them, name by name.* AMEN.

". . . Who is on the Lord's side? . . ." (Exod. 32: 26)

SIN is abroad, sin must be punished, sin shall be rooted out, and God will have His coadjutors in this stern justice. So there goes forth the summons, "Who is on the Lord's side?" They must themselves be free, these Levites, before they can be free to fight the Lord's battle, but thrice honoured are they to whom He can look to defend, or to advance, His cause. Times may be normally peaceful but perchance a sudden emergency may arise, as in this chapter, and God may call His warriors to the colours, maybe to conflict even against their own kith and kin (vs. 27, 29), for "a man's foes shall be those of his own household" (Matt. 10: 36). In such days of spiritual conflict, are we ready to declare ourselves as on His side, and to fling ourselves into the struggle for His truth? The trumpet call may one day sound, "Who . . .?" Shall the answer be, "We . . ."?

PRAYER.—*Right valiantly, O Lord, I would answer Thy call, since I am assured that "the Lord is on my side, whom shall I fear." With Thee, therefore, I will be for Thee.* AMEN.

JULY 27

"*. . . this people . . . have made them gods of gold . . .*" (Exod. 32: 31)

MANY a man has made a god of pleasure, many of success, many of popularity, many of learning and many have made gods of gold. But how sad, how silly, how sinful. It is not wrong to possess wealth; some most godly men have been rich, Abraham among them. But it is wrong to worship it. Not money in itself, but "the love of money is the root of all evil" (1 Tim. 6: 10). There is no harm in what we possess if properly gotten, but only if it possess us. Is it needless to say such things to Christians? Alas, no; for we have ourselves known of those who, weaker than John Bunyan's Christian and Hopeful, have been lured from the narrow way by Demas' silvermine. If you happen to have money, don't make an idol of it, but an instrument in God's service. All this is very different from the real meaning of the text, but it is not, I hope, an illegitimate use of the words. Anyhow, we have the authority of 1 John 5: 21, addressed to Christians, "Little children, keep yourselves from idols."

PRAYER.—*O Lord, may any gifts that we have, and any possessions, be held by us in trust to be used for Thee, and may no selfish interest cause us to betray that trust. "Take my silver and my gold, not a mite would I withhold"—it is all Thine if I am Thine.* AMEN.

JULY 28

"*. . . My presence shall go with thee . . .*" (Exod. 33: 14)

THE fact is that God does not save and help His people from a distance. For them it is always true that He is actually "with" them. What then does this, His promised presence mean for Israelite and for Christian? That He is just Behind them, for protection from the enemy, as when He stood between Israel and the Egyptians. That He is just Before them, for leading as when in the pillar of cloud He guided His people in their unknown wilderness wanderings, until, by Him, they found "rest." That He is just Beside them, for comradeship even as He befriended them all through their long trek. In the picturesque language of Exodus 19: 4, "I bare you on eagles' wings." Moses so deeply valued His presence that he begged that, if it were withheld, they might never proceed to Canaan at all. How greatly do we estimate that Presence; how richly do we enjoy it?

PRAYER.—*Our Lord, help us to "practise the presence of God" by keeping Thee constantly in mind, for we know that if we act as if Thou wert there we shall soon discover that indeed, Thou art there.* AMEN.

"*. . . be ready in the morning . . .*" (Exod. 34: 2)

IT was going to be a great day for Moses. Indeed, when you come to think of it, every day, however seemingly humdrum and insignificant, is a great day for each of us. When God wakes you first thing, and offers you His gift of a new day, who knows what it may hold in store; what opportunities, what emergencies, what problems, what responsibilities, what experiences. Why, looked at that way, every new day is an unknown adventure. And how shall we use it to the fullest and the best? "Be ready in the morning." That early tryst with the Master will prove the key, and set the tone, of the whole day. There will lie the secret of putting the most into it, and of getting the most out of it. Your circumstances may prevent your spending a long time, first thing, with God. Well, it is not the length that counts, but the depth. If it is real, even five minutes, a Word from God, a Word with God, will get us "ready in the morning," and as with Moses augur a great day.

PRAYER.—*Each day we shall meet with so many people, first thing may we meet with Thee. Each day we shall talk with many, may we first talk with Thee. Each day we shall listen to many, first may we hearken to Thee. So may we learn the secret of a good day, by being "ready in the morning."* AMEN.

"*. . . his face shone . . .*" (Exod. 34: 29)

AFTER fasting forty days with not even a drop of water to drink (v. 28), one would have expected Moses to have looked haggard. But to our delighted surprise, we observe that he looked radiant. Ah, and no wonder, for he had been in intimate touch with God, and that touch is bound to set its mark on a man. In a recent note here, we quoted the American Revised Version of Psalm 34: 5, "They looked unto Him, and were radiant!" That is the secret of the radiant moon; she keeps her face to the sun and reflects his glory. That light is not her own, she has none in herself. It is the sun's effulgence, caught and transmitted. Oh, that we might be so occupied with Him, the Sun of Righteousness (Mal. 4: 2), that whether in our face, or in our character, or in our behaviour, the glory may be seen. We shall not be aware of it; "Moses wist not," but others will.

PRAYER.—*May we company so close to Thee that we may be "changed into the same image from glory to glory, even by the Lord the Spirit." Be this the glow, and Thine the Glory.* AMEN.

". . . so Moses finished the work . . . and the glory of the Lord filled the tabernacle" (Exod. 40: 33, 34)

WHAT a work it had been! Every detail of it had been shown to Moses in pattern. Every bit of it was full of most happy and important teaching. Every piece of it was now completed and in place. Would that we all, with equal fidelity, might do the work God gives us to do. Are you a Sunday School teacher, for instance? Well, are you doing the work with uttermost faithfulness? If we, by His grace, see to the "finish," the Lord will see to the "filling." What a crowning of the work it was! "The glory of the Lord filled the tabernacle." I think that in the Old Testament that phrase, "the glory of the Lord" means "the manifested presence of God." If we will do the part that God has assigned to us, He will manifest His presence to us in our hearts, and to others through our life and work.

PRAYER.—*So, Lord, we find it emphasized again, how great a store Thou dost set by the fidelity of Thy children. We covet the words of Thy servant that "they glorified God in me."* AMEN.

AUGUST

A BUNDLE OF OLD LETTERS

Here they are, a packet of four of them, so old that they were written about 1900 years ago, yet having this remarkable quality; that they are so fresh that they sometimes seem as if they were written but yesterday, so exactly do they speak to our present condition, and so pulsating is their power still after all this long time. That is, of course, because it is not merely Paul who wrote them, but that he uttered "words . . . which the Holy Spirit teacheth" (1 Cor. 2:13). The first of the four letters was written in the midst of a busy life; the other three from the irksome confinement of prison. The prevailing vowel in their titles will help you to recall the order of their place in the Bible: a, e, i, o. May we find much joy this month in sampling some extracts from this remarkable correspondence.

AUGUST 1

"Grace be to you and peace . . ." (Gal. 1: 3)

JUST the usual greetings of an Eastern letter writer: "grace," the Greek salutation; "peace," the Hebrew. Yet in New Testament usage how infused with reality they become. A beloved Bishop once said that "grace is love in action." Perhaps we may be allowed to add that "peace is love in possession." What better wishes can any Christian correspondent convey to his friends? I only know that, from my heart, I who here write wish these two things for you who now read.

PRAYER.—*May I learn from this correspondence how great a ministry may be exercised by writing letters, and if I find it hard to speak a word for Thee, may I use my pen to say it, and always with the desire for the readers' grace and peace.* AMEN.

AUGUST 2

". . . he which persecuted . . . now preacheth . . ." (Gal. 1: 23)

WHAT a transformation! And there have been many more such by the grace and power of God. This man was so dramatically challenged on that Damascus road, in hot pursuit of his victims. The living Christ, whom he thought to be dead and done for, halted him in his mad career. And he was so drastically changed in that tremendous moment and meeting. The alteration in him was so extraordinary that Christians in Damascus, and later in Jerusalem, could not believe it, but suspected he was setting a trap to catch them. Ah, it was no trap, but glorious truth. And straight away this Paul was so dynamically charged with the message of the Gospel of the crucified and risen Saviour, and charged with the power of the Spirit to deliver the good news, that he went forth to be perhaps the most wonderful evangelist ever known. If we are thus changed, we also can be thus charged!

PRAYER.—*How shall we ever praise Thee enough for the transforming power of the Gospel. May it so transfigure our own selves that our very lives, with our lips, may become a potent influence to the changing of many.* AMEN.

"And they glorified God in me" (Gal. 1: 24)

PAUL has been writing autobiographically, and he here says that the upshot of his remarkable conversion and ministry was not that people said what a wonderful man was he, but what a wonderful God was He! Of course, if the Lord Jesus should return before you pass hence, if you are a real believer, you would have no deathbed, no coffin, no funeral service, no grave, no tombstone. You would be joyously "caught up" (1 Thess. 4: 17), but if that event be much further delayed, and you need a headstone, would you not covet such an epitaph as our text? Take pains, then, that you so live your life, that you so prepare and deliver your message, that you so do all your work for Him, that in it all you so reflect your Lord, that the people you touch may glorify God for what they know of you and see in you. "Not unto us, O Lord, not unto us, but unto Thy Name give glory" (Ps. 115: 1).

PRAYER.—*How far short we so often fall of this great ideal of the Christian life. How little of Thee is seen in so many of us. Yet, O Lord, may there be no eclipse of the "Sun of Righteousness" caused by the intervention of ourselves, that people may begin to see Thee even in us.* AMEN.

". . . the life which I now live . . ." (Gal. 2: 20)

IT is vastly different from the life I used to live, but what sort of a life is it? A life according to the flesh? Though I be a Christian "now," are my motives, my desires, my opinions, my actions governed by the lower nature which abides in me till I reach the other side? A life according to the feelings? Am I at the mercy of my moods, one day up, one day down? A life according to the fashion? Do I regulate my behaviour by the prevailing tone and habit of whatever may, for the moment, be my environment? "When in Rome, do as Rome does"; is that it? A spiritual chameleon? A life according to the faith of the Son of God? Since Paul was converted, his "now" life was the "new" life of Romans 6: 4, a life based on and controlled by, not faith in himself, but faith in Him.

PRAYER.—*Since that initial faith that brought salvation to my heart, may a continual faith actuate all my life. Relying on Thee, may I be and do all that "now" Thou requirest of me.* AMEN.

AUGUST 5

". . . the Son of God . . . loved me, and gave Himself for me" (Gal. 2: 20)

G OD so loved the world that He gave His only begotten Son" (John
3: 16). Yes, I know, and I am deeply grateful for that assurance.
The description of His love narrows: "Christ loved the Church,
and gave Himself for it" (Eph. 5: 25). Yes, I know, and I am deeply
grateful for that assurance also. Ah, but the circle comes to its narrowest
radius: "the Son of God . . . loved me, and gave Himself for me." How
can I assess or express my gratitude for that? The giving God in Christ
set His saving purpose on me individually, so that He would have done
it all if I had been the only sinner in the world. Do you remember the
publican in Luke 18: 13, "God be merciful to me the (as the Greek says)
sinner," as if he were the only one or anyway the worst one! Oh, then,
to love Him back to the utmost of my capacity, and to give Him service
to the utmost of my ability.

PRAYER.—*May it ever be, O Lord, the spring of my endeavour that "the
love of Christ constraineth" me, and in that great impulse may my service
flourish and my character flower, for Him.* AMEN.

AUGUST 6

". . . it is good to be zealously affected always in a good thing . . ."
(Gal. 4: 18)

P AUL's plea for enthusiasm! Some of us Christians are so dreadfully
"lukewarm," and we need to heed the stricture of Revelation 3: 16.
Enthusiasm is a grand quality in any "good" cause, music, sport,
business, learning, what not. How much more welcome is it in the cause
of Christ. Therein are we all too often reticent, shy, dignified, cool, calm,
and collected, too fearful of letting ourselves go. When I was a boy,
I heard a young clergyman say in a sermon, "Never mind if we sometimes make mistakes, do let's have enthusiasm." To this day I have
remembered it, and have tried to practise it. Paul would add that our
zeal is not to cool off when the mission or campaign is over, when the
evangelist is no longer with us—"not only when I am present with you,"
ends our verse. An excellent after-the-campaign slogan would be, "Keep
clean and keep keen."

PRAYER.—*Lord, when so many things around tend to cause a drop in
temperature, may Thy grace so abound in us that our zeal shall never
abate. May we always be on fire for God, content to burn out for Thee.*
AMEN.

"... *the flesh* ... *and the Spirit* ..." (Gal. 5: 17)

THE verse describes for us the Fight for holiness; "lusteth against, contrary," there is a continual antagonism, a ceaseless conflict, going on within. The Foe of holiness is "the flesh," that old sinful nature, the entail of Adam's transgression. It was born with us, and will be borne by us until the end. One of the ultimate joys of our salvation is that one day we shall lose entirely this evil principle of our present make-up. The Friend of holiness is "the Spirit." The Greek justifies us in substituting for the pessimistic "and" the optimistic "but." The foe fights, all too true, but so does the Friend! There lies our hope. Paraphrase the last clause thus! "So that ye need not do the things that ye (otherwise, without His help) would." There is no need to yield to the flesh; let Him undertake the struggle, and we shall know continual victory.

PRAYER.—*We all of us know from experience how difficult is the combat with this foe if left to ourselves, but blessed be He who knows so well how to tackle it, and how to triumph over it. May we then trust Him to do His own work in us.* AMEN.

"... *the fruit of the Spirit* ..." (Gal. 5: 22)

WHAT a lovely orchard of delectable fruits, nine varieties of excellent character. What a picture they are of the Saviour's human nature. What a power they are among men, when they are seen in any believer's demeanour. What a fulfilling they are of all requirements, human and divine, "against such there is no law." What a challenge they are to any Christian who will honestly face up to them. Are we, and to what extent are we, producing such qualities in our lives? What a secret they convey of the way in which they can be cultivated and displayed, not the fruit of our own energies, but "the fruit of the Spirit," the outcome of our allowing Him to fill our hearts and rule our lives. The results of our own efforts are like apples unnaturally tied on a tree. The results of His working within us are like apples naturally growing out of a tree. So, let Him!

PRAYER.—*Thou Blessed Holy Spirit, may nothing of self intrude here, or get in the way of Thy producing such a fruit harvest in our lives, and may all the glory be given, not to us, but to the Divine Husbandman.* AMEN.

AUGUST 9

". . . I bear in my body the marks of the Lord Jesus" (Gal. 6: 17)

A s a slave would be physically branded to mark him as belonging to the master who purchased him, so Paul carried scars of suffering by which he could be identified as the bondslave of Jesus Christ. You know, scars are in any court of law accepted as proof of identity. If we have never been called upon thus to be stamped as His, are there no other "marks" by which our allegiance to Him can be recognized? The mark of tirelessness should be ours, ever busy in God's service as He was. Oh, for grace to keep on keeping on. The mark of blamelessness should be ours; no negative shortcoming, no positive evil-doing, no active wrong influence. No blame ever attached to Him. The mark of fearlessness should be ours; utterly unafraid was He of man or devil. Of one who bore this "mark" it used to be said, "He feared man so little because He feared God so much." The mark of selflessness should be ours. "Others," not Himself (Matt. 27: 42) was ever His way, in a sense His enemies never intended. "Let him deny himself," say "No" to his self, is His own rule of discipleship (Matt. 16: 24). Bear we these "marks" of His?

PRAYER.—*May such signs of our allegiance to Thee be stamped upon all Thine own, that even the world may recognize us as Thine, and may all marks of self be completely obliterated.* AMEN.

AUGUST 10

". . . God . . . is rich . . ." (Eph. 2: 4)

H E is possessed of unimaginable and inexhaustible wealth. How infinitely good it is to have such an One as God for our Father, Christ Jesus for our Friend, the Holy Spirit for our Companion, the Triune Deity for our Storehouse of Supply. Think of the richness of mind He has; "O the depth of the riches both of the wisdom and knowledge of God" (Rom. 11: 33). He can solve all our problems and plan all our blessings. Think of the richness of heart He has; "the riches of His goodness, and forbearance, and longsuffering" (Rom. 2: 4). His heart is a purse, yes a bank, of spiritual currency, which can move out in active sympathy to meet all our distresses and sorrows. Think of the richness of store He has; "His riches in glory in Christ Jesus" (Phil. 4: 19), that is stored up in Heaven in Him. So that what His rich mind plans to do for us, and what His rich heart longs to do for us, His rich store enables Him to do for us. What immeasurable resources are at His disposal for our good!

PRAYER.—*We thank Thee that we belong to such a wealthy family. Help us to live as becomes such well-to-do children.* AMEN.

"But God . . . But now . . . But ye . . . But against . . ."
(Eph. 2: 4, 2: 13, 4: 20, 6: 12)

W HAT amazing differences do those "buts" introduce! The one
concerns our eternal destiny. We should have been and deserved
to be lost indeed, "but God" in love and mercy moved to our
rescue, and of His infinite grace and wisdom devised a just way of salvation. The next presents our changed situation. Once "far off" from God,
with all that that dread estrangement entailed, "but now" brought near
and at such a cost welcomed into the family, with all that that wonderful
reconciliation implies. The third emphasizes our entire contrast, in
character and conduct, to the worldlings. They were verily guilty of all
manner of evil, and remember "such were some of you" (1 Cor. 6: 11),
"but ye" are no longer found in such categories of wrong. That is nothing
to your credit; it all started in that first "but," which escorted you into
the second, and which properly and naturally issues in this third. Others
may be this, and that, and the other, "but ye," in the purpose and power
of God, are to be so different. And let us not forget the fourth "but,"
for our new life betokens a new warfare, under the "Captain of our
salvation" (Heb. 2: 10).

PRAYER.—*We thank Thee, O God, for all the altered relationships of the
true believer, by Thy grace reckoned as saved ones, as sons, as scholars,
as soldiers.* AMEN.

AUGUST   12
". . . together in heavenly places in Christ Jesus" (Eph. 2: 6)

W HAT a distance we have travelled since we were "in sins" (v. 5),
and what a destination we have reached, "in the heavenlies."
One of the many wonderful things which happened to us when
we "received" the Saviour was that we were then brought into union
with Him, and were from that moment identified with Him. As when,
in Old Testament days, the offerer put his hands on the head of his sin-
offering, what happened to the offering was reckoned as happening to
the offerer, so now when we put the hand of faith on Him, we are counted
as being crucified with Him, buried with Him, raised with Him, ascended
with Him, seated with Him "in heavenly places" (vs. 5, 6). Oh, that we
would "reckon" on all that (Rom. 6: 11) and live accordingly! So many
Christians live in the earthlies, occupied and distressed by earthly care.
So many others live in the worldlies, caught up in its vanities. So few
live in the heavenlies, as by faith's reckoning we should.

PRAYER.—*We think with joy, O Lord, of this truth, that is not mere fancy,
but revealed fact, that Thou, O God, dost reckon us identified in this way.
May we, on our part, reckon ourselves thus, and live on its reality.* AMEN.

". . . *we are His workmanship*" (Eph. 2: 10)

IN the margin of 1 Samuel 12: 6 we are told that "the Lord made Moses." He was not a self-made man, and neither are we who are true Christians. It is "not of works" of ours, but of "His workmanship" that we are a "new creation," as 2 Corinthians 5: 17 describes it. It is He who makes us safe, makes us holy, makes us beautiful, makes us happy, makes us fruitful, makes us useful. "Make me . . ." plans the returning prodigal to say in Luke 15: 19. "I will make you . . ." promises the Lord in Matthew 4: 19. If anyone can make anything of us, He can, and truly He has been amazingly successful even with most unpromising material; a Peter out of a Simon; a Justified out of a Publican; a Missionary out of a Legion; a Beloved out of a Boanerges. How wise we shall be to leave ourselves in His hands, malleable to His touch, a product of "His workmanship" alone, not spoiling it by the bungling craft of our own poor interfering work.

PRAYER.—*We ponder with amazement, O Lord, the wonder-working Hands that can make even of us some vessel for Thine own use, and Thine own glory.* AMEN.

". . . *speaking the truth in love* . . ." (Eph. 4: 15)

THERE is no manner of question that the Christian is called upon to do everything "in love"; that is to be his continual attitude in all circumstances. Such is the insidious craft of the enemy, such the natural tendency to error of the human character that there will in all probability come to most of us occasions when we feel we must speak out for the truth, either in the assembly or to the individual. At such a time let us ever remember to do it "in love"; love to God, whose truth is being impugned; love to truth, which has become of signal importance in our spiritual reckoning; love to the person concerned, whose utmost spiritual welfare we deeply care for. Beware of getting hard and harsh; our very zeal may make us steel if we are not careful. Let us not be so anxious to win arguments as to win adherents. Be as straight as you like, but always, always, always "in love."

PRAYER.—*Since we are glad to follow Thee as our example, may we mark how lovingly and tenderly Thou dost deal with those who are making mistakes; and since we ourselves are fallible, may we not fail to speak and act kindly, though faithfully, to those who falter.* AMEN.

AUGUST 15

". . . sealed unto the day of redemption" (Eph. 4: 30)

AN article has been purchased; the buyer does not wish to take it with him. It is left, and kept safe for him. Some later day he calls for his purchase and takes it home with him. The secret of its safe keeping till that day lies in the fact that a seal is put on it, not to be tampered with, to show it has been bought and awaits the coming of its owner. The Ephesians would know all about that Imperial Seal of Purchase. And Paul is led to use it as a parable of something which has happened to us Christians. In 1: 13 he tells us that "after that ye believed," that is on your believing, "ye were sealed," not with a thing but with a Person, the promised Holy Spirit. In this 4: 30 he says that we are then left here (John 17: 15) to await "the day of redemption," when He will come back to take us Home, "the redemption of the purchased possession," as he calls it in 1: 14. Meanwhile, as the "seal" assures the owner that his property will be guarded intact, so we are to be careful not to "grieve" the Spirit-seal by allowing ourselves to be used by any other than Him to whom we belong.

PRAYER.—*We thank Thee, O God, for the Divine Seal whom Thou hast placed upon Thy people, and we pray Thee for such grace as shall enable us to present ourselves without shame when He comes for us, because we have kept ourselves exclusively as His property.* AMEN.

AUGUST 16

". . . be filled with the Spirit" (Eph. 5: 18)

THIS is a plain command, as much so as "be not drunk with wine." If any one of us is not at any time thus "filled," he is living in disobedience. This filling is God's purpose for every Christian. Not for special people and special occasions only, as if it were Sunday's speciality, or the clergyman's sole prerogative. It is for that husband and wife, sitting together in verses 22–25. It is for that insignificant servant, as well as his master, in 6 : 5. It is for that child playing over there in 6: 1–4, no less than for his father. If you are a Christian at all, this privilege is for you. Note that in this filling rests the possibility, as the New Testament reveals, for all you ought to know, all you ought to do, all you ought to be. Moreover, the experience is not a "once for all" matter. It is "keep on being filled," a regular thing, in response to our daily surrender. And remember, it is not our having more of Him, but His having more of us.

PRAYER.—*We bless Thee that He did enter the house of our being the moment when we received the Saviour, but we desire that He shall not be confined to just one part of the dwelling, but that He may have the run of the whole house, filling every corner, every part of us, every day.* AMEN

". . . I have you in my heart . . ." (Phil. 1: 7)

THAT is better than having them on his nerves! What a man Paul was for taking people into his great big heart; and while that is evident in all his letters, it is nowhere more apparent than here when he is writing to his beloved Philippians. That affection was certainly mutual. More than once the church at Philippi had clubbed together to send him tokens of their love, and his deep feelings for them cannot here be hidden. It is when we have people in our heart that we can really long for their highest spiritual welfare as Paul did; that we can fervently pray for them that they may come to know Him, and continue to grow in Him, as Paul did. It is not enough to have them on our minds, nor merely on our lips, even in prayer. We must begin by getting them on our heart, and Romans 5: 5 will show us how.

PRAYER.—*May we live so close to Thee, dear Lord, that we really do begin to love people, even though some may be naturally not very lovable. Since Thou hast always loved the unlovely, may we not come behind in this lovely gift of the Spirit.* AMEN.

". . . the things which happened unto me have fallen out rather unto the furtherance of the Gospel" (Phil. 1: 12)

THAT "furtherance" is the passion of Paul's life, and he has always sought to take the good news to strategic points, whence it could permeate far distances. So we find him at Jerusalem, the heart of Palestine; at Antioch, the heart of Syria; at Ephesus, the heart of Asia Minor; at Athens, the heart of Greece; and now he is at Rome, the heart of the then known world. But here, it would seem, his great purpose was nullified, for he was held prisoner. Yet that is not his own view of his circumstances. If ever he could secure a very widespread "furtherance" it was now. All has turned out for the greater advancement of the Cause. During those two years he employed himself with his visitors, who will hence travel to many parts; with his military guards, who may subsequently be sent to any far-flung post of the empire; with his letters, which will reach across continents and down the years; with his prayers, which embraced a multitude and touched the throne. For the Christian, circumstances are ordered of the Lord. Let us then like Paul regard them not as opposition, but as opportunity. Happy is he who has learned to spell disappointment with a capital "H"—His-appointment.

PRAYER.—*We covet, O Lord, a like eagerness for the spreading of Thy Gospel. Help us then, that we may see and seize every opportunity to work and witness to that end, not in some fancied more favourable sphere, but just where we are.* AMEN.

". . . *your own salvation* . . ." (Phil. 2: 12)

IT was of course God's salvation, proposed, planned, purchased, and proffered by Him. But you accepted the Gift and made it "your own." Now what are you to do with it? Why, as God "works it in," you are to "work it out"; that is to translate into daily practice what of His will He causes you "to will" and enables you "to do." The point is that if you have made His salvation yours, it simply must not be allowed to remain secret. It just must come out! Not so much in what we say, though there is a proper and indeed obligatory place for that, but in what we do, and what we are. And if anyone asks how this "good purpose" of God's is daily to be fulfilled in our lives, we answer, The Holy Spirit within (one of the wondrous aspects of our salvation) makes possible the holy life without.

PRAYER.—*Lord, may we allow no obstacle to prevent our showing forth "so great salvation"—no fear of others, no selfish sloth, no careless thought, no personal inability, no hindrance at all. So to the work!* AMEN.

"*That I may know* . . . *the power of His resurrection* . . ."
(Phil. 3: 10)

WE might so profitably dwell upon the first part of Paul's longing "That I may know Him," or upon the last part, "That I may know . . . the fellowship of His sufferings," but just now I want to stress the exceeding importance of "knowing . . . the power of His resurrection . . ." We want our lives to be victorious lives, selfless lives, holy lives, fruitful lives. We certainly cannot produce such great qualities by our own power, but we certainly can by the power of the Living Christ, who lives within us if we are truly His. "We shall be saved by His life," says Romans 5: 10. We are "saved from . . ." (v. 9) all that sin means, by His death. We are "saved" unto all that sanctification means, by His life. Oh that we may all "know" that, not merely as piece of information, but as a bit of experience.

PRAYER.—*Thou Living Christ, even as Thy first disciples were completely transformed in character and galvanized into service by the glorious fact of Thy Resurrection, so may it be with us, who still have Thee as Living Presence in our hearts, as a Living Companion along the road, and as a Living Master to appoint unto us our task, with the power to do i* AMEN.

"*. . . the prize of the high calling . . .*" (Phil. 3: 14)

THE "high" is in the original the "upward" calling. At the Roman games, the Imperial box was high up above the tiers of seats, and when the races were finished the successful competitors received their "upward calling," to go up to be presented to the Emperor, and to get their prizes. So shall it be with all who "run well." When they have finished their course they shall get their "upward calling" to meet the Lord, and to obtain from His hands the "incorruptible crown" that is "laid up" for them (2 Tim. 4: 7, 8). "So run that ye may obtain" (1 Cor. 9: 24). Don't let us follow those who affect to despise the reward. Enough for us that Paul himself speaks so much about it and "presses" to receive it, and above all that the Lord so graciously deigns to offer it. True, we shall not run primarily for the prize, but we shall greatly esteem it, all the same, if by going "all out" we can but gain it.

PRAYER.—*Thou Emperor of our lives, who dost watch us as we struggle along our course, how shall we bless Thee if by Thine aid we may burst the tape victoriously, and may receive at Thy hands the emblem of conquest, and hear from Thy lips the gracious words, "Well done."* AMEN.

"*Rejoice in the Lord alway . . .*" (Phil. 4: 4)

I WOULD not accept this from anybody. The lighthearted, if not light-headed, back-slapping, cheer-up, keep-smiling brigade are an abomination unto me. Never having known trouble or loss themselves, they unfeelingly exhort those who have, to be bright and cheery. Ah, but Paul was different. He had known adversity in abundance as 2 Corinthians 11: 23–28 makes plain, and indeed this very letter was written in prison. Yet, the Epistle is full of radiant happiness, and from such a man as he I do most readily, and most wonderingly, hearken when he says, "Rejoice . . . alway." It does not jar when it comes from his lips, and it assures me that it can be done. But only "in the Lord" who Himself, in John 15: 11, could speak of "My joy," and in John 14: 27 of "My peace," even when confronting the fearful ordeal of Gethsemane, and Gabbatha, and Golgotha. Yes, then, "alway!"

PRAYER.—*Lord, we cannot forget how much cause for sorrow there is in our poor old world—such pain, such disappointment, such loneliness, such anxiety, and yet, blessed be God, when the ocean of life is troubled, the waters are at peace beneath the surface. May such joy be ours, even as it was the apostles' and the Master's. In spite of life's disturbances for ourselves and for others, may we dwell deep in Christ.* AMEN.

AUGUST 23

". . . *The Lord is at hand*" (Phil. 4: 5)

THE Second Coming of Christ was a matter very dear to the heart of this apostle. He was always looking for it. Not that he ever said that it would happen in his lifetime, but that it might. In a score of passages he speaks of it, but as a matter of fact I do not think he was referring to it here in this text. What is in his mind just now is the fact that the Lord is very close to His people, always at hand to help them, whatever be their circumstances. It is in the light of that practical and glorious fact that, to speak humanly, he feels justified in exhorting his friends that they need "be careful (anxious) for nothing," but may in everything turn in prayer to Him, who is ever so faithfully at their side, always there, always sufficient. He is never aloof, unless we keep Him at arm's length, but always alongside.

PRAYER.—*We thank Thee, our Saviour, for Thine abiding presence with us. We may not always be aware of it, but we know it is a fact. May we constantly remind ourselves that "surely the Lord is in this place" even if we know it not. May nothing spoil the fellowship, but may it sweeten care and lift the load, and cheer the heart.* AMEN.

AUGUST 24

". . . *my God . . . your need . . .*" (Phil. 4: 19)

THE other day I was hanging pictures in one of my rooms. The problem, at such times, is to match them satisfactorily. Here are two pictures, to hang on the walls of your mind, which exactly blend. The first is "Your Need." What a large canvas it is, and how full of detail. You know all its items so well. You often look at it, and are sometimes upset at what you find painted there. Yes, but here is the second, " My God." How beautifully, how exactly, how satisfactorily, it matches the first. As you carefully take in something of what is to be seen in Him you feel, as Paul felt, that there is nothing in "Your Need" that is not admirably and perfectly balanced in "My God." Never look at the first picture isolated, by itself. Stand back a bit until you can focus the pair of them together. The one alone might at times almost terrify you, with its stark realism, but the other will completely satisfy you with its powerful suggestiveness.

PRAYER.—*Great indeed, O God, is the picture of our need, but how can we falter if we keep in sight the greatness of Thy riches in glory, which so graciously and so generously are placed at our disposal. Thou dost never belittle our need, but Thou dost so gloriously overshadow it and meet it.* AMEN.

AUGUST 25

". . . *that in all things He might have the pre-eminence*" (Col. 1: 18)

CHRIST present is the mark of the third-class Christian life. If He were not there we should not be on the Gospel Train at all; we should not be Christians. Thank God if He be in our heart and life, but that would be true if we were only just Christians. Christ prominent is the mark of the second class, when we are not merely Christians but known to our fellows as such. He then holds a place in our conversation, conduct and character which makes Him evident to those who watch us. Christ pre-eminent is the mark of the first-class Christian. That He should have that "highest place" is God's purpose in creation, as this passage shows. Let it be our purpose too, who are the subjects of His new creation, thus to exalt Him over everything, and everyone, in our own lives.

PRAYER.—*Prevent us from being satisfied to travel second-class heavenwards, but may our way be blest with all the comfort, with all the provision, with all the safety, with all the fellowship of the first-class journey. May Thy purpose, our Father, be our purpose too, that "He may have pre-eminence" from the start to the terminus.* AMEN.

AUGUST 26

"*As ye have therefore received Christ Jesus the Lord, so walk ye in Him*" (Col. 2: 6)

CONVERSION is not only a stopping place, but also a starting place. It is a "walk," a progress, and that word is a favourite metaphor of the Christian life in the New Testament. Indeed, the Old Testament has the like idea, for both Enoch and Noah "walked with God." We are to walk warily, "See that ye walk circumspectly" (Eph. 5: 15), looking all around like soldiers suspecting mines, for our enemy, the devil, will be laying many traps for us. We are to walk wisely, "Walk in wisdom toward them that are without" (Col. 4: 5), lest we should lead them astray by giving them a false impression of the Christian way. We are to walk worthily, "Walk worthy of God, who hath called you unto His kingdom and glory" (1 Thess. 2: 12). Since you "received" Him you are His son, His servant, His soldier. Behave as all should who have been admitted to such a high privilege.

PRAYER.—*Save us, O Lord, from standing still or from back-sliding, but keep us by Thy Spirit always on the move, getting further and further in the Christian way. May our spiritual experience be not only profession, but also progression "in Christ."* AMEN.

149

". . . ye are complete in Him . . ." (Col. 2: 10)

"COMPLETE" is one of those picture words which abound in the Greek language. The picture is that of a ship fully equipped for the voyage. As the Christian sets sail upon the ocean of life, making for the Port of Heaven, he is as a vessel, amply provisioned in Him for the voyage, amply safeguarded in Him for any storms or difficulties which may arise, amply empowered in Him to pursue the journey to the end, amply directed in Him as the Captain of the Boat. "In Him . . . all the fulness of the Godhead" dwells as verse 9 tells us, so it is no wonder that in Him we find our full completion. Let us, then, without fear, without shame, and without misgiving, run up His colours to the mainmast, and fare forth upon our sea of life, happily aware that all our supplies are within reach because He is.

PRAYER.—*We are so well aware, O Lord, how miserably incomplete we are in ourselves, yet we do rejoice that we are not left to ourselves but positioned in Thee, and if Thou dost not promise us a smooth voyage, we thank Thee for the promise of a safe landing. Save us, then, from all anxiety, and be Thou the Captain of the ship.* AMEN.

". . . Christ . . . is our life . . ." (Col. 3: 4)

NOT merely "gives," but "is." The spiritual life is not just an "it," but a "He," a Person. Having Him is having it. In Him is its entrance. "He that hath the Son hath life" (1 John 5: 12). What a moment when He entered and we were brought from death unto life. In Him is its abundance. "I am come that they might have life, and that they might have it more abundantly" (John 10: 10). Not only barely alive, but bubbling and bursting with it. In Him is its permanence. "I give unto them eternal life" (John 10: 28). It lasts because He lasts. In Him is its influence. "Out of him shall flow rivers of living water" (John 7: 38), bringing blessing to many thirsty souls. In Him is its radiance. "In Him was life, and the life was the light of men" (John 1: 4). It was so with Him, and in our measure may be so with us. All this depends on just two conditions: One, We must have Him; Two, He must have us.

PRAYER.—*Our Gracious Saviour, as Thou hast redeemed our life from destruction, so wilt Thou make all that life the very best that Thou canst. Not for ease do we ask, but for earnestness to do Thy will.* AMEN.

"*. . . put on . . .*" (Col. 3: 10, 12, 14)

THAT is just what you did when you got up this morning; having "put off" the night attire (v. 8), you "put on" the clothes for the day. And what an extensive and lovely wardrobe the Christian possesses. "Put on the new man" (v. 10). A suit so different from the "old," so delightfully and continually fresh, and that gives its wearer more and more a striking resemblance to the very "image" of God. "Put on . . . mercies, kindness, humbleness . . . meekness, longsuffering, forbearing . . . forgiving . . ." (vs. 12, 13). What attractive garments, each piece always in the height of Heaven's fashion, all so delightful to look on. Oh, and don't forget this very becoming overcoat, "Above all these things put on charity" (v. 14). To be bound and buttoned up in this desirable finish will give you a veritable appearance of "perfection." To be sure, if he will use his well-stocked wardrobe, the Christian is a remarkably well-dressed man.

PRAYER.—*Such desirable and durable suitings of the soul shall be to the praise of Him who made them and not of him who wears them, but how they will minister to our demeanour and to our behaviour as we walk among men. So glad to be so clad!* AMEN.

"*. . . whatsoever ye do, do it heartily, as to the Lord, and not unto men*" (Col. 3: 23)

IT glorifies God when a Christian man does his ordinary job well, even as it dishonours Him if he is a shoddy workman. All work is honourable that serves the welfare of our fellows and the community, and we should put our best, and our utmost, into all such, as if we were doing it directly for the Lord instead of only indirectly, by way of our employer, or whomsoever we serve. If we were doing it for Him, how we should put our heart into it; but the consecrated Christian is to be doing it for Him! A remarkable man, the late Rev. Samuel Chadwick, would never send out a letter to anyone if it had any blots, smudges or mistakes, because he wrote as if it were going to the Master, and he said that on that account it must be cleanly and clearly written.

PRAYER.—*So may we see the spiritual side of our secular work, and may we so discharge our duties as if we were conscious that Thou wast looking on, as indeed Thou art. May we not fail in our duty towards our neighbour, lest perchance we should thus fail in our duty toward God.* AMEN.

AUGUST 31

"... *always labouring fervently* ... *in prayers* ..." (Col. 4: 12)

SUCH was the intensity of the prayers of this man, Epaphras, that it is here described as an "agonizing," according to the Greek of "labouring fervently," and such is the frequency of his intercession that he is said to be "always" at it. He cared so deeply for his converts in Colosse, he had a "great zeal" (v. 13) for them, but now that he is in far-off Rome he can do nothing for them. Can't he? What about prayer? That transcends all distance and all difficulties, and as a matter of fact we can never do anything better for another than to pray for him, if it be real prayer, of the Epaphras type. We often grow tired of praying. Do we ever get tired through praying, spent, worn out, as he did? May this grand prayer warrior lead us to overhaul our prayer life.

PRAYER.—*Our Lord, Thou hast left us so wonderful an example of what prayer should be, and Thou hast given us such encouragement to use it to the full, that we desire to give it a greater and a deeper place in our lives, that we may find the truth that "the effectual fervent prayer of a righteous man availeth much."* AMEN.

SEPTEMBER

THE RECOLLECTIONS OF AN EX-SERVICE MAN

Whether Joshua himself actually wrote the book or not, it is certainly the official record of his recollections as Commanding Officer of the Army of Israel. He had had a taste of that position some years before, at the Battle of Rephidim (Exod. 17: 8, 9), and now he is invested with the full command, and given his Commission, by his God and King. Military operations began almost at once, and the book is naturally very largely coloured by soldierly exploits until the close of the campaign in victory and post-war settlement.

SEPTEMBER 1

". . . now . . . go . . ." (Josh. 1: 2)

"Go!" "Now," in the face of calamity; "after the death of Moses." Can there be any "after," following such a devastating loss? Yes, God buries His workmen (Deut. 34: 6), but carries on His work. "Go!" "Now," in the face of opportunity; "the land." Our promised land is the land of the promises. Happy he who enters, and who leads others in. "Go!" "Now," in the face of difficulty; "this Jordan." There will be no difficulty He cannot surmount. "Go!"

PRAYER.—*We rejoice, O Lord, in so many stories in the Word concerning those who, at Thy command, went on Thy errands, though in the face of difficulty and often danger. May we on our part heed nothing but Thy will and go anywhere at Thy behest.* AMEN.

SEPTEMBER 2

". . . I will not fail thee, nor forsake thee" (Josh. 1: 5)

IMAGINE yourself, for a moment, in Joshua's position. The call has come to him to take up Moses' mantle. What must his feelings have been? There he was, with all the immense responsibilities of his leadership. He would, in all humility, feel that he might so easily "fail." There was the people that he was to command. They might, in actual reality, "fail" to follow. Failure, on both sides; yes, only too possible. How infinitely reassuring, then, was the word of God, "I will not fail . . ."! We, as he, can utterly rely on that. However weak we ourselves may be, however difficult our circumstances may be, He is our unfailing Standby. If, like Joshua, we will walk in the line of His will, we shall walk in the light of this blest encouragement.

PRAYER.—*In the light of such assurance, O Lord, help us not to fail, but enable us so utterly to rely on Thy utter reliability, that we may step out, head high, on to victory.* AMEN.

SEPTEMBER 3

". . . then thou shalt have good success" (Josh. 1: 8)

WE all of us want to make a success of our lives, not only for our own sake, but also for the sake of those dependent on us. What will you say of this young man, called to take over the control of this vast crowd of something like two million people, including many women and children? How immense are his responsibilities, how tremendous are the issues hanging over his "good success." Well, it will all depend upon what foundation he builds on. That rule holds for us, as well as for him. Good Queen Victoria, giving audience to an African prince of long ago, is reported to have presented him with a beautiful copy of the Bible saying, "The secret of England's greatness." That's it; a life that is built foursquare on the Bible is assured of success. "This book of the Law," the same old secret, was Joshua's; the Book perused, and pondered, and practised.

PRAYER.—*Make me, Lord, in every sense a Bible man, that all my life may be guided thereby, that all my strength may be drawn therefrom, that all my battles may be fought therewith—"it is written."* AMEN.

SEPTEMBER 4

". . . the Lord thy God is with thee whithersoever thou goest"
(Josh. 1: 9)

How greatly comforting is the surety of the Presence. Moses had said, "If Thy presence go not with me, carry us not up thence" (Exod. 33: 15), so enormous was his estimate of the value of His company. And now, as Joshua takes over the command, he is cheered with the assurance, "As I was with Moses, so I will be with thee" (v. 5). Relying upon that promise, Joshua felt that he could go anywhere, face anything. You too, have the Presence. Do you enter into the power of it, the peace of it, the pleasure of it? "In Thy presence is fulness of joy . . ." (Ps. 16: 11). "Whithersoever" is a large place, a long journey. It may lead us into difficult spots, and along rough ways, but the promise abides to the end of the road.

PRAYER.—*With Thy blessed whithersoever, O Lord, I am emboldened to face my varied whatsoever, and to battle with any vicious whosoever that shall cross my path, and prosper in every vagary of my whensoever. How I bless Thee for my whithersoever God.* AMEN.

"*. . . the scarlet line in the window*" (Josh. 2: 21)

THE first piece of Window Dressing of them all! It bears a threefold significance, in fact, and in type. First, Rahab has chosen her side. Somehow or other she has come to realize which is the winning side, the Lord's side, and that scarlet is the symbol of her choice. Second, she has ensured her safety. Her character did not save her, harlot and deceiver as she was; but then, neither will you be saved by your character, even though yours be good. Her faith saved her (Heb. 11: 31), even as we also secure salvation, by God's grace, the same way. Her actions testified to the reality of that faith. She believed, and risked all on it, as James 2: 25 implies. So is our faith to be followed by "works." Third, she has gathered her friends. She is not content to be saved alone (v. 13), but obeys the word to get them "in the house" (v. 19). The red line is as the red blood of Exodus 12: 13. Are we sheltered there? Are we getting others sheltered?

PRAYER.—*We adore Thee, O God, that though our sins be as scarlet, there is a scarlet covering that makes them white, so in Thy forgiving mercy, and even in Thy justice, Thou dost look upon us who believe as if we had never sinned. Thus shall we eternally bless Thee for "The precious Blood of Christ."* AMEN.

"*. . . ye have not passed this way heretofore*" (Josh. 3: 4)

THAT phrase could be applied to every fresh experience of life. How often we have thought of it at the beginning of a new year, and even at the opening of a new day. It was vividly true for Joshua at this juncture; it is always true, of all of us, for all our future. The point for the believer to lay hold of is this, that whatever the coming days may contain for him, he will discover that his Lord has been graciously acting as his forerunner, and has been on ahead preparing the way. Do you remember His word in Deuteronomy 31: 8, "The Lord, He it is that doth go before thee." It is like the pilot engine that always precedes the Royal Train, which if there were any unforeseen difficulty, any concealed danger, would meet it first and surmount it, and so the Important Personage would be spared. Fear not the future. He is just on ahead to meet it first, and so to fulfil Romans 8: 28 for you.

PRAYER.—*So would we accept from Thy Hand, O Master, any untoward circumstance of our lives, knowing that Thy hand has moulded it to our good. So shall we trust Thee, whatever comes, and be assured that all is well.* AMEN.

SEPTEMBER 7

". . . the people passed over right against Jericho" (Josh. 3: 16)

W HAT a jolt to their joy! They had just passed over Jordan, and amid all the thrill and emotion of God's miraculous dealing; and now as a cold douche to their fervour, they came at once face to face with Jericho! That experience has been a not uncommon one in the spiritual realm. Many a soul newly converted, filled with gladness over "the great transaction," beginning the new life with radiant hope, has found himself forthwith up against some big temptation, some unexpected opposition, some seemingly insuperable problem. In some cases the sudden test has been too much, and they have fallen. In other cases, these new believers have looked to "the Captain of their salvation," as Joshua did, and they have trusted Him to see them through this first onset of the enemy's antagonism. After Jordan comes Jericho; but Jesus is there all the time.

PRAYER.—*Lord, how many, and often how big, are the obstacles that cross our path, yet how small they look if seen through Thine Eyes, for Thou art the Great One who will overcome every opposition for us and in us. On, then, to victory, seem Jericho ever so great.* AMEN.

SEPTEMBER 8

". . . prepared for war . . ." (Josh. 4: 13)

" A BOUT forty thousand" of them; but tell me are you prepared for war? Let it never be forgotten that the Christian life is not a picnic. It has its times of quiet rest, of steady progress, of sheer enjoyment, but we must always be "prepared for war." Sometimes in obvious ways, sometimes from unexpected directions, sometimes in sudden emergencies, to catch us off our guard, the adversary launches his attacks. Wherever, whatever, whenever, we must always be ready for him. What a preparation is "the whole armour of God" (Eph. 6: 11ff); the girdle (which hitched up the under garments) of truth; the breastplate (which covered back as well as front) of righteousness; the sandals (which protected from irritating grit) of peace; the shield (not the little, but the large one) of faith; the helmet (giving head cover) of salvation; the sword (so sharp and piercing) of the Word; the greaves (which covered knees and legs) of prayer. Take it (v. 13) and put it on (v. 11) and you will be wondrously "prepared for war."

PRAYER.—*We know, O God, how subtle a foe we have against us, and "we are not ignorant of his devices." Neither are we ignorant of Thy all-covering and all-conquering accoutrement. We go into battle certain of the conquest under our Great Captain.* AMEN.

"... *What mean these stones?*" (Josh. 4: 21)

O H yes, the "children" would be sure to ask, such is their inveterate thirst for information. As they stood by those twelve monuments they were to be told the marvellous story of the rolling back of Jordan's waters, and the crossing of the multitude on dry ground. Moreover, they would also be told that there were other twelve stones erected on the river's bed ere the waters returned. For our own purposes today, as we look for the meaning of these stones, we recall that this passage of Jordan is a type and picture of our crossing over into the Christian life; the twelve stones buried under the water representing our being "planted together in the likeness of His death," the twelve stones erected in the open representing our rising together "in the likeness of His resurrection" (Rom. 6: 5). Upon the fountain stones of these two complementary truths rests all the possibility of the truly blessed Christian life.

PRAYER.—*May we know not merely the historical meaning, but the spiritual meaning and the practical meaning of this glorious truth, and may our innermost experience and outermost life be based and blest in Him, who is "the Living Stone."* AMEN.

SEPTEMBER   10

"... *a Man* ... *with His sword drawn in His hand* ..." (Josh. 5: 13)

T HIS "Man" was actually the One whom we now know as the Lord Jesus. We have here one of His pre-incarnation appearances in human form. Joshua had before him on the morrow perhaps the supreme test of his career, whether as man, or as soldier. On the eve of the battle, he went out alone to be quiet, and doubtless to pray, for he was that sort. And to this soldier He appeared as a Soldier, with drawn sword. How apposite! But then, it is so often like that. He comes, not only "just when I need Him most," as the chorus says, but just as I need Him most! Thus, when by the death of Uzziah the throne was empty, He appears to Isaiah as "sitting upon a throne" (Isa. 6: 1). And when He comes to Abram with an amazing proposition, beyond human dreams and calculations, He reveals Himself (Gen. 17: 1) as El Shaddai, the God Who Is Enough. So will He so often draw near to you in the guise that will best meet your need.

PRAYER.—*How many an encouragement, how many an example, how many a help, have we found in the assurance that for all Thy deity Thou wast ever so human. Thou knowest us and our experiences so well for Thou hast Thyself passed this way, and we rejoice that to the understanding sympathy of the Son of Man, is added for us the undertaking strength of the Son of God.* AMEN.

SEPTEMBER 11

". . . Captain . . . am I . . ." (Josh. 5: 14)

YES, it was our Lord Himself; and Joshua was soon constrained to recognize His deity, and to worship Him. But note that He is come to take charge. Joshua must learn, at the outset, that it is not a matter of His being on our side, "for us" (v. 13), but of our being on His side, "as Captain." We are told in Luke 2: 11 that He is a "born . . . Saviour" and in Matthew 2: 2, a "born King." No less is it true that He is a born Captain, this "Man" who in Hebrews 2: 10 is described as "the captain of their salvation." Ah, what a Captain He is, and how wise are they who take service under His command, who follow His leading, however strange, like the marching round Jericho, it may seem, and who thus enjoy His wondrous victory, which He infallibly wins for all who go about their warfare in His way, the way of faith. Joshua was to prove that up to the hilt; a multitude has proved it since.

PRAYER.—*Shall we not prove it too?—Thou has enlisted, O Captain, many an awkward squad and trained them into brave and brilliant warriors. Let us then not hold back from enrolment in the Army of the Lord, since Thou wilt enable us to "endure hardness and to fight well" as a good soldier of Jesus Christ. We rejoice that "Thine is the kingdom, and the power, and the glory, for ever."* AMEN.

SEPTEMBER 12

". . . See, I have given into thine hand Jericho . . ." (Josh. 6: 2)

THERE it was, impressively impregnable in the eyes of that time, with its massive walls so broad that houses were built upon them. How impossible of capture sometimes seem the citadels of evil that confront us: personal problems, or more open challenges. Let us learn here the secret of their conquest. Joshua is to secure his triumph, not by the arm of force, but by the arm of faith. How many a Christian faces with fear, and failure, some Jericho of besetting sin, seemingly unmindful of the Lord's word of promise, "See, I have given into thine hand Jericho." There are two elements in our spiritual success: God's side and our side. They are summed up in the words of a familiar hymn, "I take," "He undertakes." Joshua did not fight for Jericho, he just received it. God gave it into his hands. That is the secret for our continual victory. Don't fight, take. Look to Him, not to yourself. Don't attempt to make the conquest, but take it from His hands.

PRAYER.—*Lord, we thank Thee for the mightiness of faith—mighty only because it is that which takes hold of Thee, for Thou art the Almighty One, and be our faith however simple, Thou wilt accomplish the thing Thou appointest. We reiterate our earlier use of the old petition, "Lord, I believe, help Thou mine unbelief."* AMEN.

"When I saw . . ." (Josh. 7: 21)

EYE GATE has ever been a danger spot in the defence of the City of Mansoul. Quite often the enemy has forced an entry there when all other gates have proved impervious to his attacks. It was so at the very first battle of them all. Satan was repulsed at Ear Gate, when "he said"; but "when the woman saw" (Gen. 3: 6), it was all over! It was so at Peter's sudden downfall, after he had been doing so well; but "when he saw . . ." (Matt. 14: 30), it was all over! And here it is again, when the wretched Achan is compelled to tell how it all happened, he began, "When I saw . . ." How important it is to observe the injunction of Hebrews 12: 2, ". . . looking unto Jesus," that our eyes may be right. As soon as the enemy appears, waste not a moment, but look instantly to Him; not at the foe, not at yourself, but at the Victor, as Psalm 25: 15 taught us here weeks ago. If thus the moment "when I saw" is made the moment "when I saw Him", the thing is conquered.

PRAYER.—*Wilt Thou keep our eyes from beholding evil, O Lord, and keep them steadfastly beholding Thee. Thus may the sight of Satan cause us no fear, nor the sight of evil lure us to do wrong. May our military command "Eyes right" mean, for us, eyes right ahead to Thee.* AMEN.

". . . be ye all ready" (Josh. 8: 4)

WHAT a great thing it is to be "ready". The British Army used to have a regiment called the Royal Field Artillery, R.F.A. for short. Its members used to say that their initials really meant, Ready for Anything! I fancy there is just such a regiment in the army of the King of Kings. How many "soldiers of Christ" belong to it? Do you? This portion of Joshua's forces was, at this Second Battle of Ai, posted at a certain point, and told to watch for the sign of the stretched-out spear (vs. 18, 19), which would be their cue to go in to the attack. Well now, let us "all" cultivate this attitude of readiness for any service that He shall appoint, and above all, let us be on the watch for "the sign of the Son of Man" (Matt. 24: 30), for which we are exhorted, "Be ye also ready" (Matt. 24: 44).

PRAYER.—*We are never really sure where the enemy is proposing to strike, but may we be ever on the alert. We never know when the door of opportunity shall open, but may we ever be awake to the chance. We are never sure when the Lord shall wish to send us on His errands, but may we ever be at His hand to go. May we in nothing be caught unawares.* AMEN.

SEPTEMBER

". . . all Israel . . . stood . . ." (Josh. 8: 33)

IT must have been an intensely impressive occasion, ordered by God through Moses (Deut. 27: 2–8), and now carried out by Joshua in Canaan, in token of the nation's acknowledgment of God's claims. Down the valley was the Ark of the Covenant, symbol of God's presence, surrounded by the Priests and the Levites. On the side of one mountain was half the tribes, on the other, the second half. In solemn silence, "all Israel stood" while the Levites read the words of God's laws. The acoustic properties of the place are remarkable, and every word would be heard clearly. When the curses of the Law were recited, the tribes on Ebal responded, "Amen!" When the blessings were rehearsed, those on Gerizim replied, "Amen!" Thus, in most moving circumstances, God's Word was publicly read and accepted. How deeply impressed must the "little ones" (v. 35) have been. Would God that all people today "stood" in awe and acceptance of His Word.

PRAYER.—*But while we echo such a sentiment, O Lord, we pray that we ourselves may both hear and heed Thy laws, and find in our keeping of them how fraught with blessing they are. "Lord, may I love Thy law, it shall be my meditation day and night."* AMEN.

SEPTEMBER

". . . the men . . . asked not counsel at the mouth of the Lord"
(Josh. 9: 14)

THOSE elders of Israel would never have been trapped by the clever ruse of the Gibeonites if only they had sought God's will in His appointed way. He made gracious provision for their getting His "counsel" by the Urim and Thummim of the High Priest (Exod. 28: 30; Num. 27: 21). But here they elected to judge the matter by their own unaided wisdom. All the evidence showed, as they thought, the genuineness of their visitors, and the league was made, in flat contradiction of divine orders (Deut. 7: 2). How often have we also allowed ourselves to judge important matters by human reason alone, and have found ourselves in difficulties because we "asked not counsel" of Him, by the appointed means of our Urim of the Word and Thummim of the Spirit. It is a godly habit to refer every problem, every proposal, every plan, every perplexity to Him for His guidance, otherwise our subtle Gibeonites will be sure to prove our undoing.

PRAYER.—*Give to us, O Lord, that unfailing wisdom of going for our leading to the Holy Scriptures and the Holy Spirit, that what must be said and what must be done may be according to Thy direction. May we know Thy mind about things, and have Thy power to do them.* AMEN.

SEPTEMBER 17

". . . there was no day like that . . ." (Josh. 10: 14)

HAVE you got a red-letter-day in your life? This was a never-to-be-forgotten day in Joshua's experience, when "the Lord fought for Israel." The sword made its contribution to the victory (v. 11), their enemies being routed and pursued first up, then down, the precipitous ridge of Beth-horon. The stones made their contribution (v. 11), such hailstones as constituted an amazing artillery of Heaven. The sun made its contribution also (v. 13), miraculously delaying its setting that the victory might be completed and consummated, and lest normal nightfall should bring cover and escape to the foe. What a day! And your red-letter-day? Your conversion, consecration, communion, when you had your soul-stirring experience? Have you had your doubts since then? Well, go back to your red-letter-day, abide anyhow by that. Never let what you know be disturbed by what you don't know.

PRAYER.—*"Oh happy day that fixed my choice on Thee my Saviour and my God, well may this glowing heart rejoice, and tell its rapture all abroad."* AMEN.

SEPTEMBER 18

". . . he left nothing undone of all that the Lord commanded Moses"
(Josh. 11: 15)

THE acme of obedience! I rather fear that many of us Christians fail to realize how strategic a quality is obedience. It is no exaggeration to say that, for blessing in the Christian life, everything hangs on it. There is no such blessing for the disobedient Christian; there is fulness of blessing for the completely obedient. It is this completeness which today's text emphasizes, and I fancy that we all need the reminder, for we are all too prone to partial obedience, as Peter was when in Luke 5: 4 the Master said, "Let down your nets . . .", and the disciple only "let down the net" (v. 5), so that his one net broke and he nearly lost the whole catch of fish. If only he had followed Joshua's example and "left nothing undone . . .", if he had lowered his two nets, all would have been well. Let us make up our minds that our obedience shall be both prompt and perfect.

PRAYER.—*Lord, if obedience is so great a secret, how infinitely great is the one who accepts it, and as we do what we are told, may we find also how joyously gladsome a thing such obedience is. "Trust and obey, for there's no other way to be happy in Jesus"* (be anything in Jesus) *"but to trust and obey."* AMEN.

"*. . . he wholly followed the Lord . . .*" (Josh. 14: 14)

THERE was nothing half-hearted about this man Caleb. The statement is here in the first, and the second, and the third person. "I wholly followed" (v. 8), "Thou hast wholly followed" (v. 9), "He wholly followed," this verse 14. What would not Peter have given to have been entitled to say the same, but to his grievous undoing he "followed afar off." Many difficulties may have to be faced, much daring may have to be called for, but what rewards await the "wholly" people! If we will go all out for God, keeping right up with Him, He will lead us into ever deepening experiences in our own souls, into ever fascinating adventures in His service, into ever extending influence with others. Caleb started thus following when he was a young man; he is still at it at the age of eighty-five (v. 10), and still ready to adventure for God, eager to conquer a "mountain" (v. 12).

PRAYER.—*We thank Thee, O Saviour, that Thou dost follow after us until Thou dost find us for Thyself, and now we pray that we, on our part, may follow Thee up to the hilt and right to the end, keeping close by, never lagging behind for a moment.* AMEN.

"*. . . thou hast given me a land . . . give me also springs of water*" (Josh. 15: 19)

THAT seems to me a very sensible request. It was a grand thing to get the "land," with all its possibilities; but how are those possibilities to be realized without the "springs of water"? We, too, have been given a land, or more accurately perhaps are a land, inasmuch as 1 Corinthians 3: 9 says, "Ye are God's husbandry," but the harvest we produce will be very poor unless we have the "springs of water." Recollect how the Master described it as "in him a well of water" (John 4: 14) and "out of him . . . rivers of living water" (John 7: 38), which He explained as referring to the Holy Spirit. He is our "springs of water"; without His quickening refreshment the field of our Christian character will be sadly barren. With Him, that field will be full of freshness, fragrance and fruit.

PRAYER.—*May no threat of barrenness mar our experience, but may our life be crowded and crowned with golden grace. To this end, O Lord, may we be enabled to give the Holy Spirit a chance to fill and flood our being with the gracious waters of His influence.* AMEN.

"*. . . they . . . did not utterly drive them out*" (Josh. 17: 13)

THAT is asking for trouble, and it is indeed the trouble with many Christian people. We deal too leniently with things in our lives that should never be allowed to remain; sins and habits are all too often tolerated as not mattering very much. But, to parody an old saying, "Little sins grow bigger sins, and so ad infinitum." Moreover, it has been abundantly demonstrated that the diminutive chains of habit are generally too small to be felt until they are too strong to be broken. If we would know God's best, and be God's best, there is nothing for it but a clean sweep, a clean cut. Saul spared some of the Amalekites, and in the end it was an Amalekite that slew him (2 Sam. 1: 8–10). I find that just above I have mentioned "little sins," but as a matter of fact, are there any little sins? Out with everything that savours of spiritual harm, hurt and hindrance.

PRAYER.—*We feel, O Lord, that if this clean-sweep is to be brought about it must be Thou that must do it. Wilt Thou, then, graciously accept our invitation, and come in, to throw out the least and last things that may hold up the best.* AMEN.

"*. . . Why hast thou given me but . . . one portion . . . ?*"
(Josh. 17: 14)

DURING these chapters Joshua has been apportioning the land to the various tribes by lot. Everybody seems to have been quite satisfied with the fairness of the distribution except this one, Joseph. He felt that reckoning by their size and strength, they ought to have a larger inheritance, a wider scope. Their leader, however, pointed out that they had plenty of room for expansion by cutting down the thick woods of the nearby mountain, and driving out the enemy inhabitants in their territory (v. 18). Quite a lot of people get restive about their lot in life. They feel they ought to be in a place of more importance and influence, and they are inclined to grumble against God's providence, "Why hast Thou given me but" this comparatively small place? Be assured that wherever He has placed you, there are woods to clear, and enemies to clear. Do that faithfully, and happily, and perchance the greater sphere will come later.

PRAYER.—*Thy servants, O God, have so often proved that whereas it is possible to serve Thee anywhere, it can only be done best in the place of Thine appointment. Be that sphere, then, small or greater, prominent or insignificant, give us grace there to serve Thee well, leaving the future to Thy wise choice for us.* AMEN.

SEPTEMBER   **23**

"*. . . How long are ye slack . . . to possess the land which the Lord . . . hath given you?*" (Josh. 18: 3)

THE Lord purposes to give us the land of the full Christian life, but alas, our backwardness all too often robs us of that joy and blessing. We are out of Egypt, but we are not in Canaan, so we are floundering in the wilderness! Why, and how long, this slackness? Some of the tribes had already entered on their inheritance, but seven of them, as in our passage, had yet to claim their portion. What tribes of Christians are spiritually in like case. Those who are ignorant of the land, not yet aware of what blessings await them. Those who are scared by the enemy, all too conscious of the opposition they would have to meet. Those who are forgetful of the Lord who is all-sufficient to subdue their foes, and to supply their every need. Those who are content with the less; after all, they are Christians, they are free of Egypt, why worry about anything further? Come, all ye Tribes of the Tardy, "how long are ye slack?" Go in at once, and claim all that God has "given you" in Christ.

PRAYER.—*We confess, O Lord, that all too often we have failed to grasp the fulness of our inheritance, and for needless causes have held back from obtaining our legacy. May we delay no longer to hasten to claim all that Thou hast willed for us.* AMEN.

SEPTEMBER   **24**

"*. . . an inheritance to Joshua . . .*" (Josh. 19: 49)

THE day before yesterday we saw Joshua mapping out the land, but what about his own share? Let it be noted that his was the last inheritance; everyone else was provided for under Joshua's direction, and then when all others were settled the last portion was taken by him. He had been the great leader of the whole expedition; the tremendous success of the invasion of Canaan was, humanly speaking, due to him, and surely he was entitled to first choice. Let it be noted, further, that his was the least inheritance. He received no stretch of territory, but just one city. I have stayed on this incident to draw attention to what I conceive to be this man's finest quality; not his military prowess, nor his evident business acumen, but his utter selflessness. So long as others were well provided for, he, who could rightly claim the first and the best, was content with the last and the least. You know, the name Joshua is but the Hebrew form of the Greek Jesus, as Hebrews 4: 8 indicates. How like the Lord Jesus was Joshua in this wonderful selflessness.

PRAYER.—*Teach us, good Lord, this perhaps hardest of all lessons, to keep self in the background, and while caring greatly for the welfare of others, may we be ready and glad to leave our own interests in Thy care and keeping.* AMEN.

SEPTEMBER 25

"*. . . cities of refuge . . .*" (Josh. 20: 2)

THERE were six of these, "that the man slayer which killeth any person unwittingly may flee thither" (v. 3). When we come to consider them as a multiple figure of safety in Christ, we remember that by way of contrast, He gives sanctuary, not only to the unwitting sinner, but even to the guilty, who is truly penitent. The general availability of those places is a noteworthy feature. They were so situated throughout the land that one or other of them was easily accessible from any point in the country. Then, the roads leading to them were clearly signposted, and they were kept always in good repair. Indeed, everything was done to ensure that they might, without difficulty, be reached by those who needed their shelter. Is that not a striking picture of the gracious nearness of God to any sinner who turns to Him for salvation from the pursuant judgment of sin? In the Person of His Son, He "came where he was" (Luke 10: 33), that the sinner might find Him as He is: Refuge and Saviour and Friend. Do not forget that those cities were bound to provide hospitality for the fugitive until at the death of the High Priest he was finally safe. So do we find in Christ both our safety, and our sustenance.

PRAYER.—*How complete is Thy provision for the guilty sinner who runs to Thee, O Saviour, in true repentance and real faith.* AMEN.

SEPTEMBER 26

"*There failed not ought of any good thing which the Lord had spoken . . . all came to pass*" (Josh. 21: 45)

OF course, He sometimes has to speak stern things, and they too all come to pass. Let us beware of a modern tendency to think only of God's love. We cannot dwell too much on that, but we must not ignore the other side: His holiness, His justice, His hatred of sin. A famous Scots preacher, speaking on Exodus 34: 6, 7, called the phrase "that will by no means clear the guilty" the Dark Line in God's Face! Joshua had been made aware of that, but just now he is recalling the good things He spoke, the promises of good He made, and how wonderfully He made good every word of them. I wonder how many good promises of His there are in the Scriptures? We ought not to forget that almost every one of them is conditional; if we fulfil the condition, He will fulfil the promise, but only so. When we have dealt faithfully on our part, by observing His requirement, we shall be able to testify about His part, that "there failed not ought . . ."

PRAYER.—*Lord, how we wish that it could be said of our promises to Thee that we have kept them, yet how we rejoice that never a promise of Thine has gone astray, but help us to fulfil the appointed conditions.* AMEN.

SEPTEMBER 27

" . . . *an altar not . . . for sacrifice; but that it may be a witness . . .*"
(Josh. 22: 26, 27)

THERE was a rare fuss when, after returning to their possession, the two and a half tribes built this altar. There is only one legitimate altar, said the rest of the tribes, the altar in the Tabernacle at Shiloh; and they feared God would punish the whole nation for what they supposed to be a sacrilegious rival altar. It was, however, explained that no altar of sacrifice was here intended. Of course not, but only an altar of witness to their children of the oneness of the tribes east and west of Jordan. We Protestants still maintain that there is only one altar of sacrifice (Heb. 13: 10), the Altar of Calvary. What is all too commonly designated an "altar" in modern churches is no such thing. "No blood, no altar, now, the sacrifice is o'er." That all-sufficient Sacrifice has been offered once, and for all. The "table" is but the witness to our children's children of the finished sacrifice, the feast of communion of the "all one in Christ Jesus" (Gal. 3: 28), and of the final return, for as ye partake, "ye do show the Lord's death till He come" (1 Cor. 11: 26).

PRAYER.—*Resting upon that One Altar, may we see to it that our manifold testimony is ever radiant and true. May our lips ever witness to Thy grace and goodness as revealed in the One Sacrifice, and may our lives add to the testimony of the wonder of it all.* AMEN.

SEPTEMBER 28

"*Take good heed . . . that ye love the Lord your God*" (Josh. 23: 11)

THAT is part of the old leader's talk with his people, and verily it is a strategic utterance, and one all the more striking as coming from the lips of a virile soldier. Yet, on reflection, love is not a soft sentimentality, ill-becoming a hardy warrior, but is a deeply strong quality and indeed the greatest force in the world. When it is love for God no one can measure its potentiality for good. When Paul says, in 2 Corinthians 5: 14, "the love of Christ constraineth us," we recognize that he is touching the spring of all else. These meditations have, from time to time, stressed much the duties of holiness, of obedience, of service, and the demand for these is inescapable. No earnest Christian can, nor will wish to, ignore them. Well, the secret is love. "Take good heed" that you love Him, and all else will follow. How acquire that love? Relying on Romans 5: 5 ask the Holy Spirit to take you often to Calvary.

PRAYER.—*Recalling the injunction of Thy servant, that we should "covet earnestly the best gifts," we remind ourselves of his further utterance that "the greatest of these is love." "Gracious Spirit, Holy Ghost, taught by Thee we covet most, of Thy gifts at Pentecost, Holy, Heavenly Love."* AMEN.

"*. . . as for me and my house, we will serve the Lord*" (Josh. 24: 15)

THIS text was once hung upon the entrance hall of the house of a very well-off city man. It was a lovely place, containing many treasures, but to find that framed testimony meeting the eye immediately upon entering the house was, to many, the most valuable thing in this rich man's possessions, especially as it was known that he so happily lived up to it. Joshua has now settled the Israelites in their home, and he bids them choose their Master, for their new life; for his own part he has neither doubt nor hesitation. He has come to know too well the goodness of the Lord, in all the vicissitudes and ventures of his tremendous career, to allow him to choose any but Him to be the supreme Overlord of his life. Upon the entrance hall of your will and mind will you hang this as the directing motto of your life, for all, by your living of it, to see?

PRAYER.—*Lord, what other Master could we choose but Thee, who hast bought us at such tremendous cost, who hast filled our lives with such a multitude of blessings, and who wilt accompany us safely through to glory. Be Thou for me the Master of the house.* AMEN.

"*. . . the servant of the Lord died . . .*" (Josh. 24: 29)

THAT'S how we put it, but it is not the real truth about a believer's passing. D. L. Moody once said, "One day you will read in the newspapers that D. L. Moody is dead. Don't you believe it. On that day Moody will be more alive than ever he's been." How grand! His service here is finished; not till then will God call us hence. What glorious service Joshua had rendered to the end of his 110 years. His service here is blessed, its influence continued after his departure, as verse 31 tells us. Shall we leave behind us any such abiding impress, I wonder? "Serve in newness of spirit" (Rom. 7: 6), that it may be so. His service here is preparatory to service yonder, where "His servants shall serve Him" (Rev. 22: 3). Good news for eager souls: eternal busy-ness without tiredness!

PRAYER.—*We praise Thee for the blessed assurance that they which believe in Thee have entered into an eternal life with beginnings here, and continuance through the endless hereafter beyond. May we so serve Thee now that we may be trained to serve Thee then, "Whose service is perfect freedom" always.* AMEN.

OCTOBER

INFANT'S PROGRESS

*How very varied are the succeeding pages of
the Church's story, some of them stained and
blotted; some, best forgotten, some, resplendent
with golden deeds. This Book of Acts is the first
page of them all, and with fascinated interest we
peruse its contents, the record of those earliest
days of its childhood, so fresh, so adventurous,
so wonderful. That accurate historian, Dr. Luke,
is the human author, and inspiring him is the
same Holy Spirit who was behind all the life and
activity of the Church of the First Days.*

OCTOBER 1

". . . all that Jesus began . . ." (Acts 1: 1)

T HE Doctor's first book, the Gospel, had been a glorious account of the Lord Jesus. When that book closed, with His death and resurrection and ascension, it is not to be thought that that was the end. It is but a description of "all that Jesus began . . ." The Acts is the story of what He continued "both to do and to teach," during those first days and right on to these days. Lay hold on the sublime truth that what your Lord "began" to do for you, He will always continue to do. For example, the fact that He began to keep you is the guarantee that He will so continue to do.

PRAYER.—*We take heart, O Lord, that Thou hast revealed Thyself as "The Beginning and the Ending." May our spoilings never mar Thy continuings, but may we enjoy to the full Thy perfect endings.* AMEN.

OCTOBER 2

". . . many infallible proofs . . ." (Acts 1: 3)

T HERE was no doubt about His having died, but now "He shewed Himself alive." Was there no doubt about that either? Or, were these men suffering from an hallucination? No, it was no delusion. He showed that "by many infallible proofs." His voice, most difficult of human qualities to counterfeit, as Jacob found in Genesis 27: 22. Mary recognized Him thus (John 20: 16). His scars, evidence of identity in any court of law. Even in heaven we shall know Him by these (Rev. 5: 6). His keepsake, the something they were to "do" in remembrance of Him. That was how He made Himself "known of them in breaking of bread" (Luke 24: 35). His memory, He re-enacted an old incident in the miraculous draught of fishes (Luke 5: 6; John 21: 6). That was "proof" enough for the discerning mind of John. "It is the Lord" (v. 7).

PRAYER.—*We thank Thee, O Lord, that to meet the weakness of Thy children Thou dost take pains to bring them, and us, such certainty of Thy Rising by these simple things. O God, warm our hearts, steel our wills, hasten our footsteps, foster our witness, by "The power of His Resurrection."* AMEN.

OCTOBER 3

". . . ye shall receive . . . and ye shall be . . ." (Acts 1: 8)

HERE in this verse we have the Great Charter of World-Wide Evangelism. In the Book of Acts as a whole you have the Missionary Magazine, the first of them all, with its notes of recruits, dismissal meeting, news of stations, converts, native churches, medical missionary, furloughs, reports meeting. In our particular verse is the Missionary Medium, "ye." Not to angels but to us believers is committed the privilege and responsibility. The Missionary Mandate, "shall be"; this is not a choice but a command, and His last command. The Missionary Method, "witnesses"; we are to tell not what we think, nor what others say, but what we ourselves know from personal experience. The Missionary Message is "unto Me," truly an inexhaustible theme. The Missionary Map includes "both in . . . and unto . . .," beginning at home and spreading ever onwards and outwards. That's what "ye shall be," and now for the Missionary Might, "ye shall receive," the power of the Holy Spirit, so utterly needed for such a task, and so completely sufficient.

PRAYER.—*May we, O Lord, who are privileged to go upon Thy errands, look ever to the Holy Spirit for our guidance and power.* AMEN.

OCTOBER 4

". . . this same Jesus . . . shall so come in like manner as ye have seen Him go . . ." (Acts 1: 11)

HE Himself had told them, "If I go . . . I will come again" (John 14: 3), and now comes this corroboration from the heavenly visitants. His return to earth is to be as definite as His return to Heaven, and "in like manner." Visibly so, "they shall see the Son of Man coming"; materially so, "in the clouds of heaven" (Matt. 24: 30); corporeally so, "His feet shall stand"; geographically so, "on the Mount of Olives" (Zech. 14: 4). Those who spiritualize the promise of His return are up against the very plain statements of Scripture. Such people have said that His Second Coming took place at Pentecost or at the Fall of Jerusalem, overlooking the fact that the promise is still being repeated after both those events have taken place. Or, say they, His Second Coming took place at the Resurrection, or in trouble, or at death. Yes, indeed, He does come at such times, but do any or all of these fulfil the details of such a passage as 1 Thessalonians 4: 16, 17, or our text of today?

PRAYER.—*How blest a day will that be when Thou our Sovereign Lord wilt come back to earth, to take Thy power and reign. Prepare us, Lord, for that Day.* AMEN.

174

OCTOBER 5

". . . they were all filled with the Holy Spirit, and began to speak . . ."
(Acts 2: 4)

NEVER mind, for the moment, about those "other tongues." It is your own tongue that you are troubled with. You have so often longed to say a word for your Lord, but you are so shy, or reserved, in this matter. Over and over again you have felt urged to give some witness to the saving and keeping power of the Master, but you are held back by the crippling thought that you wouldn't know what to say. Maybe, you have been asked to teach a Sunday School class, but you have always said that speaking was not in your line. Now, will you bring all that out into the clear light of our text? It is here evident, isn't it, that if you were filled with the Holy Spirit you would begin to speak. You know you ought to speak for Him, you really want to speak for Him. Then throw open your whole being to be filled by Him, and watch the result!

PRAYER.—*"Take my lips and let them be filled with messages from Thee. . . . Take myself, and I will be, ever, only, all for Thee."* AMEN.

OCTOBER 6

"And they continued stedfastly . . ." (Acts 2: 42)

THEY don't seem to have been over careful in those early revivals concerning the counting of heads, for the converts are reckoned as "about three thousand" (v. 41), and later as "about five thousand" (Acts 4: 4). But my point today is that all these "continued." You see, the work was very definitely the operation of the Holy Spirit. It was not just emotional excitement, or mass hysteria, breeding a great, sad crop of so-called backsliders. It is said in Daniel 1: 8 and 21 that "Daniel purposed . . . and Daniel continued." So was it with these early believers. The explanation lies in their faithful use of the appointed means of grace: "The apostles' doctrine," the Bible School; "The fellowship," a definite article should be read before each of these things, the Church family; "The breaking of bread," the Lord's Table, and "The prayers," the Prayer Meeting. In such things is to be found the secret of a holy and happy continuance.

PRAYER.—*We thank Thee, O God, that Thou hast been so mindful for our progress in the Christian life as to arrange for us such means of grace. Help us to be so faithful to use them, that we may, without wavering, 'continue."* AMEN.

"*. . . all that believed were together . . .*" (Acts 2: 44)

TODAY's meditation is to be a plea for Christian togetherness. How much is involved and included in the word! A common heritage in Christ is in it. There is no distinction nor difference there, "neither Jew nor Greek . . . neither bond nor free . . . neither male nor female . . . all one in Christ Jesus" (Gal. 3: 28). A mutual care for each other is in it. While we are to have a heart of sympathy, hand of help, for all, yet that is to be "especially unto them who are of the household of faith" (Gal. 6: 10). A single front against the enemy is in it. Do you know that bit in the margin of Zephaniah 3: 9, "Serve Him with one shoulder," an army marching "eyes right," moving as one man, one shoulder. How weakened is our Christian advance by reason of internal discord. A united testimony to the world is in it. What a grand message early believers and all believers have to give. Oh, that it might be delivered not in isolated units, but in Christian togetherness!

PRAYER.—*Lord, as Thou hast called us to be "labourers together with God," so help us in that service to be happy workmates with one another, happy to sink immaterial differences in essential unities, even as we are many Regiments in one Army of the Lord.* AMEN.

"*. . . expecting . . . something of them*" (Acts 3: 5)

A PAIR of churchgoers, so of course the outsider expects something of them. This particular man got more than he expected. He asked alms, he got legs! But does the world always get what it expects from us churchgoers? They expect us to be different from themselves, and surely they are right. They expect us to be straight in all our dealings, but, alas, I have heard of not a few cases in which business men have been shocked by the shady behaviour of a man who professed to be a Christian, and was a leading light at his church. They expect of us a high standard of personal consistency, that life and lip shall exactly tally They expect us to show sympathy with their needs, as these two did In fact, sometimes the worldly folk are perplexed that some churchgoers seem to be so little concerned for their spiritual needs. "No man cared for my soul," they would say with Psalm 142: 4.

PRAYER.—*And, dear Lord, if others have such expectations, what shall we say of what Thou dost expect of us. Dost Thou not come expecting "fruit" and so often finding nothing but "leaves." God forgive us and put us right.* AMEN.

176

". . . beholding the man which was healed standing with them, they could say nothing against it" (Acts 4: 14)

THE most convincing argument for Christianity is a changed life. What a change had been wrought in this "man." Forty years a cripple, carried about by others, compelled to beg for a mere existence, then of a sudden utterly transformed with a new power in his legs, a new hope in his heart, a new light in his face, a new song in his mouth, a new life in his future. What was the use of enemies saying that Christ could not heal and save? There was an instance of it right there before them. There was nothing more to be said. Theoretical objections cannot stand against practical objects of His grace and power. What He is looking for is changed men and women, cripples become miracles, whom He can set down in offices, workshops, homes, circles, for such are still the best arguments in the world. Let us finish with this challenging question: Am I a good argument for Him?

PRAYER.—*Lord, it is our great desire that we shall be changed into Thy likeness and charged with Thy power, that indeed it may be so obviously Thee that has done it, that foolish tongues may be stopped, and that many shall seek a like change at Thy hands.* AMEN.

". . . great power . . . great grace . . ." (Acts 4: 33)

HOW refreshing it is to go back to the days and doings of the early church. Here we see their preachers at work and note two outstanding qualities of their ministry, remembering that we, each of us, have a ministry to exercise for the Lord. It was a ministry of force, "great power." They spoke with the force of conviction, the force of inspiration, all of which is greatly to be desired for modern preaching. But note a second characteristic. It was a ministry of favour, "great grace." Some have power without grace, and that is likely to make them hard and harsh in their work. Others have grace as well as power, each balancing the other, the combination resembling what is said of the Master, that He was "full of grace and truth" (John 1: 14) the gentler and irradiating quality winning for the message a favour that mere power may fail to secure. In all our work for God, let us pray for a mixture of power and grace.

PRAYER.—*Lord, Thou hast set us in our generation to be representatives of Thine. Give us we pray Thee, that dual touch that shall accomplish much for Thee. May our words and ways be marked with sweetness as well as with strength.* AMEN.

". . . sold . . . but God . . ." (Acts 7: 9)

So does Stephen recognize the overruling providence of God in the affairs of men, but Joseph himself went even further when, as in Genesis 45: 8, he recognized the controlling providence of God in his affairs. Happy indeed is that man who can thus see his circumstances as ordered and planned by His fatherly hand, and who can believe that in the light of Romans 8: 28, all those circumstances however seemingly unfortunate shall turn to his ultimate good. We might cite a score of instances in Holy Scripture, and indeed from daily life, to show how God uses circumstances. Through them He would teach us some lesson, foster some quality, manufacture some blessing, prepare some opportunity. Joseph is "sold," with all the distress that that implies, "but God" uses that very fact to bring about Joseph's great service to men. Put, therefore, this "but God" into all that happens to you, and you shall learn that however painful, "nevertheless afterward" (Heb. 12: 11), it shall prove greatly fruitful.

PRAYER.—*We are so slow to learn the deep lessons that Thou, O Master, wouldst teach us, this amongst them, that Thy overruling hand is over all that happens to us. So may our Text be a constant comfort in all our conditions.* AMEN.

". . . a man . . . some man . . . some other man" (Acts 8: 27, 31, 34)

THREE men in a carriage. The first man is the seeker, nationally a man of great importance in his own country, religiously, I imagine a Jewish proselyte returning from worship in Jerusalem, where he had bought a copy of the Greek LXX Version of Isaiah, spiritually, seeking further light. The second man is the soulwinner, come at God's ordering from the revival crowds of Samaria to reach this one soul in the desert. Like all successful soulwinners, he uses the Bible to do his work. "Beginning at that same Scripture," which the Ethiopian was poring over, "he preached unto him Jesus." The third Man is the Saviour. Verily, we can begin at any Scripture and preach Him therefrom. The Master Himself began at Genesis (Luke 24: 27). And what a Saviour to preach; what depth of love He displayed in going to "the slaughter" (v. 32); what heights of blessing He ever brings to trusting hearts, even as He sent this African "on his way rejoicing" (v. 39). Will you be "some man," to reach "a man," for this "some other Man"?

PRAYER.—*"Lord, lay some soul upon my heart and bless that soul through me, and may I humbly do my part to bring that soul to Thee."* AMEN.

". . . a man named Ananias . . ." (Acts 9: 12)

Aᴺᴰ what a lovely name to have. It means "one to whom God has been gracious." In that happy sense, every one of us is an Ananias. But unfortunately some people disgrace their honourable name, like Ananias, the deceitful (Acts 5: 1ff). He was concerned not, like Barnabas, for others' good, but for their praise. Love of popularity; what a snare! Then there was Ananias, the disgraceful (Acts 23: 2ff). He was High Priest, and should therefore have known better. When Paul was brought before him, he was not prepared to listen. After his unworthy behaviour, it is little wonder that Paul did not recognize him as the High Priest. Ah, but here in our text is Ananias, the delightful. How delightful was his eventual complete obedience to God; how delightful his subsequent love for "brother Saul" (v. 17). How gracious should we be to whom He has been so gracious. Be a worthy Ananias!

Pʀᴀʏᴇʀ.—*If there should be an errand on which Thou wouldst send us, wilt Thou make Thy wish clear to us, and grant that we may be instantly and gladly obedient to Thy call, even if sometimes it looks forbidding.* Aᴍᴇɴ.

". . . a chosen vessel . . . to bear My name . . ." (Acts 9: 15)

Oɴᴇ thinks of a waterpot, chosen down at the potter's house, bought for a price, carried home, and used by the owner to bear water from the well to thirsty and needy people. Such a "vessel" was in figure this man Saul. When first we meet him he was sadly "marred," but he has just been "made . . . again another vessel" (Jer. 18: 4), and now, blessedly regenerated as he has become, the Lord has "chosen" him, and "bought" him (1 Cor. 6: 19, 20), to be the medium for carrying to famishing souls "this water that I thirst not" (John 4: 15). His "Name," that is, all that He is, is the saving and refreshing water of "everlasting life." What a wonderful water carrier Paul afterwards became. And my dear Christian reader, whether you be a big pot, or a little pot, you also are chosen to be a waterpot, to bear His name as living water to those who without Him must forever thirst.

Pʀᴀʏᴇʀ.—*Save us, O Lord, we pray Thee, from the sin, that while having the Water of Life we keep it to ourselves. So many around us are athirst, and we can help if only we would. May we then give to others as Thou hast given to us.* Aᴍᴇɴ.

". . . when he . . . had seen the grace of God . . ." (Acts 11: 23)

JOSES was his real name (Acts 4: 36). The apostles nicknamed him Barnabas, "son of consolation," because he was such a kindly soul, a great encourager of others, always looking for the best in people, and he had a rare eye for "grace." He would spot it, if there was any of it present. He found it in Mark, in spite of his desertion, when there was very little sign of grace about him, but "Barnabas took" him (15: 39). He found it in Saul, when fearing he was laying a trap for them, Christians in Damascus and Jerusalem gave him the cold shoulder, "but Barnabas took him" (9: 27). And in today's passage, the Jerusalem authorities, hearing of a revival movement in Antioch, and wishing to know if it were good and sound, sent Barnabas to the area. He would quickly discover if "the grace of God" was in the campaign. And how "glad" this good man was to find it there all right. Some of us might be happily employed if we were to go about looking for "grace" in people.

PRAYER.—*May we indeed by prospectors for this Godly gold of grace, discovering it even if it is wrapped around or hidden within the ore of earthly weakness. May we have a blind eye for the faults and failures of men, and a keen eye for anything, however little, that is of God.* AMEN.

". . . but prayer was made . . ." (Acts 12: 5)

WHAT was the good of that? Why not a petition to the king, or even an attack on the jail, "but prayer was made." What could that do? These people could do nothing else for Peter, but then they could do nothing better than to pray. The story, like a thousand others, discloses that prayer moves the Hand of omnipotence. This is the Hand that here puts soldiers to sleep, that struck chains off the prisoner, that unlocked stout doors and unbolted iron gates, that set the condemned man free. And all this because "prayer was made." Is there not an unhappy multitude desperately imprisoned today? So often our preaching fails to reach them, nothing seems to help, but what if, by a concerted intercession for individuals, as in Peter's case, "prayer was made without ceasing of the church unto God" for them, one by one, name by name. What mighty releases would thus be effected!

PRAYER.—*Enlarge our understanding, O Lord, of the mighty power of prayer, whether in person or in assembly, and let us exercise this enormous ministry with a pure heart, with a confident assurance, and with a single eye to Thy Glory, in the blessing of many.* AMEN.

". . . bind on thy sandals . . ." (Acts 12: 8)

GOD never wastes energy. He never performs unnecessary miracles. He never does for us what we can do for ourselves. Peter could not unlock his chains, nor his cell door, nor his prison gate, so God did all that for him. But he could put his own shoes on, so God did not do that for him. The Master observes that same principle. He makes the wine, but the servants can bring the water. He feeds the multitude, but the disciples can find the loaves and fishes, and distribute them. He raises Lazarus, but the friends can unwrap him. So we arrive at the thought of a very blessed partnership in the Great Service: we are expected to do what little bit we can, and He undertaking to see to the rest. He will look after the chains and doors, but we must look after the sandals.

PRAYER.—*We are not worried, O Lord, about Thy side of the matter, but we are often anxious lest we should fail in our part. But even as we believe that Thou wilt tell us what our part is, so we ask for grace to do it, and then, as Thou dost condescendingly take us into partnership, may we have the joy of entering into the blessed accomplishment.* AMEN.

". . . when they . . . saw him, they were astonished" (Acts 12: 16)

IMAGINE that earnest, urgent prayer meeting in this good lady's house. One after another they pray: "O Lord, deliver Peter out of prison!" Then came the interrupting knock at the door, and little Rhoda rushes in excitedly where still they are praying, O Lord, deliver Peter out of prison! "It's Peter," she says, "he's at the door." They tell her she's mad, but she persists, until they conclude she has seen a ghost. At last, Peter is admitted, and "they were astonished." But I thought they had been praying for this very thing. Yes, but, alas, that is so often the way we pray, with such little belief in its efficacy that we are "astonished" when the answer comes. How we need the word of Mark 11: 24, "When ye pray, believe that ye receive . . . and ye shall have . . ." Other conditions being satisfied, this believing before receiving is a mighty prayer secret. Of course, their astonishment may have arisen from a different cause. Perhaps they had prayed only that Peter might be comforted and strengthened, never dreaming of his being released. In that case, God gave so much more than they asked, which is so often His way.

PRAYER.—*Lord, why should we ever be surprised or astounded at Thy work, for have we not a wonder-working God. Let us, then, rather expect "great things from God," and in prayerful dependence upon Him, "attempt great things for God." Blessed be such prayer!* AMEN.

OCTOBER

19

" . . . *John* . . . *returned to Jerusalem*" (Acts 13: 13)

So that finishes him! He had started out on a missionary career with such enthusiasm, and while they were in Cyprus, John Mark was full of earnest purpose. But when they landed at Perga, a malaria-infested district, his courage failed, and we see him "departing from them." Personally, I think Paul did catch malaria there, which was ever after his "thorn in the flesh" (2 Cor. 12: 7). Paul was right in refusing to take Mark on the return tour. How could he exhort believers to loyalty with such a disloyalist on the party? Barnabas was right in taking him back to Cyprus, for there he had been loyal enough (Acts 15: 39). Did I say his desertion finished him? How wrong, for see how later he returned to Paul's grateful assistance (2 Tim. 4: 11), and see how God entrusted him with the writing of the Second Gospel. If a Christian stumbles and fails his Lord, he always gets another chance, as Mark did, and as Peter did, and as Jonah did.

PRAYER.—*Great comfort this, for all who once were true but long since have failed Thee. Teach us that a worse thing than falling is not getting up again, and help us to come back, to stand up, and once more, to go forward in Thy service.* AMEN.

OCTOBER

20

" . . . *We* . . . *are men of like passions with you* . . . " (Acts 14: 15)

HAVE you sometimes felt, when reading the exploits of Bible men, that such things were all very well for them, they were not ordinary people like us? Today's text reminds us that that was not so. We get the same caution in James 5: 17 concerning that remarkable man, Elijah, and his remarkable prayer-power. He was lifted out of the ordinary only because he surrendered himself to be utterly at the disposal of God. So was it with Barnabas and Paul here; absolutely yielded to God as they were, He could use them to do great things, as this wonderful cure at Lystra. But let no one suppose that they were, in essential manhood, anything more than their fellows. Indeed, their own disclaimer seems to find illustration in something very like "passion" in their "so sharp" contention in Acts 15: 39. Seeing, in the Scriptures, what God can do with very ordinary people, we ordinary folk can take heart and hope.

PRAYER.—*Most of us, Lord, are ordinary folk, but we have not an ordinary God, and if we are His we have not ordinary work to do. May we then do the seemingly ordinary things with the extraordinary grace of God, that our lives may prove to be out of the ordinary.* AMEN.

". . . They returned again to Lystra . . ." (Acts 14: 21)

JUST a simple statement, scarcely worth bothering about, do you say? I agree, on the surface, but looking deeper, what amazing courage is here. Lystra; why that was where Paul had been stoned, and left for dead by the roadside. On the very next day, this tough and intrepid warrior is on the move again, proceeding to Derbe, the last point in his planned itinerary. Retracing his steps for home, it might have been expected that he would by-pass the scene of the attack on his life, but not he! There were new "disciples" now in Lystra (v. 22), and he was not going to desert them for any danger to himself. Yet we so often crumple up at the least sign of opposition, ridicule or ostracism. This same Paul was led of the Spirit to write, "Endure hardness, as a good soldier of Jesus Christ" (2 Tim. 2: 3). He surely was entitled to say it, and we surely should be ready to fulfil it.

PRAYER.—*Give us, good Lord, a good courage, for such a gift would mean so much to our work and witness. So much of our service is spoiled by fears of varied sorts. Yet since the Lord is round about us, why need we fear?* AMEN.

". . . they caused great joy unto all the brethren" (Acts 15: 3)

THE little deputation was travelling up from Antioch to Jerusalem to put before the authorities a matter of great, indeed fundamental importance. And as they "passed through" various cities on the way, they told the little bands of believers how God was adding to their number in the Gentile world, with the result that wherever they passed, they left behind them a trail of gladness. What a happy feature of the "first days" of the Church this was. You find it over and over again on this "first page" of the history. For instance, "There was great joy in that city" (Acts 8: 8). Amongst us Christians are some who always seem to bring the miseries with them. People avoid their company, if they can. Others always seem to bring the merries with them. People cultivate their presence, if they can. Which of the two, think you, bring the more glory to God?

PRAYER.—*Help us, O God, to be so occupied in mind with our mercies, that our miseries will be crowded out, and because of Thy remembered goodness to us may we bring gladness wherever we go, an infectious joyousness which many shall catch from us.* AMEN.

". . . the Spirit suffered them not" (Acts 16: 7)

ALREADY the apostle had experienced the blessing of the guiding hand of God when "they were forbidden of the Holy Spirit to preach the Word in Asia" (v. 6), and now, once more the Spirit prevented their going to Bithynia. This latter was Paul's intention. He was planning in terms of Asia, but God was planning in terms of Europe, as was presently apparent when the missionary party was led on to Troas, Philippi, Athens, Corinth, and the rest. The children of God may, if they will, always have the leading of the Spirit, as Romans 8: 14 teaches, not always consciously perhaps, but surely their feet will be directed in the ways of His will, step by step. We are not told how the Spirit made His way plain to Paul, nor may I suggest how He will guide you. I only know that if we are truly surrendered to Him, we shall be directed aright; a door shut here, a door opened there.

PRAYER.—*We thank Thee that our God is expert in doors, shutting and no man opening, opening and no man shutting. Right gladly and right confidently do we leave the affairs of our life with Thee, who wilt take us right through to the end.* AMEN.

". . . what must I do to be saved?" (Acts 16: 30)

HOW would you answer if you were suddenly asked that question? Paul's reply is of course precise. "Believe"; not the "about" of historical assent, not the "in" of mental acquiescence, but the "on" of personal commitment. But, would you be justified in giving the same answer to anyone who made this inquiry of you? Look on to Acts 20: 21 where this same Paul recalls what have been the two notes of his Gospel preaching as "repentance toward God, and faith toward our Lord Jesus Christ." I feel sure that one reason for the disappointing weakness of much modern Gospel testimony is the all too frequent absence of that first note. In the Philippian's case there was no need to introduce it, because it was obviously there. Something has brought him real conviction of sin. Paul would never have answered as he did if the jailor, as some say, was anxious only to be "saved" from his awkward predicament. The proper answer to this question lies usually in these two notes.

PRAYER.—*Help us, O Lord, to be able to answer the inquiries of men, and to know especially how to lead them to Thyself. Help us, we pray, gradually to acquire that knowledge of Thy Word that shall enable us to point them to the Way of Heaven.* AMEN.

"These . . . searched the Scriptures daily, whether those things were so"
(Acts 17: 11)

NOBLE fellows, these Bereans! They would not take the sermons for granted, even though the preacher was Paul. Every day they tested his utterances by the Scriptures so as to be quite sure that he spake according to truth. They listened carefully, "with all readiness of mind," but only when it passed the Bible test did they accept it. Would that we modern Christians would bring all to that test. False teachings would stand little chance if only we used our Bible. That, of course, is the problem, that if we are to use the Scriptures we must know them, and that is not done in a day. The word "daily" in our text gives us the clue. A real study, day by day, of a bit of the Book will give us a growing grip of it, so that we shall be able gradually to acquire such a knowledge that we shall know almost instinctively whether "those things" taught are truth. Be Bereans!

PRAYER.—*Make us, we pray, O Lord, to be diligent students of Thy Word, that it may become our test of the truth, our arm in the conflict, our mirror of the soul, our guide for the way, and our strength for the life.* AMEN.

". . . Jesus, and the resurrection" (Acts 17: 18)

I HAVE no doubt Paul's theme in that Athens discourse was the light that Jesus shed on the resurrection, and truly He "hath abolished death and hath brought life and immortality out into the light . . ." (2 Tim. 1: 10). But our meditation today shall be on the light the resurrection sheds on Jesus. It vindicates His Word. "He is risen, as He said," the women were reminded in Matthew 28: 6. If He can keep that promise, most difficult of all, He can keep every other word. It guarantees His work. He made claims for His death, that it was "a ransom for many" (Matt. 20: 28), but how may we be sure that the price was acceptable and sufficient? The Cross is the payment, the Resurrection is the receipt. It enhances His worth. Not His intrinsic worth, of course, but His worth to us. He is not merely a lovely Memory, a beautiful Example, a pervasive Influence, but a living Saviour, Master and Friend.

PRAYER.—*Our Risen Master, help us to live in the light of Thy life and in the power of Thy Resurrection, and in the joy of Thy full salvation.* AMEN.

". . . whose house joined hard to the synagogue" (Acts 18: 7)

JUST a matter of propinquity, but perhaps a matter of consistency as well. Follow with me these hypothetical steps: the house next to the church, the place where he lived next to the place where he worshipped; the day of the week near to the day of the Sabbath; the practice of the life near to the profession of the lips. There are members who live a long way from the church, spiritually. I hope and expect that with this man Justus, in Corinth, church and home coincided. It would mean a new atmosphere in the home. Brother Lawrence used to say that he felt Him "as near in the kitchen as in the chapel." It would mean a new consistency in the life. Our religion would not be put away with the Sunday clothes. It would mean a new power in the witness, for nothing so impresses the world as a really consistent Christian life. If any of us have been living a long way from the church, let us move nearer, and let us ask:

> And help us this, and every day,
> To live more nearly as we pray.

PRAYER.—*We thank Thee, Lord, for the hints we have of Thy behaviour in the home, and we ask that in our home relationships, and in all our relationships, we may show ourselves as true followers of Thee, who art the Head of our home and the Master of our life.* AMEN.

"Many . . . brought their books . . . and burned them" (Acts 19: 19)

"LET'S have a bonfire," said a small boy one time just before November the 5th. What a bonfire they had here in Ephesus! By the way, you remember they once had a bonfire in the churchyard of London's St. Paul's Cathedral to burn up all the Bible books. But, of course, you cannot burn the Bible away (Jer. 36: 28). But the books of our text were fortunately entirely consumed for that was the only way to deal with such rubbish. I wonder if you have any books that need to be burned? Anyhow, let's have a bonfire of other things; horrid grudges, bad habits, stupid prejudices, groundless fears, and such-like—on the fire with the lot of them! Isaiah 4: 4 speaks of "the Spirit of burning" who will, if we let Him, burn out the Dross and, thank God, burn in the Pattern.

PRAYER.—*We often think, O Lord, that the Christian's chief problem is not so much sin, as self—or is self a sin? May the Holy Spirit so work in us that there may be the very minimum of self and the maximum of Thee. May our practised motto be "Not I, but Christ."* AMEN.

"*. . . that I might finish my course with joy . . .*" (Acts 20: 24)

PAUL is making his touching farewell on the Miletus beach. It is an affecting scene. And he looks ahead to the time when he shall bid farewell to life itself. He reveals to these elders of Ephesus what is the ambition of his heart, that at that day he may have no regrets. "Bonds and afflictions" (v. 23) may await him on the road, but what are they if only at the end he may arrive at the finish with joy in his heart, though with scars on his body. Let us exhort one another and help one another that it may be so with us: no regrets, all joy! There is no doubt that the secret is that as we pursue our "course," our whole being, all we are and all we have, shall be utterly His. Thus shall we know budding joy on the journey and bursting joy at Journey's End.

PRAYER.—*Lord, how we thank Thee if we have left the course of this world and have set foot in the Way of Life. Wilt Thou guide our footsteps, hasten our progress, accompany us on the road, guard us from stumbling, and at the end, forgiving our failures, welcome us Home with joy.* AMEN.

"*. . . God, whose I am, and whom I serve*" (Acts 27: 23)

PAUL is on that ship, bound for Rome, in charge of a Roman centurion, probably like most a fine specimen of humanity, proud to be in the service of his Emperor. But for all his lack of inches, I suspect Paul is the prouder of the two, inasmuch as he serves the Greatest Emperor of them all. With what a confident ring does his confession sound forth from the midst of the storm. He is under His ownership, "whose I am." Years before he wrote, "Ye are not your own" (1 Cor. 6: 19). Here he acknowledges it of himself. His; to use as He will, to mould as He will, to treat as He will. "Is it not lawful for Me to do what I will with Mine own?" (Matt. 20: 15). He is under His orders, "whom I serve." How he rejoiced to call himself "the bondslave of Jesus Christ." How devoted he was to that service, how fruitful in it, winning many for his Lord. Are we as rightly proud to make, whether in storm or sunshine, the same grand confession?

PRAYER.—*Our way through life may often be tempest-tossed, but we bless Thee, O God, that whatever the circumstances we are under Thine observation—Thou knowest our circumstances and meetest our needs. May we, then, never be afraid or ashamed to be known as Thine.* AMEN.

"*. . . some believed . . . and some believed not*" (Acts 28: 24)

THAT is only what our Lord led us to expect, in His parable, when He told about the disappointing results of three parts of the seed sown. The phenomenon appeared even in His own ministry, and we are not surprised to meet it in Paul's case. There was great and glorious harvest in the apostle's service, but there were failures, too. It was the same all through, as here in Rome; "some believed, and some believed not." So, Christian worker, don't be too downhearted if you see less success than you hoped. Go on faithfully sowing the seed, and you will be found one day fruitfully reaping the harvest. It was an important conference that Paul called. The agenda consisted of "the things which were spoken," all about Jesus, and one way or another all had to vote. The Ayes "believed," with all the results accruing. The Noes "believed not," with all the consequences ensuing. Of course, I know how you would have voted.

PRAYER.—*Praise be to Thee, O God, for all we have believed on Thy Name, and who are numbered among Thy privileged and grateful adherents. May we be proud to acclaim our allegiance far and wide, for Thine is no secret ballot. AMEN.*

NOVEMBER

EXTRACTS FROM THE ROYAL ARCHIVES

Strictly speaking, of course, the History of the Kings begins with 1 and 2 Samuel, where the times of Saul and David are dealt with. 1 and 2 Kings opens with Solomon, and after the disruption, we have the nineteen kings and one queen (Athaliah, 2 Kings 11:1) of the South, and the nineteen kings of the North. All of the latter were bad; a few of the former were in varying degrees good. Hezekiah was the best of them all. He reigned twenty-nine years, and the history and literature of his reign occupy no less than 77 chapters of the Bible. Let us turn the pages of the records for our meditations this month.

". . . *the Lord . . . that hath redeemed my soul . . .*" (1 Kings 1: 29)

SUCH is the testimony of the old King David, at the end of a long and adventurous life. It has been a life packed with interest and incident, including much "distress." And now one more distress is added to his last days. Adonijah is seeking to oust Solomon from the succession to the throne. David now takes action, and his first words are those of this testimony. It is upon this fact of his being a "redeemed" man that he rests all else. Let us also learn to begin everything there, that God will surely care for those He has redeemed with His precious blood.

PRAYER.—*Let us never forget, O Lord, that it was no easy thing for Thee to forgive and redeem and save us, but that Thou didst accomplish it at such tremendous cost. How gladly, therefore, should we be ready to offer these our redeemed lives to Thy service, even if it should cost us something to do it.* AMEN.

". . . *they saw that the wisdom of God was in him . . .*" (1 Kings 3: 28)

IT all started, of course, that night when God came to him at the outset of his reign and said, "Ask what I shall give thee" (v. 5). It was a tremendous moment, alike for Solomon and for his kingdom. He must have been strongly tempted to ask for long life, great riches, military prowess, but one after another, he put them from him. Realizing what would be the demands his position and people would make upon him, he asked simply for "a wise and an understanding heart." (v. 12). This he received in striking measure, and God added those other things also for which he refrained from asking. It is so often His pleasure to give more than we ask, "more than we desire or deserve." So people "saw" the answer to his prayer, and they "saw" as well the application in his practice, in the grand and almost humorous story of the disputed baby. In the light of James 1: 5, 6, people should come to see that the wisdom of God is in us.

PRAYER.—*Lord, we have learned that God gives the best to those who leave the choice to Him, so we ask Thee that Thou wilt endow us with whatever Thou seest we need, in order that we may be the best for Thee. We make it our choice that Thou shalt choose for us.* AMEN.

". . . prove him with hard questions" (1 Kings 10: 1)

WHAT a blessing it is to have someone to whom we can bring our problems. Because of Solomon's great and wide reputation for wisdom, the Queen of Sheba came a long distance to consult him, and she got the solution to all her perplexities. "And behold a greater than Solomon is here" (Matt. 12: 42). Happy and wise are the people who have formed the habit of bringing their "hard questions" to Him. To such an age-long question as, How can I get into right relationship with God? He will tell us, "I am the Way . . ." (John 14: 6). Or this, How can I find rest in this restless world? He will answer, "Come unto Me . . ." (Matt. 11: 28). Or again, How can I live a really Christian life? His solution is "the Spirit . . . shall be in you" (John 14: 17). And so with all your "hard questions," such as those mentioned, or those of your more daily problems, "prove Him" with them all.

PRAYER.—*We thank Thee, O Lord, that Thou art always so accessible to Thy children, and that we may with every confidence bring our difficulties to Thee, whether our query be "What ought I to do?" or "What ought I to say?" or "What ought I to be?" We shall know the answer if we ask in a confident and obedient spirit.* AMEN.

". . . right in the eyes of the Lord . . ." (1 Kings 15: 5)

IT was said of certain people away back in the old Book of Judges (17: 6) that "every man did that which was right in his own eyes." There are others whose standard is what is right in other people's eyes. They are scared of doing anything their acquaintances would not approve. When in Rome they are all for doing as Rome does. They are slaves of convention. The happiest and wisest folks are they who seek to do only that which is right in God's sight, whose estimate of any line of conduct is, "How will this look in His eyes," who seek to regulate their whole life by that rule. I can so well imagine that many a tough problem would find happy solution if we considered it not only from the angle of what we think or what others think, but what He thinks. Take this test for your talisman.

PRAYER.—*Master, may I act this way this day, and at day's end may it be that I shall have pleased Thee in everything. Nothing shall please me more.* AMEN.

". . . hide thyself . . . shew thyself . . ." (1 Kings 17: 3, 18: 1)

THE public life of this man showed him to be a man of implicit obedience to God, a man of grand courage, a man of isolated testimony, a man of tremendous challenge, a man of holy fire. What a picture of magnificent public service for God. Yet he could never "show" himself like that, to king and nation, unless he first "hide" himself in the quiet privacy of a hidden life which shall fit and feed him for his open ministry. There will be no Carmel if there be no Cherith. By the brook Elijah shall learn the all invigorating and inspiring lesson of the utter dependability of God, and in that truth he shall venture forth to do and dare anything for Him. There in the hiding place, he and we shall be tended, with food from Heaven (17: 6); tested, to find the reality of our trust (17: 7); and taught, "the word of the Lord" (17: 8), ere we go forth to serve Him. Get alone before you get about.

PRAYER.—*Lay it ever deeper upon our hearts, O God, that the Quiet Time with Thee is of so strategic importance. May every day begin there, and every service find its roots there.* AMEN.

". . . I have commanded a widow woman there to sustain thee"
(1 Kings 17: 9)

THREE things are here of high importance for all God's children. One, God has a plan for every emergency. "The brook dried up" (v. 7), God's selected brook! Now what is Elijah going to do? What can he do? Have you ever been there, at Wit's End Corner? Be at rest; God has a plan. Two, God has a worker for every plan. He does not need our aid, but He generally employs it. Such is our privilege. We may, in ourselves, be as insufficient for the task as was this "widow woman," who was quite unable to "sustain" this man in this time of drought. But God "commanded" and she obeyed, and in the doing she found she could do what before she knew she could not do. Three, God has a rule for every worker. "Me . . . first" (v. 13). Elijah spoke not so much for himself, but as the representative of God. If our rule be "God first," everything else will fall into its right place, and the impossible service shall become gloriously possible.

PRAYER.—*We beseech Thee, O Lord, that Thou wilt grant us the excessive privilege of being Thy instruments in the service and blessing of others, and to that end enable us to relegate self to the background, and to regulate our life to Thy pre-eminence.* AMEN.

"Then the fire of the Lord fell . . ." (1 Kings 18: 38)

WHEN? When the altar was repaired (v. 30). There is no fire of the Holy Spirit till God is reinstated in His rightful place. When the offering was made (v. 33). There must be a complete surrender of ourselves to Him, all the "pieces" of our being on the altar of sacrificial abandonment to His purpose. When the water was poured (vs. 33–35). There shall be no chance for any spurious, man-made fire, no false emotion, no energy of the flesh. When the prayer was offered (v. 36). There must be a definite seeking for God's blessing, an earnest supplication for the baptism of fire. When the motive was purged (v. 36). There can be no thought of self being exalted. Is there here a slight pause at the end of verse 36? In the first part of Elijah's prayer, self has a place; in the second part, self is entirely eliminated. "Then . . ."!

PRAYER.—*How often we long for some outpouring of mighty blessing to fall from heaven, and are disappointed if it never comes. May we search to see if the fault lie in any sense with us, for we know that if our offering be right Thou art ready to open the windows of heaven and pour down the blessing in overflowing abundance.* AMEN.

". . . There is nothing . . . there ariseth a little cloud . . . there was a great rain . . ." (1 Kings 18: 43–45)

"DON'T stop praying" is the moral of this story. After the three and a half years' drought (Jas. 5: 17), Elijah now set himself to pray for rain (v. 42), but how naturally he might have given up, for no less than six times over (v. 43), the result was "there is nothing." Have we not all had experiences of that sort, when we have prayed again and again and nothing has happened? Yet Elijah encourages us to keep at it, for at the seventh time "there ariseth a little cloud." Can this be at last the beginning of the answer? Note that it was "like a man's hand" (v. 44), as if the intensity of his prayer-uplifted hand (1 Tim. 2: 8) had stamped itself on the very sky. It is, indeed, the harbinger of an abundant answer, for soon "there was a great rain" (v. 45). Verily, God always answers prayer. Sometimes He says, "Yes"; sometimes He says, "No," and sometimes He says, "Wait!" So don't stop praying!

PRAYER.—*We are so grateful, O Lord, that in Thy gracious condescension Thou dost allow us to persist in importunity, thus testing the earnestness of our desire, and the reality of our faith. In our praying, as in our living and in our working, may we keep on keeping on.* AMEN.

"*. . . What doest thou here . . . ?*" (1 Kings 19: 9)

ELIJAH ought never to have been under that juniper tree dispirited and dejected, especially as he had just had that great and exhilarating triumph on Mt. Carmel. But the strange thing is that our glad victories are sometimes followed by sad defeats; the excitement and emotion of the conquest have taken a big toll of our nervous strength and left us, unless we are watchful, the prey even of lesser foes. So Elijah ran away at the threats of Jezebel and lay downcast and done. That is no place or condition for a prophet, or for a Christian. All the attributes of Deity are on our side, His omnipotence, His omniscience, His omnipresence, His omniexistence, so why should we ever be depressed? Trees are very wonderful, generally very beautiful, things, but some are to be avoided. For instance, never, in any circumstance, have anything to do with the juniper tree!

PRAYER.—*Lord, wilt Thou especially guard us at times of physical strain or mental stress lest we should be found out of place, and may no frustration, no opposition, cause us to lose the gleam in gloom.* AMEN.

"*. . . a still small voice*" (1 Kings 19: 12)

THE Lord does sometimes speak in the wind, the earthquake and the fire, to invididuals and even to nations. And persons and peoples are wise to seek to hear His voice at such times. But what can compare with the sweetness of His "still small voice"? It is thus that He would ever choose to speak to His children, and it shall be our wisdom and our pleasure to catch His faintest whisper. Of course, if we are going to enjoy that privilege, we shall need to keep very close to Him, and we shall have to see that no obstruction comes between to blunt His accents, and we shall have to eschew the many and often strident voices of the world around us which would inevitably distract our attention from Him. He may have to whisper rebuke, as to Elijah, or guidance or comfort or encouragement or what not, but oh, to have ears so sensitive, so attuned, to catch each word, as in Isaiah 50: 4.

PRAYER.—*Our Heavenly Father, may Thy children be always so obedient that Thou shall never need to raise Thy voice to us, nor tell us a second time. May we allow nothing that shall spoil the sweet fellowship that Thou dost allow.* AMEN.

"*. . . as thy servant was busy here and there, he was gone . . .*"
(1 Kings 20: 40)

ACCORDING to the story as told by a prophet to a king, a very important prisoner of war was left in the charge of a certain soldier. This military gentleman was restively disappointed at being thus immobilized when the battle was on, and placing his captive on parole, he sought adventure elsewhere on the field. Alas, when he returned to what was after all his place of duty, he found his charge had flown. Some of us find it hard to stick to unexciting, humdrum duty. We prefer to turn to something more thrilling and exhilarating. The campaign is more interesting than the church engagement. God seems to attach great importance to fidelity to little tasks, hidden tasks, dull tasks, and to be gravely disappointed if we fail in them. Plain duties precede fair delights in importance. Being "busy here and there" in more attractive things, we may all too easily find the reward of faithfulness "gone."

PRAYER.—*If we yearn and pray, as we do, for faithfulness, help us to remember that ordinary things are embraced within that category as well as extraordinary things, and being faithful in that which is least, may we be fruitful also in much.* AMEN.

NOVEMBER   12

"*. . . ours, and we . . . take it not . . .*" (1 Kings 22: 3)

WHATEVER were the rights and wrongs of the matter of the ownership of Ramoth-Gilead, whatever the nature of the claims of Ahab to that city, whatever the reason for the decision of Jehoshaphat to join in the battle for it, there can be no question at all about this, that we Christians have a claim to a Promised Land, that is the Land of the Promises. It is "ours," all of us, but "we . . . take it not," some of us. How many things of spiritual blessing offered to us "in Christ," we fail to "take," either from ignorance of the fact that they are ours for the taking, or from indolence that will not bother to stretch out the hand of faith to take what is ours by His promise and purchase, by the price He paid to give them to us. Let us learn to "take" and use all that is "ours" by His grace.

PRAYER.—*Save us, good Lord, from being content with possessing anything less than the utmost of Thy covenanted blessing. May nothing spoil our appetite for the abundant fare of Thy provision, and may nothing keep us back from entering into our full inheritance, in Christ.* AMEN.

NOVEMBER 13

". . . bring me a minstrel . . ." (2 Kings 3: 15)

A MAN must be in a right frame of mind, in a proper mood, if he is to be the recipient of the Lord's message, to get the touch of His hand. He must be in tune. We are all differently constituted, and what helps one is perchance useless to another. Like many since, Elisha evidently found that music had a way of bringing him heart's ease and quiet rest of soul, so that he could discern the voice of God. The threatening situation which had here arisen could not be satisfactorily handled in turbulence of spirit, and music was the palliative of mind which would bring him peace and poise. Some find music a great aid to worship; others find it only a distraction. Whether or not, let us learn this, that we cannot rush at worship, that we cannot hear God speak if we are in a turmoil of heart, and that we should foster whatever it is that quiets us. "Bring me a minstrel," whether yours be music or some other medium. "Study to be quiet" (1 Thess. 4: 11), if you aspire to be taught.

PRAYER.—*Once again, O Lord, dost Thou here impress upon us the importance of Thine adage, "be still and know." "Speak, Lord, in the stillness while I wait on Thee, hushed my heart to listen, in expectancy."* AMEN.

NOVEMBER 14

". . . Make this valley full of ditches" (2 Kings 3: 16)

IN a time of widespread spiritual drought, we long for the mighty waters of revival. If the dried-up river beds made a deep problem for these armies of Israel and Judah, in their projected attack on Moab, their spiritual counterpart is an even deeper concern to the armies of the Lord of Hosts in their campaign against the forces of Satan. Yet these waters of revival cannot be engineered by man; only God can give them. But we can and must prepare the way for His moment. We must "make this valley full of ditches"; the ditch of earnest concern, the ditch of persevering prayer, the ditch of unswerving loyalty, the ditch of unconquerable faith, the ditch of faithful service, the ditch of personal testimony, the ditch of consistent behaviour, the ditch of utter surrender. We must "make this valley full of ditches" into whose expectant spaces the waters of His grace shall flow in their lifegiving fulness.

PRAYER.—*We recognize, O Lord, that these movements of revival blessing are in Thy Sovereign Will, but we recognize, too, that there is a part that we must play—all of us, each of us. May we not be found wanting in the spadework, getting ready for when the tide shall roll in from the ocean of Thy love.* AMEN.

NOVEMBER   **15**

". . . what hast thou in the house? . . ." (2 Kings 4: 2)

HERE is a poor lady in great distress. Her boys are likely to be sold as slaves to clear her of her late husband's debts. The sum total of her assets is one pot of oil. What is to be done? Well, God will cause a miracle for her, but He must first have what she has got. Then the boys "borrow" all kinds of empty pots and jars from the "neighbours" and lo, the widow's little oil is multiplied to fill them all, and out of the great store she is able to pay the debts, and sustain the family. Ah, thou hast a great God in the heavens, but "what hast thou in the house?" The two must come together. God can do wonderful things with your little pot of oil, but you must give it up to Him. Five little loaves: "what are they among so many?" (John 6: 9). Yes, but "bring them hither to Me" (Matt. 14: 18), and see what they can do! Your small capabilities, let God have them and He will once again multiply the oil.

PRAYER.—*We would search our being to see if there be in us anything as yet unyielded, and may we bring to Thee every smallest vessel, that Thou mayest fill us completely with the oil of the Holy Spirit, that we may live thereby.* AMEN.

NOVEMBER   **16**

". . . I perceive that this is an holy man of God which passeth by us continually" (2 Kings 4: 9)

WHAT is it that constitutes a "man of God"? Doubtless here it was something of a title, an office, but this man so fully lived up to the name. (1) A man of God is a man who believes on God, that is, of course, the fundamental basis of all else. No one can doubt that Elisha possessed this qualification (2: 14). But what of us? (2) A man of God is a man who belongs to God. Elisha was so much God's property that he was absolutely at His beck and call. What a privileged position for any of us. (3) A man of God is a man who behaves like God. No one can claim to be a "man of God" who is not "an holy man." Elisha's predecessor had been recognized as having this office by reason of a great miracle (1 Kings 17: 24). Elisha himself was to perform the very same miracle, but he had not yet done so; it was just his holy behaviour which earned him the name. Fancy earning such a testimonial from his landlady! Read again the conditions of membership of this godly confraternity, and tell me, do you belong?

PRAYER.—*Certainly, Lord, we desire to be, and we beg Thee to show us whereinsoever we fall short, that believing with all our heart, and belonging with all our life, we may be seen to be holy through the Holy Spirit's working within us.* AMEN.

" . . . *the child sneezed seven times* . . ." (2 Kings 4: 35)

D EAD people don't sneeze, so this was the first sign of the new life which came to the child who was dead. There is always something which betrays the new life in Christ if it is really there. There is the sign of appetite, as when the Saviour said of Jairus' daughter that "something should be given her to eat" (Mark 5: 43). There is the sign of speech, as when Nain's young man "began to speak" (Luke 7: 15). There is the sign of liberty, as when it was commanded concerning Lazarus, "Loose him, and let him go" (John 11: 44). Yes, a new taste for spiritual things, a grateful word of testimony, a true release from bondage are some of the tokens of real regeneration, or maybe, some homelier evidence like a sneeze, some little unexpected difference in ordinary behaviour. Wherever there is a supposed conversion we may look for some practical mark by which we can test its genuineness.

PRAYER.—*Lord, before we criticize others, may we search ourselves to find what evidence we show of the reality of our conversion to God. May that evidence in us be not just some little thing, but a whole life of difference.* AMEN.

" . . . *Abana and Pharpar* . . . *may I not wash in them, and be clean?* . . ."
(2 Kings 5: 12)

W ELL, it depends how deep you want the cleansing to go. If just the surface, Abana and Pharpar will do admirably, but they cannot cleanse away the root trouble, the deep-seated leprosy. Only Jordan, because God has chosen to plan it so, can do that. How splendid, for their purpose, are the rivers of social amelioration, good housing, good schools, good health services, good working conditions, good recreational facilities, and the rest. But they cannot touch man's deepest needs, the needs of the soul. Yet, be it noted that Abana and Pharpar actually rise in the Anti-Lebanon range of mountains, the very same range as does Jordan. Care for the body and the mind flows from the same source as the care for the soul, from the mountain and fountain of God's love. But let us not confuse the function of each: Abana and Pharpar for outer cleansing; Jordan, figure of "the stream that flows from Calvary's mountain," which alone can cleanse the heart.

PRAYER.—*Those who have had their leprosy of sin washed away never cease to praise Thee for the Precious Blood that did it for us. We are grateful for those other rivers of social benefit, but we never forget the eternal boon of that first stream of Thy wondrous grace. "Be of sin the double cure, cleanse me from its guilt and power."* AMEN.

NOVEMBER **19**

". . . his flesh came again like unto the flesh of a little child . . ."
(2 Kings 5: 14)

JUST as if he had become born all over again it was. Naaman was a fine type of man, like many a worldling. Some of them, although not Christians, are delightful and splendid people, as was this grand soldier, "but he was a leper" (v. 1), a type of a sinner. Like so many of his spiritual counterparts, what mistakes he made. He tried the wrong plan, with his silver and gold and raiment (v. 5), thinking he could buy his cleansing which, picture of the spiritual, was to be free. He appealed to the wrong person, the king instead of the prophet (vs. 6–8), like those who think that a priest can save them. He depended on the wrong power; "surely . . . stand . . . strike . . ." (v. 11); no emotional, theatrical energy of the flesh is called for. He sought the wrong place, "Abana and Pharpar" (v. 12), when only Jordan would suffice, picture of the "fountain opened . . . for sin and for uncleanness" (Zech. 13: 1). Naaman went away in a rage, but came back in a rapture: cleansed, cured, child-skinned, as if born again!

PRAYER.—*For all the glories of our new birth, we give Thee thanks, O Lord, and pray that we may be as new creatures in Christ Jesus.* AMEN.

NOVEMBER **20**

". . . he went out . . . a leper . . ." (2 Kings 5: 27)

SIN is so serious, yet you may have thought this servant's sentence over severe. Well, there is, I think, a special point here. Naaman had brought gold and garments to pay for his cure, but Elisha had refused them. Naaman, immensely grateful that he was cured and that he was cured free, decided to set up in Syria the worship of Elisha's God. Then came Gehazi to "take somewhat of him" (v. 20). As Naaman expected, it wasn't free, after all. I think this made an unfortunate impression on Naaman, and we never hear that the worship of Jehovah was set up in Syria. And besides Gehazi broke the "type." It was all a picture that salvation is free, and he had spoiled the picture. Moses did the same when he struck the rock the second time (Num. 20: 11). The Rock needs be smitten but "once for all" (Heb. 10: 10), thenceforward only asked to give forth His water of life. Moses was severely punished, as was Gehazi, for God seems to have cared much even for the type foreshadowing the reality.

PRAYER.—*We have learned long since that we have nothing to pay for our salvation. Nothing that we are, nothing that we have, nothing that we do, could purchase the gift. And now we pray that we may never cause anyone to misunderstand the true nature of Thy saving plan, but point them ever to the One who has fully paid the price.* AMEN.

NOVEMBER 21

". . . *Alas, master! for it was borrowed*" (2 Kings 6: 5)

THE vivid little story is full of spiritual suggestion. The responsibility of the lent life is here. This man should have been more careful with borrowed property. And don't forget, "ye are not your own . . ." (1 Cor. 6: 19). Your life is lent you, to serve God's purpose. The tragedy of the lost life is here. It used to be so keen, so sharp, so bright, so useful, but now it is so different. The axe is damaged, the work is hindered, the owner is saddened. This speaks, not of a lost soul, but of a lost life, a Christian, but now "good for nothing" (Matt. 5: 13). The glory of the lifted life is here. Rescued through the tree, the cutdown "stick" (v. 6) is a picture of Calvary's "tree" (1 Pet. 2: 24). Raised by miracle, "the iron did swim" (v. 6). Like the regeneration of the unbeliever, the restoration of the backslider is always a miracle. Restored to its former usefulness it was; "take it up to thee" (v. 7), not again you may be sure to be used by that careless wielder, but now given back to the keeping and service of its rightful owner. "Yield yourselves unto God . . . and your members as instruments of righteousness unto God" (Rom. 6: 13).

PRAYER.—*It is our life after conversion that is here brought home to us. May we be so careful that it may be yielded to Thy hands, and used to the full in Thy service. Keep us clean and keen.* AMEN.

NOVEMBER 22

". . . *open his eyes, that he may see* . . ." (2 Kings 6: 17)

THIS "young man," Elisha's servant, Gehazi's successor, was very frightened. His master was being hunted by the Syrians, but up till then they could not find him. Through the previous night, however, having discovered his whereabouts, they had quietly surrounded him, and when his servant arose early that morning, his eyes met this sight which thoroughly unnerved him. Elisha's prayer was that "his eyes" might behold another sight, and the miracle being granted, "he saw . . ."! Human eyes saw what in the next chapter (7: 6) human ears heard, the heavenly armies. Normally they are neither heard nor seen, but they are there. "The angel of the Lord encampeth round about them that fear Him" (Ps. 34: 7). What grand reinforcement is this against the force and guile of the enemy of souls. What glorious security is this against the coming to us of anything which would really harm us. Things hurtful may, for our good, be permitted to come, but nothing harmful can penetrate that cordon of love.

PRAYER.—*How greatly we value our outward eyes; yet often are little aware of the importance of our inward sight. May these "eyes of our understanding" be enlightened by the Holy Spirit, that we may apprehend spiritual things, and live "as seeing Him who is invisible."* AMEN.

"*. . . this day is a day of good tidings, and we hold our peace . . .*"
(2 Kings 7: 9)

A GOSPEL day! The people were starving in Samaria; there was plentiful provision in the Syrian camp. These four lepers had discovered it, and feasted themselves on its abundant supply. Suddenly they realized how criminally selfish they were in not publishing the news in Samaria. "Which things are an allegory," as Galatians 4: 24 would say. The people are starving for want of the Bread of Life. The Father's house has "bread enough, and to spare" (Luke 15: 17) and we Christians have found in Him that Bread "which endureth unto everlasting life" (John 6: 27). Yet some of us "hold our peace," and no one hears from our lips the wonderful "good tidings." What criminal neglect of plain duty, what strange callousness of others' dire straits, what base ingratitude to Him who has saved us, and bidden us preach this Gospel to all whom we can reach.

PRAYER.—*We so often pray, and we pray again, that Thou wilt give us tongues to tell, and hearts to burn, and feet to hurry with the glad tidings, that none shall lay it to our charge, whom we ought to have reached, that we never cared enough to do it.* AMEN.

"*. . . Is thine heart right, as my heart . . . If it be, give me thine hand . . .*"
(2 Kings 10: 15)

So inquired Jehu of Jehonadab, and on the affirmative answer the two of them rode together on the expedition. Are we thus riding in "the chariot" of God, as He goes forth to the accomplishment of His mighty conquest? Two things will answer that. First, the heart will answer it. Is it in tune with Him, "thine heart . . . as My heart"? Is our love called forth by His love, our purpose in line with His purpose, our will happily embracing His will? Then, the hand will answer it. This will assuredly, even inevitably, follow the heart, a hand yielding to His servitude, a hand giving to His work, a hand doing all for His glory. If the heart is right, the hand will be right. Where there's love there's service. Should you meet with an idle Christian, don't blame his hand, blame his heart. For our part, let us with heart and hand join "the chariot" on the divine mission.

PRAYER.—*Oh glad adventure, to ride out with Thee, O Lord, in Thy chariot. Take us in, then, and may our hand be made strong by the hand of the mighty God of Jacob.* AMEN.

" . . . *they gave the money . . . to repair . . . the house of the Lord . . .*"
(2 Kings 12: 11, 12)

How interesting this passage will be to any whose God's House has to be built or rebuilt. On the human side there will needs be a great effort to gather in the large sum of money to complete the work, and much prayer will surround that effort. I like that "chest" with "a hole in the lid" (v. 9), so similar to the modern collecting box. I like that testimony to the workmen, that "they dealt faithfully" (v. 15), so that there was no need to be overcareful in "reckoning" the money. I like that announcement that the money was to be used for the building itself, not for any of the furniture, the "vessels" of verses 13 and 14. Well, now the purpose of this note is to remind ourselves of what some church members are inclined to forget, the spiritual responsibility of our "money," and our duty to see to the material welfare of our own God's House.

PRAYER.—*Our Master, Thou hast taught us that "it is more blessed to give than to receive." As we come to our Christian Assembly may it be first to give, and we shall assuredly get. Help us then to give Thee the worship that is Thy due, the praise of our grateful hearts, the prayer to the Throne, the attention to Thy Word, and the gift of our substance, then to go home to a life that corresponds to it all.* AMEN.

" . . . *Thou shouldest have smitten five or six times . . .*"
(2 Kings 13: 19)

It was a kind of "Let's Pretend" that Elisha was playing with King Joash, in reference to the enemy he had to face. With him, it was Syrians; with us, it is sins. So the bedridden prophet bids the king do three things. He bid him open the window (v. 17). Let's pretend the enemy is out there. He bid him shoot the arrow (v. 17). Let's pretend that is the arrow of victory and deliverance God is going to win. He bid him strike the floor (v. 18). Let's pretend you now have the enemy on the ground at your feet, and you are smiting him. Ah, but he strikes only three times, at which the angry prophet tells him that his victory will be incomplete and inconclusive. If he had shown greater persistence and determination by smiting "five or six times," his triumph would have been decisive and final. Determine to be not just a Three Victory Christian, but a Six Victory Christian, utterly routing the sins that confront you.

PRAYER.—*We bless Thee for Thy purpose that we should become more than conquerors. Give us then, not just a few little victories, not just temporary conquests, but a deliverance that lasts and that leaves no foe undefeated.* AMEN.

". . . *the bones of Elisha* . . ." (2 Kings 13: 21)

ACCORDING to Romans 15: 4, there must be some lesson in it for us, but what a queer little story it is. One's first reflection is that a man's influence lives after him. Elisha had exercised a very gracious influence during his lifetime, and even when he was dead, it hadn't died, since his bones gave life to another. Though not in this material sense, yet in a spiritual way, we too may leave a beautiful, lifegiving influence behind. Shakespeare said, "The evil that men do lives after them, the good is oft interred with their bones." Oft, but not always, as our story suggests. Compare this with "he, being dead, yet speaketh" of Hebrews 11: 4. But a further reflection comes to mind, that a man's life depends on another's death. It was by the contact with Elisha who had died that this dead man lived. What a parable! There could have been no resurrection to eternal life if He had not died for us. Have we made saving contact with Him by faith?

PRAYER.—*We are so concerned, O Lord, that as we pass through this world, and indeed, as we pass out of it, we may exercise a living influence for Thee upon other lives. May not our dead body, but our deathless being, be such as to have a living effect upon those around us, and those after us.* AMEN.

". . . *a piece of brass* . . ." (2 Kings 18: 4, margin)

IT was a most interesting relic. The first part of its history was a story of need, man's sin, repentance and prayer; a story of grace, God's provision for man's rescue, a something which all could see, all could do; a story of salvation, as they looked they lived (Num. 21: 4–9). The foolish part of its history was that what had been kept as a memorial and thanksgiving came to be an object of worship, as if it, and not He, had saved them. So, it had to be destroyed in Hezekiah's reformation, who called the relic only "a piece of brass." The finest part of its history was that our Lord used it as a parable (John 3: 14) of His own lifting up in saving sacrifice, that all who exercised the "look" of trust should be cured of sin's serpent bite (Gen. 3: 1), and made to live everlastingly. Having "looked" ourselves, let us urge others to look and live.

PRAYER.—*We praise Thee, O Lord, for the saving efficacy of the Cross whereon "the Prince of Glory died." We thank Thee, too, that we were even drawn to look to Him and be saved. We thank Thee, also, that Thou hast commissioned us to bear to others Thy gracious invitation. May we, then, go forth with alacrity to bid sin-stricken ones to look and live.* AMEN.

"*. . . he began to reign . . .*" (2 Kings 22: 1)

THE phrase comes over and over again in the Books of Kings. Some of these sovereigns like Manasseh (21: 2) "did . . . evil in the sight of the Lord." Others like Josiah here (v. 2) "did . . . right in the sight of the Lord." But today I leave all that on one side to ask, Have you begun to reign yet? You see, in Romans 5: 17, there is a word which says, "They which receive abundance of grace, and of the gift of righteousness, shall reign in life by . . . Jesus Christ." That is the evident purpose of God for believers, since He "hath made us kings . . . unto God" (Rev. 1: 6). In the millennium, some Christians will "reign" with Him over people (Rev. 20: 6), but meanwhile we are to reign, not over lands and people, but over feelings and moods and nerves and habits and temptations and emergencies and circumstances and, of course, sins. Why should these things be allowed to rule us when, by His righteous gift and abundant grace, we may exercise a daily lordship over them?

PRAYER.—*Write upon our hearts, O Lord, the amazing privilege of our royal descent as sons of the King. And as Thou hast guaranteed to us supply of grace to live up to such a high degree, may we not fail in this, Thy loving purpose for us, but may we enjoy a regnant life with Thee.* AMEN.

"*And his allowance was a continual allowance given him of the king, a daily rate for every day, all the days of his life*" (2 Kings 25: 30)

FOR thirty-seven years Jehoiachin has been a prisoner. But now, from Evil-merodach, he meets with grace, "spake kindly unto him" (v. 28); he is given release, "did lift up the head" (v. 27), he is suitably clothed, "changed his prison garments" (v. 29); and he is given a throne, "set his throne" (v. 28). All of which is strikingly parabolic of us Christians. But how is he, how are we, to keep up the new position? This king of Babylon saw to that, too, as does also our King of Kings. Mark the daily rotation, "daily . . . day . . . days"; whatever the day's needs, always sufficient sustenance to live up to the new circumstances, to meet the new demands. Mark the daily ration, His grace, "as thy days, so . . ." (Deut. 33: 25); His Word, of royal origin, of remaining quality, of regular use. As each day we open our Bible we sit at His board and partake of the royal dainties to strengthen us for the day's life.

PRAYER.—*Give us, we pray, a healthy appetite for the food of the soul. Beget in us the habit of daily feeding, and cause us thereby to become ever stronger in spirit, and ever fitter for Thy service all the days of our life.* AMEN.

DECEMBER

LOVE'S GOOD NEWS

It seemed only right to match our last month with some other last thing in our Meditations, and thus this last Gospel suggested itself. What a glorious Volume of the Divine Library it is. We approach it with deep reverence for its majestic unveiling of the divine glory, with enraptured appreciation of its sheer beauty, with profound thankfulness for its portrait of the Master.

". . . *the Word* . . ." (John 1: 1)

A WORD is the expression of a mind. What a person thinks is conveyed to us usually by what he says. So here, as this Gospel opens, the Lord Jesus is introduced to us as "the Word," the expression of the Mind of God. In the late Archbishop William Temple's words, He is "the self-communication of the Father to His children." If we would know God's Mind, we shall find it in Christ. "He that hath seen Me hath seen the Father" (14: 9). As, then, we turn the pages of this wondrous Scripture, let it be our eager desire to hear, and to heed, such a Word.

PRAYER.—*We are ever thankful, O Father, for the words that "This Man spake," but especially for the Word that He is, as telling us of Thyself. Truly we see in Him the expression of Thy power, Thy holiness, Thy love, Thy grace. May that grace enable us to heed.* AMEN.

". . . *Thou art . . . thou shalt be* . . ." (John 1: 42)

I T is a far cry from the shifting sands Simon to the stable rock Peter. Yet upon His first sight of him the Lord made this promise and prophecy of Simon's enormous transformation of character. Such a transfiguration is by no means an isolated case. He has done the same for a multitude, not only as recorded in Holy Scripture, but also in the story of the Church right down through the ages. What mighty alteration is that which changed a Jacob into an Israel, or the drunken sailor, John Newton, into the saintly author of "How Sweet the Name." But what about you and me? Are we sad and disappointed that we are so little like our Lord Jesus? "Thou art" such a bad portrait. Yes, but if yielded to Him, "thou shalt be" such a good presentment. "Changed into the same Image," says 2 Corinthians 3: 18, while telling us how.

PRAYER.—*We have proved, O Lord, that our strong resolutions, our mighty efforts, our earnest intentions, our religious observances could never change us into the Image, but we thank Thee that the glorious alteration can be achieved by the Holy Spirit who dwells within the believer. So to Him would we surrender our whole being that He may work in us, and out of us, the pattern of our Example.* AMEN.

DECEMBER

"*. . . whatsoever He saith unto you, do it*" (John 2: 5)

SUCH was Mary's advice to these people in their difficulty. It was, I think, an advice born of experience. When her husband had died, she was left with her "First Born" (Luke 2: 7), and with the younger boys and girls, Joseph's children (Mark 6: 3). And as Jesus grew older, she found herself often turning to Him for help in the home, and always she discovered that things turned out all right if she did as He said. We, too, shall find the same. The "whatsoever" may sometimes be surprising, as here when He told them to fill the pots with water. It was not water they wanted, but wine! The "whatsoever" will never be impossible. All these people could do toward the miracle was to bring water, so He asked them for that. He ever asks for what you can do, never for what you can't. The "whatsoever" will always be fruitful, as in our story. You see, what really matters is, not our ability, but our obedience.

PRAYER.—*We are sure that if we will do what Thou sayest, we shall be what Thou desirest. Make us then, completely obedient to every word of Thine, even to the things that we would not have chosen of ourselves, but which, because Thou sayest them, we know will be best, and blest.* AMEN.

DECEMBER 4

"*. . . His disciples believed on Him*" (John 2: 11)

OF course, did you say? Alas, there is no "of course" about it. All too often His disciples do not believe on Him. The root trouble with the Church is probably this, that there are so many un-believing believers. They have believed on Him for the saving of their souls, but they have then believed in themselves for the running of their lives, whereas the all-over secret of the living of the Christian life is faith in Him. Our very salvation is "through faith" (Eph. 2: 8); so is our progress, "we walk by faith" (2 Cor. 5: 7); our understanding, "by faith we understand" (Heb. 11: 3); our victory, "this is the victory . . . even our faith" (1 John 5: 4); our sanctification, "sanctified by faith that is in Me" (Acts 26: 18); our calm, "how is it that ye have no faith?" (Mark 4: 40). Verily, revolutions would be wrought if only "His disciples believed on Him" today. Take any promise of His, observing its conditions. Put your finger on it; come now, do you believe it? Truly?

PRAYER.—*The very question humbles us, O Lord, for, alas, we know that so often we do not really believe Thee. We would not say it quite like that, but we realize that it is not just a promise that we disbelieve, or a word, but it is Thee, Thyself, that we distrust. Save us, O Lord, from such disloyalty, and lead us into the joyous life of faith.* AMEN.

"... *Ye must be born again*" (John 3: 7)

WHO must? A poor wretch, down in the gutter of sin. Of course, that would be his only chance. You can't improve him. If ever he is to be any good, he will have to be born all over again. Yes, but Nicodemus was not that sort, and Jesus said he "must." This man had been brought up in a godly home. He had been an assiduous Bible student, and was now the leading expositor of his day, "the (Gk.) master of Israel" (v. 10). He was a good and important citizen, on the Council, "a ruler of the Jews" (v. 1). He was a prominent office bearer in the church, and yet, the Lord said he had not even begun. He "must be born again!" What a challenging thought. Well, have you been born again? However religious you may be, however respectable, however anything, "ye must be . . ." If you are not sure, will you act on John 1: 12 now?

PRAYER.—*Lord, wilt Thou make this eternal necessity plain to any one of us who is not clear about it, and cause that any such may turn repentantly to receive Thee into their heart and life, that they may thus become the sons of God, believing on His name.* AMEN.

DECEMBER 6

"... *He must needs go through Samaria*" (John 4: 4)

WHY "must" He? To go from Judea up into Galilee, as He was planning to do, one would normally cross over to the eastern side of Jordan, journey up north through Perea, and then, thus bypassing Samaria, recross Jordan, and so into Galilee. This was the longer way, but it was the pleasanter, because Jews and Samaritans were at loggerheads (v. 9), and it was asking for trouble for a Jew to go up through Samaria. Yet He elected to go by that direct route, and why? He had an appointment with Need, and nothing will keep Him away when that is the case. He walked on the water to go to His distressed disciples (John 6: 19). He walked in the fire to be with His loyal three (Dan. 3: 25). He walked through bolted doors to go to be with frightened believers (John 20: 19). He walked through Samaria to meet this woman, through her to bring revival blessing to Sychar. Be assured that your need is a very magnet to His loving heart. Whatever your trouble, you will find Him there, to meet it, and you!

PRAYER.—*Thy Word is full of this beautiful truth, but even that Word apart, we have, so many of us, and so often, known the blessedness of it in our own experience. Truly we were in need, truly Thou didst take heed, and because Thou wast there, we came through.* AMEN.

DECEMBER 7

". . . he that soweth and he that reapeth may rejoice together"
(John 4: 36)

WERE you rather disappointed, a little jealous even, that you were not allowed to bring those souls to Christ upon whom you had, this long while past, bestowed much labour? You were such friends; you did so long that they might be the Lord's. You had been so careful to live consistently and happily before them. You had prayed so often and so earnestly for them. You had so hopefully spoken the word of testimony. And after all this, someone else stepped in, and had the joy of leading your friends to Him. Yes, but all your sowing was as essential a part of the harvest as the other one's reaping. Verse 38 puts that quite clearly. In harvesting souls, the reaper may be the more conspicuous, but the sower has a no less vital ministry. So cheer up. "He that soweth and he that reapeth may rejoice together." God has His reapers, and God has His sowers.

PRAYER.—*We can never be too thankful that Thou hast given us our part in the Harvest Field. Help us to be faithful in the discharge of that part, that whether in one way or another, we may have a vital share in the fruit that shall abound, and "bearing precious seed" we shall be found in that day "bearing His sheaves."* AMEN.

DECEMBER 8

". . . the fever left him" (John 4: 52)

THE father had asked what time his boy "began to mend," imagining that the fever's cure would take its normal and natural course, the patient getting better and better. When did he take that initial turn for the better, and how long would the convalescent stage be? Ah, but the Lord Jesus doesn't do things like that. All of a sudden, and all in a moment, the fever "left" him; one instant ill, the next well! That is how He would cure the disease of sin. "Let him that stole, steal no more" (Eph. 4: 28), not steal gradually less and less until he is quite rid of the nasty habit, but instantly and completely done with. Whatever the sin, He does not contemplate a gradual improvement. He nowhere promises to make us better, but He does undertake to make us quite well at once.

PRAYER.—*How needless then, that a Christian should dally over some besetting sin, since the victory over it that Thou hast envisaged is not partial or gradual, but at once and all at once. May such complete triumph be always ours, in Him.* AMEN.

"... *Wilt thou be made whole?*" (John 5: 6)

THAT seems a strange question to ask of any ill person. This man had been a more or less helpless invalid for thirty-eight years, and it would appear to follow, as a matter of course, that he wished to get well. Yet, believe it or not, any experienced doctor could tell of patients who did not want to be cured. It is literally true that some people enjoy bad health. And certainly when you make spiritual application of it, there are people who are afraid of what it might involve them in if they were saved from their sin. Indeed, there are some who so enjoy a besetting sin that they just don't want to be "made whole." Well, let it be faced squarely, there is no cure, no victory, for anyone who does not really want it. Anyone can have victory who truly wants it, but not unless. So "wilt thou?" is His first question.

PRAYER.—*Thou Great Physician of the Soul, Who dost so truly diagnose our case, wilt Thou proceed with Thy healing work, and do Thy miraculous cure of our whole being, that we may arise perfectly fit for Thy service.* AMEN.

"*He was a burning and a shining light . . .*" (John 5: 35)

WHO does not want to be a shining light? Indeed, so long as the idea is not to glorify oneself but Him, the desire is a laudable ambition. But let us remember that there is no kind of light without some sort of combustion. To take the simplest level, a candle can only give light as it gives itself. One recalls John the Baptist's word about the Master, "the Light of the World," that "He must increase but I must decrease" (John 3: 30). Thus we hear the Lord's testimony concerning him, "He was a burning and a shining light." Was it not the famous missionary, Henry Martyn, who said he was going to India to burn out for God? If then we would shine for the Lord in this dark place of a world (Phil. 2: 15), we must make up our minds that self must be consumed. As self goes, He glows.

PRAYER.—*We remember, Lord, that Thou hast said "Ye are the light of the world," so we pray that nothing may darken our light nor dim our shining, but that we may irradiate the true light to many who are in darkness of sin, sorrow or anxiety.* AMEN.

DECEMBER

". . . *Jesus took the loaves* . . ." (John 6: 11)

THE loaves are pictures of lives, and when the Lord takes either, wonderful things happen to them. Follow out for a bit this figure of the loaves. They are a symbol of partnership. The Master is to feed the multitude. He could have called down "bread from Heaven" (v. 32), but instead He called earthly agency into partnership; the apostles, the little lad, the loaves, even as He calls you and me. They are a picture of insufficiency. "What are they among so many?" (v. 9). What, indeed, are we that He should be able to use our small help? They are an intimation of sacrifice. He "brake the loaves" (Mark 6: 41). We need to be broken, if we are to be of full use to Him. They are a medium of power. It is not we, in our impotence, but He in His omnipotence who is to feed the multitude of hungry souls around us. Our part is to let Him take us, and break us, that He may make us His instruments.

PRAYER.—*Lord, it is our great desire that Thou wilt do this for us and with us. Of ourselves, we can be of so little use in the face of a world's hunger, a soul's distress, but Thou canst employ even us as the medium of Thy blessing. "Oh use me, Lord, use even me, just as Thou wilt, and when and where."* AMEN.

DECEMBER 12

". . . *Gather up the fragments that remain, that nothing be lost*"
(John 6: 12)

GOD doesn't waste His wonders, and He will have nothing lost. Neither must it be supposed that He had created more than was wanted. Remember, these "fragments" were not the crumbs left over, they were the pieces He had broken in the miracle; twelve little baskets more of them than the crowd needed. Yes, but what of the twelve apostles, who had been helping in the distribution? Were they not to be fed? Oh, yes, in the service of God, those who feed others will themselves be fed. That is why the old Law ran, "Thou shalt not muzzle the ox when it treadeth out the corn" (Deut. 25: 4). So, one basket of the pieces for Andrew, who had brought the little chap (not "lad") to Jesus; one basket for his brother Peter, and so on; one for each. Thus nothing was "lost." He had made exactly the right quantity, which is ever His way.

PRAYER.—*Lord, we do not serve Thee for what we get out of it, but we find that we get out of it just what we need. We bless Thee for this loving care for the sustenance and sufficiency for Thy servants, and we pray that these, Thy supplies, may but strengthen us to serve Thee further.* AMEN.

DECEMBER

13

". . . *I am . . .*" (John 6: 35)

IT is the very Autograph of the Almighty (Ex. 3: 14), and when the Lord Jesus used it, in John 8: 58, the Jews recognized the divine significance of it, and were for stoning Him for blasphemy, but He who "thought it not robbery to be equal with God" (Phil. 2: 6), thought it not forgery to use His signature. And how delightfully He attached it to the supply of our needs. "I am . . ." what? Seven times it comes in John's Gospel (6: 35, 8: 12, 10: 7, 10: 11, 11: 25, 14: 6, 15: 5). It is as if we are offered a signed blank cheque to be filled in by us for the sum which shall be required. "I Am . . . the Bread of Life, the Light of the World, the Door, the Good Shepherd, the Resurrection and the Life, the Way, the Vine," and whatever else you need. It is the signature which gives validity to the promise in the Royal Bank of Heaven, "according to His riches in glory by Christ Jesus" (Phil. 4: 19).

PRAYER.—*How vast, O Lord, are Thy riches, how great Thy bounty, how more than sufficient the open cheque of Thy generous provision. May we not fail to endorse the cheque with our personal faith and appropriation, and live on the proceeds.* AMEN.

DECEMBER

14

"*If any man will do . . . he shall know . . .*" (John 7: 17)

I SHOULD think that a great number of Christians are more perplexed about guidance than about any other problem of the spiritual life. There is, of course, no room to discuss the subject here. One thing only engages our attention just now, and that straight out of our text. As in so many matters, one of the big secrets of knowing divine leading lies in the will. It is surprising how much of spiritual experience and blessing waits upon our really wanting it. So here the infinitely desirable knowledge we speak of is specifically linked up with a man's willingness to do what is revealed. If we ask guidance with the secret proviso that we will do it or not, in accordance with whether it coincides with our own wishes, we shall get no guidance. If our mind is first in tune with His, our sole purpose in wanting to know His will is to do it, then "he shall know." In His own time and way He will disclose His direction.

PRAYER.—*Our Master, all that we know of Thy will prompts us and urges us to will it for ourselves. We would tell Thee beforehand that we are going to do what Thou art going to say, and so our purpose coinciding with Thy purpose, we shall rejoice in that "good and acceptable and perfect will of God."* AMEN.

DECEMBER 15

"The neighbours therefore . . ." (John 9: 8)

I AM afraid that when it comes to spiritual things we think all too little about our neighbours. But have no doubt, if we make any profession of allegiance to Christ, they think a good deal about us. They know us so well; passers-by knew something of this blind man, but the neighbours knew so much more, and they saw all too clearly the effects of his blindness. They know, at once, if there's a change; the alteration wrought in this man by the Lord Jesus was so marked that they scarcely recognized him. "Is not this he . . . ?" They know if it lasts; it did in this case, but neighbours would have seen at once if he had backslidden into blindness again. If our eyes have been opened, if our lives have been changed, if our profession has endured, "the neighbours" will be aware of it. What do our neighbours see, and think, and say about us who profess to be Christ's? And ought we not to be seeking "the neighbours" for Him? Let us sum it up by exhorting one another to live neighbourly.

PRAYER.—*Cause us then, Lord, to be deeply concerned that we shall witness a good conversion before those "near-by us," whether in the family, in the office, in the circle, in the street, or over the garden fence, that we may put none off, but draw some in for Thee.* AMEN.

DECEMBER 16

". . . one thing I know . . ." (John 9: 25)

THOSE learned people, who hated the Master, tried to embroil this simple man in an argument about Him. They tried, so as to weaken the undoubted impression that had been made by this cure, to get the subject of the miracle to declare publicly that He was an undesirable character, and no Messiah. Into all this the man refused to be drawn. In any case, he couldn't follow what all the bother was about. It was all very wonderful, but very simple to him. He knew nothing about all these seeming quibbles of the leaders. One thing he knew, and that was clear and plain to him, and to anyone who knew him: "Once I was blind, now I see." No amount of arguing could shake him out of that; no scepticism of theirs could alter that fact. I daresay that concerning religion there are many things you can't understand, many mysteries which baffle your mind, but can you say, "One thing I know . . ."? By His mercy, though once you were "blind" and lost, now are you saved, and "see"?

PRAYER.—*Lord, may we never allow what we know to be upset by what we do not know, and if by Thy mercy we have come to know Thee as our Saviour, Lord and Friend, may nothing deter us from our loyalty, or disturb the peace and joy of our fellowship with Thee. Whatever the problems, let us, anyhow, cling on to what we know of Thee.* AMEN.

"*. . . I am come that they might have life and that they might have it more abundantly*" (John 10: 10)

NOT just a rivulet, but a river; not just a spark, but a fire; not just alive, but fully alive. How like the Saviour, who always does things, and gives things, in a superlative degree! We are too often content with so little when He is prepared to give us so much. If, according to 1 John 5: 12, we have "life," let us ask ourselves what degree of life we have. Go to any hospital to see the difference. That patient, desperately ill, has almost no strength, is scarcely breathing, only just alive. That nurse, thoroughly fit and strong, bursting with energy, is alert and alive to her fingertips. The latter is a picture of what every Christian should spiritually be. Alas, all too frequently, it is the former which is the truer portrait. Oh, for "life . . . more abundantly," giving us joy of life ourselves, and enabling us to give service to the unfit around us.

PRAYER.—*Our God, for any degree of physical health we have, we give Thee thanks. May we have the fullest degree of spiritual health. As Thou hast called us to life, may we not be invalids, but may we be virile in ourselves and valiant in Thy service. AMEN.*

"*My sheep . . .*" (John 10: 27)

THE Old Testament refers constantly to the shepherd ministry of the Lord, and in the New Testament we find the Master Himself frequently employing the figure, the two great complementary passages being, of course, Psalm 23 and John 10. How gloriously wonderful it is if He looks upon us and says, "My sheep," and if we can say of Him, "My Shepherd." Thus He guarantees to us three things: Our progression: the Shepherd going before the sheep, and leading them in the way. Our protection: wild beasts, or Bedouins, may snatch ordinary sheep out of the shepherd's care, but none shall "pluck them out of My hand" (v. 28). Blessed safety! Our provision is assured to us, all we need, for all the days, as He leads us to "green pastures" and "still waters." Thus, all the responsibilities of the Shepherd are His, and our part, and wisdom, is just to follow in His track.

PRAYER.—*In the light of this exceeding blessedness, keep us ever mindful that "other sheep Thou hast which are not of this fold," and may we devote our lives to be amongst those who will go and find them, the many sheep who are straying far from the Saviour's fold. AMEN.*

"*. . . The Master is come, and calleth for thee*" (John 11: 28)

H E was late, wasn't He? Oh dear, no, He is never late. If ever He seems so, it is only that our clocks are fast. We shall have occasion, in a later Meditation, to speak about His punctuality. The sorrowing sisters thought He was altogether too late. Each of them in turn made the same remark to Him when He arrived at last. "If Thou hadst been here," the dreaded thing would not have happened. Yet, I suppose that when it was all over, and the three of them could dispassionately look back on the whole incident, they would greatly rejoice that He had not "come" earlier, before the appointed time. That "looking back" will be one of the happy employments of Heaven, when we shall see how right He always was, and how always on time. Still to the home of sorrow, or difficulty, He comes at the right moment, calling the troubled soul to Himself for the comfort and strength He so wondrously can give.

PRAYER.—*We rejoice, O Lord, in remembrance of the day when "the Master is come" to call us to salvation, and now we rejoice in every occasion when Thou art come to comfort our distresses, and even to seek our help. May our response ever lead many to glorify Thee, for all that Thou art to, and doest for, Thine own, in Resurrection Power.* AMEN.

"*. . . by reason of him many . . . believed on Jesus*" (John 12: 11)

W HAT a grand tribute to have paid about anyone. The strange thing is that he doesn't seem to have been a preacher. Not a single word that ever he spoke has been recorded, as if to emphasize that whatever influence he exercised was the result not of what he said. The influence of some does lie in their spoken word, but not so with Lazarus. In his case, it was simply and solely that he was a new man; being dead, he had been "raised to newness of life" (Rom. 6: 4), a picture of a man with the new birth, about which we meditated a fortnight ago. This being "born again" is always a miracle; and where it is the real thing, as manifested by the new character, the new behaviour, the "new man" (Col. 3: 10), it always deeply impresses those who had known the old, and observe the change. Many a soul has "believed on Jesus" by reason of what they have seen in a real Christian. I wonder, is our new life of such a quality?

PRAYER.—*We yearn, O Master, that this may be the summing up of our life as Christians, that we may be indeed such Christians, so Christ-like, that many shall find Thee because of us. We do not ask that we may know it now, but that it shall be revealed when we and they gather together round Thee in that Day.* AMEN.

". . . *Sir, we would see Jesus*" (John 12: 21)

I THINK it was not mere curiosity which prompted the inquiry. The whole passage has about it an air of deep seriousness. Perhaps these were people who had come out of paganism to be Gentile proselytes, and then, still dissatisfied in soul, had wondered if in this new Teacher they could find the rest of heart and mind they sought. How typical it was of Andrew that when Philip consulted him about these Greeks' request, he forthwith brought them to Jesus. That was the way he dealt with people, beginning with his own brother (John 1: 41). How greatly this Gentile approach to Him rejoiced the Saviour's heart, drawing from Him the prophetic word about His death, "I . . . will draw all men unto Me" (v. 32); not all without exception, of course, but all without distinction, Gentile as well as Jew. His mission had been largely national to "the house of Israel" (Matt. 15: 24, 10: 5), but it was to be universal, embracing "every kindred, and tongue, and people, and nation" (Rev. 5: 9), all who would be "drawn" to Him. By the way, are there not many anxiously inquiring of us Christians still, "We would see Jesus"?

PRAYER.—*May we acquire the Andrew habit of introducing others to Thee, O Lord, "no mission could be nobler nor fraught with greater joy." May we think none too good to need Thee, nor too bad to find Thee, but may we ever be on the lookout to fetch "all" we can.* AMEN.

". . . *What I do thou knowest not now but thou shalt know hereafter*" (John 13: 7)

T HE feet washing must have caused considerable puzzlement to the disciples, and certainly Peter got greatly tangled up about it, but they were promised complete understanding later on. Now that is a principle of the godly life, that present bewilderment shall be followed by future enlightenment. We are confident that all which happens to us, His children, is allowed of God, or even planned by Him, and yet we sometimes find ourselves rebelling at His providences. Trouble comes; sorrow, disappointment, loss; and somewhat petulantly we ask, "Why?" Often the answer lies in the words of our text. The day of His coming will, amongst many other wonderful things, usher in the unravelling of all our problems, and meanwhile He asks us now to trust where we cannot trace. He always attaches a present blessing to every trial, but the blessing is actually received only by those who accept the trial trustfully.

PRAYER.—"*Shall not the Judge of all the earth do right?*" *Of course Thou wilt, and right gladly will we accept as from Thy hand the circumstances of our lives, and Thy hands never make a mistake.* AMEN.

DECEMBER 23

"*. . . He dwelleth with you, and shall be in you*" (John 14: 17)

Nᴏᴛᴇ here the important distinction between "in" and "with." They mark a dispensational difference. Up to Pentecost, the Holy Spirit was "with" these disciples; after Pentecost, He came to dwell "in" them. That is the intimate relationship which exists now for all true believers. The special thought for today then is that we should seek to be living on the indwelling; hold it, not merely as a truth to be believed, but as a fact to be practised. Therein lies our only hope of holy living, our only hope of growing likeness, our only hope of spiritual knowledge, our only hope of effective service. Though He is "in" every Christian, it is all too possible, as 1 Corinthians 6: 19 shows, to live as not reckoning on Him, which means an unsatisfactory, even an unholy, Christian conduct, bringing shame on Him whose Name we bear, when we should and could bring glory.

Pʀᴀʏᴇʀ.—*When we think of all that Thou, blessed Holy Spirit, art meant to be in us, to us, for us, we wonder that we fall so far short of what is Thy plan for us. In Thee we are so rich. May we live up to our position, and find in Thee our power to live thus—find it in Thee because Thou art found in us.* Aᴍᴇɴ.

DECEMBER 24

"*He shall glorify Me . . .*" (John 16: 14)

Tʜᴀᴛ is, if I may "speak after the manner of men," the overmastering passion of the Holy Spirit is to glorify the Lord Jesus. Let me suggest three of the chief ways in which He does it. The Spirit glorifies the Lord Jesus by writing a Book about Him, the Bible, of which He is the Author. It is all about Jesus; the Old Testament is the Preparation, the Gospels are the Presentation, the Acts is the Proclamation, the Epistles are the Personification, the Revelation is the Predomination. The Spirit glorifies the Lord Jesus by finding a Bride for Him, of which Eliezer's search for Isaac's bride in Genesis 24 is a picture. So is the Spirit in this age seeking and preparing the Church to be His Bride. The Spirit glorifies the Lord Jesus by making a Believer like Him. Every Christ-like Christian brings glory to His Name, and that is a quality of character which only the Holy Spirit can produce, the last phrase of 2 Corinthians 3: 18. It is what Galatians 5: 22 calls "the fruit of the Spirit."

Pʀᴀʏᴇʀ.—*We believe that so much could happen if our purpose coincided with Thy purpose, O Lord, and so we pray that we may be possessed of a passion like to the Holy Spirit, a passion that the Lord Jesus shall be glorified. May this, then, be the over-ruling desire with us, as with Him.* Aᴍᴇɴ.

DECEMBER (Christmas Day) 25

"... God ... gave ..." (John 3: 16)

PART of the joy of Christmas is the presents we give, and get. And they all started from the wonderful Gift, which marked the first Christmas, when "God . . . gave" us His only begotten Son. That Gift reveals God's love. It was because He "so loved" that He so gave. That Gift meets man's need of "everlasting life," and all else besides; a whole lot of smaller packages wrapped up in the all-inclusive parcel of the Love Gift. "He that spared not His own Son . . . how shall He not with Him also freely give us all things?" (Rom. 8: 32). That gift becomes our example. "If God so loved us, we ought also to love one another" (1 John 4: 11). That Gift demands our thanks; "thanks be to God for His unspeakable gift" (2 Cor. 9: 15). In writing your letters of thanks for your presents, don't forget the Giver of the First and Best; only thank Him, not with a letter, but with a life!

PRAYER.—*May the jollity of this great Day never overshadow its blessedness, and may we ever rejoice in, and share with others, Thy loving, living, lasting Christmas gift to us.* AMEN.

DECEMBER 26

"... Behold, I bring Him forth to you, that ye may know that I find no fault in Him" (John 19: 4)

I HAVE found fault with others, sometimes alas in an all too critical spirit. I have found many faults in myself. They are, I fear, all too apparent. But "I find no fault in Him." Pilate was, of course, unconsciously fulfilling type. It was said of the Paschal Lamb, "your lamb shall be without blemish" (Ex. 12: 5). And now that "Christ our Passover" (1 Cor. 5: 7), "the Lamb of God" (John 1: 29) is come to His sacrifice, He too is carefully scrutinized, and given the required certificate, "No fault." From any point of view, was there ever a Christian who ever found any fault in Him? If there be any fault, it is all on our side, never on His. So let us, in effect, "bring Him forth" to the world with our glad testimony to our spotless, peerless Lord.

PRAYER.—*Our Gracious Lord, how truly we can echo the words, for never has there failed one word of Thine, never hast Thou failed one iota of Thy perfection, never has there failed one degree of Thy matchless love. Oh, to be more worthy of Thyself.* AMEN.

". . . finished . . ." (John 19: 30)

THE other Gospels tell us that just before His death, the Saviour cried out something in a loud voice, but they do not tell us what it was He said. It is left to John to record the actual utterance; just this one word, "Finished." What was finished? The vinegar, yes, but more than that. The suffering, yes, but more than that. The life, yes, but more than that. It was His work of expiation of "the sins of the whole world." The plan of salvation, long devised and love inspired, is at last completed. It is now a finished work. Thank God, there is nothing for us to do but to accept it. Though there is plenty for us to do after we have accepted it; "not of works . . . unto good works," as Ephesians 2: 9, 10 puts it. The phrase, "the finished work of Christ," was the means of the conversion of the boy Hudson Taylor, who afterwards founded the China Inland Mission.

PRAYER.—*We thank Thee, O God, that there is nothing we need do for our salvation, for indeed there is nothing we can do about it, except to turn from our sin, to take the Saviour as our own, and to trust Him alone. Now, therefore, let us strive to do everything we can in His service.* AMEN.

". . . supposing Him to be the gardener . . ." (John 20: 15)

ACTUALLY, of course, she was wrong, but spiritually, what a wonderful Gardener of the soul He is. The seeds He plants are His own precious words, "words of life and beauty," as the hymn says; not all of them taking root, as He Himself warned us (Matt. 13: 4–8), but where they do, so rich in result. The water so needful for the seedlings' proper growth is the Holy Spirit, as He explained in John 7: 39, giving freshness and fragrance to His plants. The pruning knife, which may be called for, is our sometimes unpleasant circumstances, which will deal with an excess of wood, too much self, or a too prolific foliage, without fruit, profession without practice. Always the rose will find the pain pays. "It is good for me that I have been afflicted" (Ps. 119: 71). The sun which adds health and warmth and colour to the whole is "the Sun of Righteousness" (Mal. 4: 2) which is Himself, the radiance of whose presence will help the garden to be worthy of the Gardener.

PRAYER.—*Wilt Thou, O Lord, weed out all noxious growths from the soil of our soul, and tend the seed Thou hast Thyself planted, so that "beauty of holiness" may be seen in this human garden, that people may praise the Divine Gardener.* AMEN.

"*. . . then came Jesus . . .*" (John 20: 19, 26)

THUS, in three simple words, is enshrined the most dramatic incident in a day filled with drama. How much is packed into such little words. There was His personality. It was the same Jesus who went from them in sadness on Good Friday, and returned to them now in gladness on Easter Day. True, there was a resurrection change in Him, but it was the same Person. "It is I Myself" (Luke 24: 39). There was His punctuality, "then." They were alone. They had one another, but they were bereft of His presence; without Him now they felt so lonely. They were afraid, not knowing what the Jews would do further. Perhaps it would be their turn next. They were adrift. They had "left all"; now, it would seem, they had lost all. "Then," just when I need Him most! There was His potentiality. What a change He wrought in these men. All was not lost, all was won! So is it with all into whose hearts and lives the living Christ is come.

PRAYER.—*Thou Risen Saviour, we do not always recognize Thy Presence with us, still less do we always reckon on it. Help us to understand that no doors of difficulty can ever shut Thee out from our lives, but that in spite of fear or failure or anything, Thou art there, to be found, and trusted.* AMEN.

"*. . . written, that you might . . . have life . . .*" (John 20: 31)

JOHN tells us the reason why he wrote his Gospel, and also why he wrote his Epistle. The first was "that ye might . . . have life"; the second, "that ye may know that ye have . . . life" (1 John 5: 13). In this Gospel, he leaves us in no doubt as to our natural condition, in danger, in darkness and in death, but then he tells, so clearly and so sweetly, of Him who came to give liberation from danger, light for darkness, life for death. Through this One who died all may have eternal life, whether the poor, sinful Samaritan, at one end of the scale (John 4), or the distinguished, well-bred Nicodemus at the other (John 3). "There is no difference" as to the need (Rom. 3: 22, 23), and "there is no difference" as to the way (Rom. 10: 12, 13). The Gospel, starting from Bad News, brings Good News; and let trembling souls take note that on their belief they may and should know their safety in Christ.

PRAYER.—*Lord, if it depended on our own worthiness how uncertain we should rightly be of our salvation, but because it depends upon the worthiness of our Saviour, we may be unshakably sure, since by the Work of Christ, and the Word of God, and the Witness of the Holy Spirit, we may "know."* AMEN.

DECEMBER

". . . what is that to thee? Follow thou Me" (John 21: 22)

PETER has been reinstated, recommissioned. The blessed interview closed with the words he had first heard all that long time ago by the waters of Galilee, "Follow Me" (Matt. 4: 18, 19). It assured him that all the sin and shame of recent days was washed out, and that he might begin all over again. It was at that moment that, noticing John near by, Peter asked what was to be his future, to which the Master in effect replied, Never mind his future, you give full attention to your own future. And then, once more, came the old, renewing, challenging words, "Follow thou Me." A little before he had "followed afar off" (Luke 22: 54), hence the sad disaster, but from now on he followed close up, right on to where it led him to a cross, and a crown!

So as we come to the close of our year's Meditations, and as we look out, and step out, on to a New Year tomorrow, our living, loving Lord would bid us give urgent priority to this, that we "follow," and follow close, all the way.

PRAYER.—*We know, O Lord, that Thou dost not mean us to have no concern for the welfare of others, yet we also know that if we are to help them we must ourselves first be right. As we now review another year past, wilt Thou forgive all the wrong, and help us indeed to follow Thee.* AMEN.